Sundae Best

Sundae Best:
A History of Soda Fountains

Anne Cooper Funderburg

Bowling Green State University Popular Press
Bowling Green, OH 43403

Copyright 2002 © Bowling Green State University Popular Press

Library of Congress Cataloging-in-Publication Data

Funderburg, Anne Cooper.
    Sundae best : a history of soda fountains / Anne Cooper Funderburg.
        p.   cm.
    Includes bibliographical references and index.
    ISBN 0-87972-853-1 (cloth) -- ISBN 0-87972-854-X (paper)
    1. Soda fountains--United States--History. I. Title

TP635.F86 2001
394.1'2'0973--dc21

                                                            2001043423
Cover design by Amy Smolar

FOR MURRY,

ELLEN, AND CHRISTOPHER

CONTENTS

INTRODUCTION

Not so very long ago, most American towns had at least one soda fountain, where weary shoppers paused for coffee, workers grabbed a bite for lunch, and teenagers hung out after school, drinking cherry Cokes and blowing straw wrappers at one another. Today, the few remaining old-fashioned soda fountains are a curiosity and a nostalgia trip. At a time when standardization has run amuck in fast food outlets and shopping malls, marble-and-chrome soda fountains conjure up memories of the corner drugstore, which was one-of-a-kind and didn't look just like a hundred other stores with the same floor plan and the same merchandise. The remnants of another era, old-fashioned soda fountains represent yesterday's Main Street USA.

The rise and decline of the soda fountain reflected momentous developments in American life: urbanization, the temperance movement and Prohibition, the Great Depression, technological progress, the decline of Main Street and Center City, the Car Culture, and the growth of suburbs. The fountain's evolution was also closely tied to trends in retailing, food service, and the decorative arts. Because selling soda water was a business, the fundamental driving force behind the soda fountain's evolution was always profitability. From primitive beginnings in the early 1800s, the soda fountain grew into a major business in the late nineteenth century and continued to thrive until the late 1960s. It continually evolved to satisfy the changing needs of American consumers and, throughout all the changes, was a distinctly American institution. While many American trends mimicked what was happening in Europe, the United States' fountain industry was home-grown and the soda fountain was a uniquely American phenomenon.

The history of the soda fountain reveals that its evolution was circular. In the beginning, soda fountains were plain, gooseneck-shaped spigots that dispensed unflavored carbonated water, which purportedly had medicinal benefits. Some early merchants, hoping to increase sales, decided to make their fountains more attractive. So, they began to dispense carbonated water from ornamental urns and decorative marble columns. Soon, the fountain's working parts were hidden inside marble boxes, which steadily became larger and more ornate. These showy fountains often incorporated the latest trends in the decorative arts, such as Victorian gingerbread and Art Deco streamlining. Beginning in the

1

late nineteenth century, ornate soda fountains dominated drugstore interiors, as merchants vied to have the biggest, most elaborate fountain. Before and during the Depression, many soda fountains expanded their menus to serve complete meals. After World War II, as marble soda fountains became unprofitable, stark stainless-steel, bobtail fountains became the norm. Today, fast-food outlets dispense soft drinks from metal boxes that are the descendants of marble soda fountains but bear little resemblance to them. Like the first gooseneck spigot, today's metal box is a utilitarian dispensing apparatus devoid of ornamentation.

From the beginning, some merchants realized that encouraging customers to socialize at the soda fountain increased profits. They wanted their clientele to view the fountain as a gathering place where customers could bump into friends and hear the latest local news. As soda fountains proliferated, this social aspect became even more important to their popularity and, hence, to profitability. In large cities, soda fountains often had a clubby atmosphere because they catered to the surrounding residential neighborhood or business district. The regular customers knew one another, and the proprietor and employees also knew the regulars by name. In small towns, there was often only one fountain, which was patronized by virtually everybody in town. Whether in a city or a small town, the neighborhood soda fountain was an important public space that fostered a sense of belonging. It was a place to stay in touch with the neighborhood.

The soda fountain was an urban phenomenon because its clientele lived or worked within walking distance. When many Americans bought cars and moved to the suburbs, soda fountains began to lose their customers. Suburbanites had new places to shop and new forms of entertainment. Taking a stroll to the soda fountain for an ice cream soda wasn't nearly as exciting as cruising in a convertible or watching westerns on television. Moreover, suburbanites didn't go to the soda fountain to buy soft drinks or ice cream. They went to the supermarket for bottled drinks and cartons of ice cream. When they wanted a quick lunch, they didn't head for the soda fountain. They went to a drive-in restaurant or a roadside stand. Soda fountains simply didn't fit into their lifestyles anymore. Like many other Main Street institutions, the drugstore's marble-and-chrome soda fountain was headed for extinction.

History

WILD SPIRITS AND WATER CURES

Mankind's first encounter with carbonated water went unrecorded, but the earliest references to it indicate that primitive societies were fascinated by the waters bubbling up from underground spas. Moreover, they believed that these special waters could cure diseases. Perhaps an ailing caveman drank from a spa, was magically cured, and like a modern faith healer went forth to spread the word. Whatever the reason, for centuries people believed that effervescent waters were healthy. Some ancient cultures regarded spas as a sacred gift from God, who sent forth angels to stir the waters, thereby giving them mystical powers. Others believed that bubbling spas were inhabited by *spiritus silvestri* (wild spirits) and lost their powers when these spirits were allowed to escape.

Long before anyone figured out how to saturate water with carbon dioxide to make a pleasing drink, Europe's early philosopher-scientists theorized about the powers and composition of effervescent waters. In the fourteenth century, Giacomo de' Dondi theorized that salts were the essential elements in mineral waters and recommended that they be extracted for medical use. In the sixteenth century, Paracelsus studied the characteristics of bubbling mineral waters in his native Switzerland and speculated about their medical benefits. The alchemist Thurneysser made an early attempt to duplicate natural mineral waters in the mid-sixteenth century. Libavius, a German chemist, conducted similar experiments and described them in *De Judico Aquarum Mineralium* in 1597.[1]

In the seventeenth century, Englishman Robert Boyle recorded his observations on bubbling waters in *Short Memoirs for the Natural Experimental History of Mineral Waters* and theorized about how mineral waters might be replicated by chemical means. Boyle's Law on the physics of air was a direct result of his early experiments in pneumatic chemistry, including the effervescence of mineral waters. Friedrich Hoffmann, one of Boyle's German contemporaries, also wrote a treatise on mineral waters and identified five categories—alkaline, salty, bitter, ferrous, and sulphurous. He proved the presence of carbon dioxide in effervescent waters, but his method for replicating them was never tested. Also in the seventeenth century, Jean Baptiste Van Helmont, a Belgian physician, built upon the work of Paracelsus, focusing on the vapors that characterized natural springs. He coined the word "gas" to describe these vapors, but the exact chemical composition of this gas would not be determined until Antoine Laurent Lavoisier came along in the late 18th century.[2]

Hermann Boerhaave, who published a major treatise on chemistry in 1732, extracted carbon dioxide from chalk. In the early 1740s, William Brownrigg identified a substance he called "mephitic air" and stated that it was responsible for the effervescence of the natural waters from Spa and Pyrmont, two famous mineral springs. In a paper presented to the Royal Society of London, Brownrigg described a means of producing imitation Pyrmont water. In 1750, at the French Academy of Science, Gabriel F. Venel demonstrated his method for duplicating natural mineral waters, producing a slightly saline, effervescent liquid that he called "aerated water." A few years later, Joseph Black proved that limestone contained air that differed from "common air." He called his discovery "fixed air" and theorized that it was responsible for fermentation.[3]

David Macbride, a prominent Irish surgeon, noted the presence of carbon dioxide in the human blood stream and theorized about its functions. He was among the first to attribute substantial antiseptic and antiscorbutic properties to carbon dioxide and CO_2-saturated waters. In 1764, he published *Experimental Essays on Fermentation of Alimentary Substances and on the Nature and Properties of Fixed Air*. Two years later, Henry Cavendish presented a paper on *Factitious Airs* to the Royal Society of London. After explaining how water absorbed gas, he outlined a means for measuring the amount of the gas absorbed by the water and described an apparatus for impregnating water with gas. Thomas Lane, a London apothecary, fabricated an apparatus like Cavendish's and used it to dissolve iron in water.[4]

In the 1770s, Swedish chemist Torbern Bergman learned to imitate natural effervescent waters, which he believed could cure colic, and presented his findings to the Royal Academy of Science in Stockholm. Bergman's *Treatise on the True Proportion and Artificial Production of Bitter, Seltzer, Spa, and Pyrmont Waters* outlined his method for making various mineral waters and described the apparatus he used. His procedure was so simple and efficient that it became popular throughout his homeland, even in the most isolated Swedish provinces.[5]

Joseph Priestley—the noted British scientist, theologian, and political theorist—was familiar with Black's work with fixed air and, while residing near a brewery in Leeds, noted that there was a plentiful supply of the gas above the vats of fermenting liquor. He soon began simple experiments of his own and discovered that water poured into a shallow dish suspended over a fermentation vat acquired a pleasant, acidulous taste reminiscent of Pyrmont or Seltzer mineral waters. When he poured water from one vessel to another near the top of a vat, it quickly became effervescent.[6]

In 1772, Priestley dined with the Duke of Northumberland, who showed him a bottle of distilled water. Some British naval surgeons felt that distilled water would be beneficial on long voyages because they believed it could prevent scurvy. However, its flat taste was unlikely to appeal to the average sailor. Priestley immediately remembered his experiments in the brewery and felt that he could improve the taste of distilled water. Using equipment very similar to that utilized by Cavendish and Lane, he impregnated distilled water with carbon dioxide in a demonstration for the Lord Commissioners of the Admiralty, who were favorably impressed and decided to experiment with saturated waters on Captain Cook's vessels, *Resolution* and *Adventure*, which were lying at anchor, taking on supplies for a voyage. Before setting sail, both of these ships were supplied with equipment to distill seawater and impregnate it with CO_2.[7]

Shortly thereafter, Priestley published *Directions for Impregnating Water with Fixed Air, in Order to Communicate to It the Peculiar Spirit and Virtues of Pyrmont Water, and Other Mineral Waters of a Similar Nature.* The appearance of this pamphlet caused a stir in both England and Europe. Years later, looking back on his career, Priestley stated that producing artificial mineral water had been his "happiest idea," even though it had the least scientific merit of all his discoveries.[8]

John Mervin Nooth improved Priestley's apparatus and demonstrated it to the Royal Society of London in 1774. Historians believe that Thomas Henry, who owned an apothecary shop in Manchester, was the first British merchant to see the commercial potential in artificial mineral waters. It is uncertain when Henry began selling artificial waters in his shop, but in 1781 he published a pamphlet describing an apparatus that was similar to Nooth's and could produce larger quantities. This booklet also contained recipes for Artificial Pyrmont Water, Artificial Seltzer Water, and Mephitic Julep.[9]

In France, Pierre Joseph Macquer collaborated with Lavoisier on the study of effervescence and devised methods for purifying effervescent water after generating it from alkalis. Before Lavoisier met his untimely death by guillotine during the French Revolution, he determined the proportionate chemical composition of carbon dioxide. Other French scientists, including M.J.A. Chaptal and Antoine deFourcroy, shared Lavoisier's curiosity about the properties of mineral waters. In

1790, Chaptal published *Elements of Chemistry*, which summarized the existing knowledge about the medicinal qualities of effervescent waters and the methods for making them.[10]

In Britain, the first patent for a method of impregnating water with carbon dioxide was issued to Henry Thompson in 1807. Two years later a patent for a device for making aerated waters was granted to William F. Hamilton, whose system for carbonating and bottling water was widely used in Britain for a brief period. Yet another system was invented by Joseph Bramah and improved after Bramah's death by his apprentice, William Russell, who started a company to manufacture equipment for making artificial mineral waters. Another of Bramah's apprentices, John Matthews, emigrated to the United States and played a crucial role in popularizing soda fountains in America.[11]

American interest in artificial mineral waters stemmed from belief in the curative powers of natural spas. In Colonial America, wealthy families frequented spas where their afflictions, real or imaginary, were treated by taking the water cure in a fashionable setting. Although the waters provided by nature's pharmacy often had a caustic taste and acrid smell, these balneological meccas drew crowds of affluent invalids who bathed, sipped, strolled, danced, and played whist (a popular card game similar to bridge). The waters were reported to produce many health benefits, especially regularity, or "purging . . . both by siege and by urine," as one writer described it.[12] Thus, at a very early date, Americans established the connection between latrines and leisure that would be the trademark of many fashionable resorts and sanitariums.

Parson Samuel Peters, a loyalist historian, reported that Connecticut's Stafford Springs was a fashionable spa "where the sick and rich resort to prolong life, and acquire the polite accomplishments." Chemistry professor Thomas Cooper, who realized that the psychological powers of the waters were at least as potent as their medicinal powers, wrote that people frequented spas "partly on account of ill health, and partly for the sake of amusement, company, and variety." He also stated that "laxative and tonic salts in small doses are frequently beneficial; but far more of the cures . . . are owing to good society, good scenery, amusement, novelty, change of air, incitements to pleasurable exercise without fatigue, and though last not least, to faith in the efficacy of the waters."[13]

As American spas became more popular, they also became the target of social critics who felt that they encouraged idleness and frivolity. Washington Irving declared that spas were a rendezvous for "fashionable, dashing good-for-nothing people . . . who had rather suffer the martyrdom of a crowd than endure the monotony of their own homes, and the stupid company of their own thoughts." Philip Hone visited a famous New York spa where he saw "a crowd of queer strangers, dragging out a tiresome day of artificial enjoyment." After visiting a fashionable spa, Methodist evangelist Francis Asbury wrote, "Thank God that I was not born to riches."[14]

Whatever the social merits of spas, American scientists and physicians were intrigued by the medicinal properties of mineral waters. In 1773 Benjamin Rush, a Philadelphia physician and university professor, wrote two papers about spas: (1) *Experiments and Observations on the Mineral Waters of Philadelphia, Abington, and Bristol, in the Province of Pennsylvania* and (2) *Directions for the Use of the Mineral Waters and Cold Baths of Harrowgate, near Philadelphia.* Rush enthusiastically recommended the consumption of natural mineral waters, including the pungent water from a well in a backyard at Sixth and Chestnut streets in his hometown. Philadelphians, convinced that water which tasted so foul must be medicinal, flocked to this well to cure their ailments. When the overutilized well ran dry, efforts to renew the flow revealed a direct connection with a nearby privy—apparently the source of the unusual flavor![15]

In advertisements for the Harrowgate spa, proprietor George Esterley exploited endorsements given by several prominent Philadelphia physicians, including Rush. He also promised "the best of liquors of all and every kind." (Undoubtedly, some guests found the whiskey more invigorating than the water.) Bristol Spring was another Pennsylvania spa that profited from endorsements by Philadelphia physicians, but for many years the state's most popular spa was Yellow Springs in Chester County. In the summer, up to 300 people per day frequented this resort, which boasted enclosed baths, pump rooms, shady walkways, and rustic scenery.[16]

While many Americans believed in the benefits of the Pennsylvania waters, others thought that the waters at Saratoga and Ballstown in upstate New York were even more potent. According to tradition, British Major-General William Johnson was the first white man to visit Saratoga Springs, having been directed there by Indians. Later, a prominent Schenectady physician inspected these waters and declared that they offered medicinal benefits. Samuel Latham Mitchill performed experiments on Saratoga water and published his findings in *The American Museum* in 1788. General George Washington, while waiting for the peace treaty to be concluded at the end of the Revolutionary War, visited Saratoga Springs and was favorably impressed.[17]

In 1793, Valentine Seaman, who had studied at the University of Pennsylvania, published *Dissertation on the Mineral Waters of Sara-*

toga . . . also a Method of Making an Artificial Mineral Water Resembling That of Saratoga. Two years later, Peter Vandervoort published *A Treatise, on the Analysis of Ballston Mineral Spring Water.* The 1805 edition of *The American Universal Geography* by Jedidiah Morse did much to popularize Saratoga Springs, describing the waters as "brisk and sparkling like champagne. In drinking they strike the nose and palate like bottled cider, and slightly affect the head of some people, by their inebriating quality."[18]

Bottlenecks and Goosenecks

While other American scholars were content to publish scientific treatises on mineral water, one impoverished professor saw a business opportunity. Benjamin Silliman, a struggling young chemistry professor at Yale, believed in the therapeutic value of mineral waters because he had gone to Saratoga to recover from a bout of depression. After recuperating, he wanted to get married and start a family but couldn't afford to do so on his teaching salary. As an undergraduate, Silliman had been taught that the purpose of an education was to benefit mankind. By synthesizing mineral waters, he saw an opportunity to benefit both himself, financially, and mankind, by providing healing waters for people who couldn't travel to a spa.[19]

In 1806, Silliman purchased a Nooth apparatus for impregnating water with gas, at a cost of $25. In a matter of only weeks, he created a market for artificial mineral water in New Haven by bottling it and selling it at a local apothecary. Heartened by this success, he decided to undertake large-scale production and to ship some of his output to other cities. Since small quantities of British bottled waters were already being imported into the United States, there was a precedent for his scheme.[20]

In order to expand his business, Silliman needed a larger apparatus as well as a dependable source of bottles. Acquiring a new apparatus proved to be a simple task, since Silliman had the expertise needed to design one and had no trouble locating the necessary materials. However, finding the proper bottles proved to be a formidable challenge. Silliman ordered batches of bottles from three local potteries, and all leaked. He concluded that, even though the manufacture of suitable bottles required a low level of expertise, the technology simply was not available in Connecticut.[21]

In a letter to a friend, Silliman complained, "I cannot procure any glass bottles which will not burst, nor any stone ones which are impervious to the fixed air." Meanwhile, the demand for his product was growing steadily. "Bottles only are wanting to make this a great business," he lamented. Until he could find a satisfactory source of new bottles, he decided to buy used British bottles and recycle them. However, this would slow down his expansion plans since used bottles were scarce and became even more so after Congress passed a law prohibiting the importation of any commodity in glass bottles.[22]

Because Silliman's finances were strained and he needed capital for expansion, he entered into a partnership with three friends—Yale mathematics professor Jeremiah Day, attorney Stephen Twining, and New York apothecary Noyes Darling. Although it is uncertain exactly when this partnership was initiated, it was formalized, or perhaps renegotiated, in a contract signed in March 1809. At any rate, Twining was already involved in April 1807 when he went to New York to find a reliable source of bottles but was ultimately unsuccessful. Since this was a major obstacle to Silliman's expansion plans, the chemistry professor focused on writing a book and lecturing at Yale.[23]

While Silliman concentrated on his academic pursuits, he did not entirely give up his dream of making a fortune. He produced small quantities of mineral water with his new apparatus and sold it in used bottles whenever he could obtain them. Although he could not secure enough bottles to expand rapidly, he nevertheless hoped to increase his business gradually. Accordingly, he began to advertise in local periodicals, including *Connecticut Journal*, where he boasted that his artificial mineral waters were better than the real thing because chemistry allowed him to omit harmful or useless ingredients and add beneficial ones.[24]

Although Silliman was confident that his knowledge of chemistry would allow him to replicate any type of natural mineral water, he initially produced only two—soda water and Ballston water. The latter was difficult to make because it contained iron in solution with carbonic acid. If the proportions were not correct, the iron formed a red oxide and the water became rust-colored. Silliman promoted soda water, which had a pleasant taste and did not cause nausea, as a remedy for stomach acidity and indigestion and as a palliative "in cases of calculous concretions." He chose to make Ballston water because Ballston Spa, New York, was an expensive resort for the wealthy and he wanted to democratize the Ballston cure by making it available to the masses. Once again, he was trying to combine money-making with altruism in order to benefit both himself and humanity.[25]

When demand for Silliman's waters expanded, he and his partners decided to hire a man to run the apparatus full-time. Soon their new employee was filling up to 430 bottles of water per week. Next, the partners decided to open a shop near a popular tavern in New Haven, where the water would be drawn from fountains and sold to patrons in glasses.[26] This plan, which was probably prompted by the shortage of bottles, foreshadowed the future development of the American soda fountain. Unlike Britain, where most mineral water was sold in bottles, the American bottled drink industry would expand slowly and for many years Americans would buy their soft drinks at fountains.

Despite Silliman's high hopes, the New Haven fountain shop stubbornly refused to turn a profit, taking in only $200 in six months. Silliman told his family that the mineral-water business was breaking even, but Day wrote his brother that the New Haven operation had lost $800. Whatever the partnership's financial status, Silliman and the others decided to open two fountains in New York City because they had heard rumors that a Philadelphia operation similar to theirs was eyeing the New York market and they wanted to get a head start. In the spring of 1809 they chose two New York sites: the City Hotel, where Darling would open a pump room with fountains, and the Tontine Coffeehouse, where the proprietor would operate the fountains as a sideline to his other business. The financial stakes were high because they had to spend nearly $1,000 for new equipment and rent was expensive at the City Hotel.[27]

First, Darling installed the fountains at the Tontine, which was one of the city's busiest establishments, located at the corner of Wall and Water streets. The Tontine was named for a famous Italian banker, which was appropriate since the building housed the New York stock exchange and business offices as well as a dining room, tea room, and coffeehouse. The Tontine, which had been financed by the sale of subscriptions at $200 per share, was resplendent with crystal chandeliers, mahogany furniture, a public bath, and water closets. When the coffeehouse's fountains were in place, Darling began preparations at the hotel. He wrote his New Haven partners that their fears about competition had been valid. An Irishman named George Usher was already selling artificial mineral waters in New York City. In addition, Joseph Hawkins, who had experience with soda water in Philadelphia, intended to open a shop. Despite the competition, Darling embarked on his new job with a great deal of optimism.[28]

At the Tontine Coffeehouse, the apparatus was placed in the cellar and, via a manual forcing pump, the water was saturated with CO_2. The resulting pressure raised it through block-tin tubes to the bar upstairs. For decorative purposes, the tubes were encased in mahogany pillars. On top of each pillar sat a gilt urn, labeled with the name of the water it dispensed—soda, Ballston, or seltzer. These urns were placed at one-foot intervals, with the middle one slightly elevated above the others. The Tontine's clientele was primarily merchants, traders, and ship owners who discussed business while they ate and drank. On opening day, the coffeehouse proprietor was disappointed by the slow sales of mineral water but attributed it to bad weather. After a few days, it became apparent that his customers preferred the waters as mixers, and he printed "recommended to be used with mineral waters" on some bottles of wine. Nevertheless, sales remained sluggish.[29]

The Tontine business received a small boost when the well-known and highly respected Dr. Samuel Latham Mitchill, editor of the *Medical Repository*, visited the coffeehouse and expressed his satisfaction with the mineral waters. Silliman was delighted when he heard that Mitchill had called the fountains "a public benefit" and had suggested that New Yorkers drink the waters to prevent yellow fever.[30]

Although the medical endorsement was encouraging, Silliman's New York venture had stiff competition. Usher's rival fountains were situated so that patrons could utilize a nearby "park for taking the necessary exercise, in the intervals of drinking the waters," according to an advertisement. In addition, Usher supplied free newspapers and novels for his patrons to read while they sipped their water in his "elegant and fashionable lounge for ladies and gentlemen." Silliman preferred to serve men only at his fountains but reluctantly agreed to accommodate women in order to compete. Accordingly, his City Hotel shop was advertised as a "genteel room . . . fitted up, for the reception of Ladies, and private parties."[31]

Because Silliman saw mineral waters as medicine, he failed to understand the social nature of the business. While Usher promoted his shop as a fashionable place for socializing, Silliman's advertisements emphasized that his waters were formulated by "correct chemical science." Fortunately, Darling understood more about marketing than his partner did. When designing the fountains for the City Hotel, Darling insisted that mahogany pillars would not be ornate enough and decided to add the gilt urns. He wrote Silliman that "something more ornamental, something that will totally eclipse" Usher's shop was necessary. Darling was more in tune with the faddish nature of the business and wanted to cater to the whims of fashionable New Yorkers. "Style, I find, has many devout worshippers," he wrote to Silliman.[32]

When the New York fountains opened, a controversy arose that would plague soda fountain owners for the next century: should they be open on Sunday? Darling and Silliman were on opposite sides of this question. In order to compete with Usher, who did a brisk business on Sunday, Darling wanted to operate on the Sabbath, but Silliman was adamant that the fountains be closed. Darling argued that it would be morally and ethically acceptable to operate on Sunday since the waters were medicinal. But Silliman was not persuaded and Darling agreed to close on the Sabbath, writing his partner that he hoped "in our endeavor to be righteous, we may not become righteous overmuch."[33]

Despite Silliman's faith in chemistry, Usher's waters enjoyed a better reputation with the public because they were very cold and bubbly. So, Silliman decided that his fountains must serve colder water. In order to produce a high level of effervescence, low temperatures were necessary. But ice, which was harvested from ponds and lakes in the winter and stored for use during hot weather, was a very expensive commodity in New York City and Silliman was operating on a shoestring. He suggested that the water be poured over ice in tumblers, but Darling warned that this would be disastrous because much of the city's ice supply came from stagnant ponds and New Yorkers were loathe to consume this ice in drinks. Therefore, Silliman had no choice but to close the Tontine fountains temporarily and install large tubs for ice, to chill the water before it was pumped up to the fountains.[34]

It was surprising that consumers preferred chilled soda water, because there was a general distrust of cold drinks. Doctors often warned patients not to drink cold water, and local governments routinely prohibited the consumption of cold foods and beverages during epidemics. An oft-recited bit of doggerel summed up the general fear of iced water:

> Full many a man, both young and old,
> Has gone to his sarcophagus,
> By pouring water, icy cold,
> Down his hot esophagus.

As late as 1814, one of the stated objectives of the Humane Society of Wilmington, Delaware, was to aid those "recovering from apparent death" caused by drinking cold water. The society published guidelines to prevent fatalities from consuming frigid H_2O, and many Delawareans faithfully imbibed hot rum to avoid the dreadful consequences of cold water. Some people poured cold water over their wrists before drinking chilled beverages, presumably to cool off their bodies and avoid shock when they swallowed the liquid. Mineral water may have escaped this cold-water phobia because it was purported to have medicinal benefits. Whatever the reason, consumers wanted chilled soda water, and Silliman had to cater to the market.[35]

In addition to solving the problem of keeping his waters cold, Silliman had to cope with another technical difficulty in manufacturing Ballston water. Because the wooden storage casks could not be made perfectly airtight, the water began to turn rusty after two or three days, as the iron oxidized. Then it became as dark as ink and lost all its bubbles.

Silliman told Darling to explore the possibility of manufacturing porcelain storage jugs, but once again American technology was not up to the job because extremely high temperatures were needed to achieve a glaze impervious to the pressurized waters and no kiln in New York was capable of generating enough heat.[36]

Unfortunately, this was not the end of Silliman's technical troubles. Uniformity of product was another challenge. Since the pressure was difficult to regulate, the waters from his fountains sometimes boasted a visible mist of tiny bubbles leaping from the surface but at other times hardly foamed at all. This was not surprising considering the primitive, temperamental equipment being used. In one letter to Silliman, Darling gave a long list of faulty components, including defective pump pistons and leaky stopcocks, that made every day a challenge.[37]

As if Silliman did not have enough to worry about, his rival Hawkins had been issued a patent for "imitating natural mineral water" and had decided to sue his competitors for patent infringement. Hawkins' lawsuit ultimately failed because Silliman had actually been making mineral water in New Haven for several months before Hawkins had submitted his application to the patent office. Nevertheless, it was one more vexation for the beleaguered chemistry professor. Perhaps even more frustrating to Silliman were Hawkins' advertisements stating that he would fill orders for bottled water. Apparently, Hawkins had found a source of suitable bottles. Meanwhile, all Silliman's attempts to procure a steady supply of bottles failed, and one effort even resulted in another lawsuit, filed by a potter whose wares had proved to be unsatisfactory. Although Silliman won in court, this was yet another hassle and another expense.[38]

Despite all his problems, Silliman's faith in his venture was apparently unshaken because he decided that the time was finally right for taking a wife. On September 17, 1809, he married Harriet Trumbull, the daughter of Connecticut's governor, and left for a honeymoon in Newport, Rhode Island. But even his newlywed bliss was interrupted by reports of business problems in New York. Suddenly, soda water was no longer exempt from the public's fear of cold beverages. Darling wrote that the death of a midshipman had been attributed to drinking chilled soda water and this was hurting sales since sailors had been among their best customers. Rumors about the dangers of artificial mineral waters were circulating around the city, and the outlook was grim.[39]

While Darling awaited instructions from Silliman, Usher reacted decisively, sensing that drastic measures were necessary to reassure the public. He began by replacing his wooden casks with copper ones, which yielded a more attractive, bubblier product because they were airtight, easy to chill, and could withstand high pressures. Usher's quick action restored public confidence in his artificial waters, especially after a prominent physician stated that copper, taken in small quantities, was an excellent tonic. Usher's share of the market increased, while Silliman and Darling watched theirs plummet. Even Usher's sudden death did not significantly change the situation because his widow took over the business. In October 1809, Darling reported to Silliman that they did not have enough money to pay the rent for November. Twining, who had been largely a silent partner, went to New York City to check on the situation and immediately recommended that they close the fountains.[40]

The failure in New York ruined Darling financially, and he was never able to recover from his losses. In desperation, he became involved in unethical business deals and risky speculation. After losing at least $40,000 of borrowed money, he wrote a letter hinting that he had decided to kill himself because he was "a ruined man." It was widely assumed that he had committed suicide, but he later surfaced in Pittsburgh, reportedly on his way South.[41]

Meanwhile, Silliman's partnership sold some of its equipment to Hawkins, who took over the City Hotel site and erected an elaborate Italian marble fountain where three types of water poured out of the mouth of an eagle. Silliman, still optimistic despite the dismal failure in New York City, wanted to open a fountain in Baltimore. He convinced his remaining partners to hire a New Haven man, Mr. Eld, who moved to Baltimore and opened a fountain under his own name. Only weeks after opening, this new venture was in serious trouble. Since Silliman could not leave New Haven at the time, Day was chosen to travel to Maryland to salvage the business.[42]

When Day arrived in Baltimore, he found that Eld was seriously ill and that the fountains were not operating properly due to broken parts. Even when Eld's equipment was working properly, which was rare, his water compared poorly with the competition's, which was made in copper casks. Day learned that three other establishments were making mineral waters in the city and that British bottled waters were also sold there. One of the competing establishments was owned by Hawkins and his brother, who had already brought suit against Eld for patent infringement and had the hapless man arrested.[43]

Day spent much of his time trying to hire competent workmen to repair Eld's equipment. Since the wooden casks were rotting, finding a cooper who could produce airtight casks was a top priority. After unsatisfactory dealings with several coopers, Day wrote Silliman a gloomy letter, indicating that he had lost all faith in the soda-water venture. In explaining the appeal of a competitor's product, he wrote, "I doubt whether his water has much medicinal quality, but it is calculated to be popular with those who drink mainly for pleasure." Day returned to Yale, leaving Eld with no hope of success.[44]

The Baltimore debacle marked the end of Silliman's efforts to produce mineral waters on a large scale, but he kept an apparatus in the basement of his home and continued to make soda water for his family and friends.[45]

Although Silliman played a very important role in the early attempts to commercialize mineral waters, Hawkins was at least as important. In 1808, Philadelphia's *Register of the Arts* identified Hawkins as the man who had introduced artificial mineral waters to the City of Brotherly Love. He was also a pioneer in the soda water business in Baltimore and New York City. Hawkins, who had formerly served as secretary to the American ambassador in Paris, made artificial waters in Philadelphia as early as 1807, using machinery of his own invention. A published description of Hawkins' first pump room stated that the mineral water was manufactured in the cellar, collected in a reservoir, and forced upstairs through metal tubes encased in wooden columns. Water was drawn by turning a stopcock at the top of the column.[46]

With Abraham H. Cohen, Hawkins first established Cohen & Hawkins on Chestnut Street in Philadelphia. In 1807, newspaper ads stated that prominent physicians, including Benjamin Rush and John Syng Dorsey, recommended Cohen & Hawkins' soda water. But the Cohen-Hawkins partnership lasted only about two years because Cohen decided to open his own mineral water business on South Second Street. Hawkins found another partner and opened as Shaw & Hawkins at a different Chestnut Street location, selling artificial seltzer, soda, Pyrmont, and Ballston waters at six cents per glass. A thrifty customer could buy a fountain subscription, entitling him to one glass daily, for $1.50 per month or $4 per quarter.[47]

In 1812, *The Emporium of Arts and Sciences* stated that the use of artificial mineral waters was "very general" in America's large cities, "both as medicine and luxury" and that the residents of rural areas were "very desirous of having a method of preparing them." Therefore, the *Emporium* published a blueprint for an apparatus similar to Nooth's but smaller, sturdier, and cheaper—one that could be used by soda-water entrepreneurs in small towns. Two years later, the same periodical gave details of an apparatus developed by Robert Patterson and James Cloud. Although the prototype of this apparatus had been successfully demonstrated at the United States Mint, attempts to duplicate it had not worked. So the periodical printed improvements to it suggested by James Cutbrush, Apothecary General of the U.S. Army, and an associate.[48]

In 1814 in *The American Artist's Manual,* Cutbush detailed the composition of various mineral waters and described machinery for making artificial waters. Chemists "have succeeded so well in making accurate analyses of mineral waters, and consequently in re-composing them, that it has given birth to a new art, of no small importance to mankind, being employed as a remedy in a considerable number of diseases," he wrote.[49]

Adlard Welby, an Englishman who visited the United States in 1819, reported that artificial mineral waters, especially soda, were popular in Philadelphia during the summer. These soda waters were sometimes flavored with syrups to improve their taste. According to Welby's journal, every American who could afford it drank a glass of soda water each morning. "Many houses are open for the sale of it, and some of them are fitted up with Parisian elegance," he wrote. Welby's journal is especially interesting because it proves that flavored soda water was available only a decade after the first fountains opened.[50]

It is unclear exactly when soda water became a standard feature in drugstores, but apothecaries were the logical retail outlet because of its purported medical benefits. Pharmacist John Hart reportedly began selling artificial mineral waters at his Philadelphia drugstore prior to 1810, at the suggestion of Dr. Philip Syng Physick. George Glentworth, who opened a drugstore in Philadelphia in 1812, worked with Cutbush on designing a soda water apparatus and may have used it in his store. Another Philadelphia drugstore, Smith and Hodgson's, founded in 1828, sold soda water flavored with fruit syrups.[51]

Although the early history of American pharmacy is sketchy, it is obvious that the number of drugstores increased as the population expanded. It is unknown what percentage of apothecaries sold mineral waters, but dispensing them became a significant moneymaker for many druggists. The first fountains were relatively simple, with the carbonating equipment in the cellar or underneath the counter. In order to generate soda water, two ingredients were essential: an acid and a carbonate. Trial and error proved that sulfuric acid was superior to any other for making soda water. Early manufacturers experimented with various materials for the carbonate, including pulverized marble, whiting (powdered calcium carbonate), and bicarbonate of soda; ground marble eventually emerged as the preferred material.[52]

In 1814, Cutbush wrote, "Soda water is nothing more than four or more grains of soda, contained in a pint or more of water, and saturated with carbonic acid." But, at some point, soda was deleted from the recipe. In 1831, Dr. John Bell noted that the liquid sold at apothecaries under the name of soda water had "a wrong appellation" because it contained no soda. Later, the writer of a technical manual agreed, saying soda water was an "accidental and inappropriate name." He predicted that the word "carbonade" would "be universally adopted in a few years." Aerated water, marble water, and carbonic acid water were also promoted as more precise terms, but the public was accustomed to soda water and didn't care that it was a misnomer.[53]

In the early decades of the nineteenth century, soda water was dispensed through columns, urns, and gooseneck spigots. From the description of Hawkins' Philadelphia pump room, it appears that his first fountains were simply metal tubes encased in wooden columns. Silliman's fountains in the Tontine Coffeehouse were somewhat more elegant because they were wood columns topped with metal urns. Decorative marble columns gradually replaced the wood columns, and urns continued to be used in some locations until the late nineteenth century, but the gooseneck was the most common dispenser in the early years.[54]

Essentially, the gooseneck fountain was a vertical metal pipe that protruded above a counter and was attached to a tank of soda water hidden underneath the counter or in the basement. Cheaper models were made of lacquered tin, but bronze and silverplated versions were also available. Because the pipe was bent in a semicircular shape, it resembled a goose's neck. At first, these pipes were plain, unadorned, utilitarian fixtures with no decorative value. But someone soon decided to make the gooseneck more attractive by adding eyes and a beak, to make it look more like its namesake, with the soda water pouring out of its bill. These first decorative efforts evolved into more elaborate models that assumed the shape of a swan, complete with ruffled feathers. This was a logical evolution since swans were associated with water and were a popular motif on the Empire-style furnishings in vogue in the early 1800s.[55]

Manufacturers continued to sell goosenecks for many decades, even though more elaborate fountains became the norm in big cities. Goosenecks were usually purchased by small-town merchants who could not afford the latest fad in soda fountain decor. In addition to having limited design possibilities, goosenecks had technical restrictions. A gooseneck could dispense only one type of water, requiring a druggist to install more than one if he wanted to sell a variety of mineral waters. Another problem was the difficulty in regulating the water pressure. When the spigot was opened, the water gushed out, spraying the dispenser and anyone else who happened to be nearby. To prevent messes, clerks learned to place a narrow-necked bottle tightly against the faucet, fill it, and then pour the water into a tumbler.[56]

A typical urn fountain had a footed pedestal, a classic vase shape, and a tightly fitted, removable lid. It had an advantage over the gooseneck because two or three faucets could be attached to the vase portion. As soda fountain design became more fanciful, the urn's spigots were sometimes disguised as elephant's trunks, fish, or other animals. Like a gooseneck, an urn was merely a dispensing apparatus, connected to the carbonating equipment underneath the counter or in the cellar, but the urn could be packed with ice, keeping the soda water frigid as it passed through the pipe to the spigot. Urn fountains were usually made of bronze or silver-plated metal, but cheap iron models, painted to resemble marble or a costlier metal, were also available. Often the urns were decorated with moldings and topped with figurines.[57]

Marble column fountains, which were less popular than urns and goosenecks, resembled architectural pillars or elongated fire hydrants. The typical marble column fountain had two spigots and a fitted, removable lid. In some marble-column fountains, the soda water traveled through block-tin coils surrounded by ice, keeping the water very cold and effervescent. Marble had an advantage over metal because it retained cold and the ice did not melt as quickly.[58]

The soda fountain industry remained relatively primitive during its first two decades, but the stage was set for advancements. Although the first experiments with artificial mineral waters had occurred in Europe, Americans were taking mineral-water manufacturing in a new direction. In the newly independent United States, the soda water industry was forging ahead on an independent path. Bottled waters were popular in Britain, but Americans were drinking carbonated water in pump rooms, drugstores, and coffeehouses. Silliman and his competitors were not only replicating the waters from fashionable spas, they were imitating spas by inviting customers to socialize while they sipped. The transformation of soda fountains from merely utilitarian, functional objects to decorative objects had also begun. The first attempts to make fountains more attractive by encasing the working parts in columns or urns were only a hint of the ornate forms to come. Soon, inventive entrepreneurs would appear onstage to take advantage of the fountain's tremendous potential and create an industry as vibrant as the bubbly waters.

FROM TREATMENT TO TREAT

When purveyors of mineral water began to flavor it, the transformation from a drug to a treat was under way. Gradually, consumers stopped buying soda water to cure their ills and started buying it just because it tasted good. In 1831 soda water was deleted from the *U.S. Pharmacopeia*—an indication of both its limited medical benefits and its changing role in society. The transformation from drug to treat was accompanied by changes in both fountain design and technology. In a relatively short time, the soda fountain mutated from the unpretentious, utilitarian gooseneck into a showy marble monument befitting its status as a fashionable social center. During the same period, advances in technology produced better drinks and more efficient service. By the mid-nineteenth century, consumers were drinking soda water purely for pleasure and were reveling in the sensory delights of ornate, gaudy soda fountains. These marble fountains changed the ambiance of the entire drugstore, and many pharmacists updated their decor by removing traditional drugstore curiosities, like ugly snakes or organs preserved in tall bottles of alcohol.

The Major Manufacturers

Two firms that would become major soda fountain manufacturers entered the business in the early 1830s. John Matthews, an apprentice to the English inventor Joseph Bramah, immigrated to New York City and set up a shop on Gold Street in 1832. That same year, John Lippincott, who manufactured copper machinery in Philadelphia, decided to design and market his own apparatus for carbonating water.[1]

Matthews, who had learned to make carbonic acid gas from Bramah, was soon manufacturing carbonating machinery, urn fountains, and soda water, which he wholesaled and retailed in New York City. His carbonating equipment was simple: a cast-iron box, lined with lead, where carbonic acid gas was generated by the action of sulfuric acid on marble dust or marble chips. He purified the gas by forcing it through a water-filled rectifying chamber, and then it passed into a tank partially filled with cool water. To saturate the water with gas, he rhythmically rocked the tank, which was suspended on trunnions in a cast-iron frame.[2]

Bramah had used whiting (powdered calcium carbonate) and chalk to make carbonic acid gas, but Matthews found that marble chips were cheap and easy to procure in New York. At one point, the enterprising entrepreneur arranged to buy all the marble scrap from the construction of St. Patrick's Cathedral. Matthews used some of this scrap himself and sold the remainder for $2 per barrel. It has been estimated that these chips produced 25 million gallons of soda water before the supply was exhausted. In addition to procuring marble scrap from buildings, Matthews bought leftover marble from sculptors and tombstone cutters.[3]

Because pressure is always a hazard in gas manufacture and Matthews had no accurate way of measuring it, noisy explosions were common in the beginning. After some trial and error, he hit upon an effective but unusual method of gauging the pressure. One of his first employees was Ben Austin (sometimes spelled "Austen"), a freedman from North Carolina. As a plantation slave, Austin had proved to be very intelligent, hard-working, trustworthy, and religious. As a result, he had been promoted to house slave and had been given special responsibilities and privileges. When his master died, the widow freed Old Ben, as he was generally called, and sent him to New York because she knew that he would have more opportunities in the North. Soon after arriving in the city, Old Ben married a freedwoman and went to work for Matthews. One of his duties was acting as a pressure gauge by holding his thumb over the pressure cock. When the pressure became so great that it blew Old Ben's thumb away, Matthews declared that the water was fully charged.[4]

Old Ben and his thumb became a legend in the soda water industry. He also became a familiar face to many New Yorkers because he pushed a portable fountain around the city, selling soda water. This fountain was suspended on trunnions attached to the frame of a two-wheeled pushcart. By rocking the fountain back and forth on the trunnions, Old Ben saturated the water with carbonic acid gas. When he became too old to work on the streets, he was given duties in the shop where Matthews fabricated fountains. During the anti-war riots of 1863, when angry mobs roamed the streets of New York City, robbing and killing Negroes, Old Ben had a narrow escape. A mob chased him, but a friendly butcher came to his aid and smuggled him to a police station. Then he was hidden in one of Matthews' shipping crates and sent to Blackwell's Island until the chaos subsided.[5]

Another of Matthews' early employees was William Gee, an apprentice who quickly mastered the fundamentals of soda fountain technology and left to start his own business. Gee was a prolific inventor who created many devices that were widely used in the industry. His numerous patents included a draft tube, a nozzle, a syrup-dispensing device, a soda-water generator, a forcing pump, and a blow-off cock for generators. Because he was particularly concerned about the reaction between carbonic acid and the metals used in fountains, several of his inventions related to the materials and linings utilized in fountain components. He also invented the Monitor Crystal Spa, a central cylinder with syrup tanks and ice compartments surrounded by a revolving caster holding glass bottles of syrup. Gee manufactured his own fountains and also sold Matthews the right to use some of his inventions. When Gee retired, Matthews purchased his entire business.[6]

A few years after Matthews started his business, he bought out four rival firms, including one owned by Sophia Usher, the widow of soda-water pioneer George Usher. Another of these businesses belonged to the widow of Robert Boston, who had held three of the earliest soda fountain patents. Over the years, Matthews acquired other firms and expanded his factory until it was the largest in the industry, prompting a newspaper to call him "the Neptune of the trade" in 1868. At that time, his company employed 100 men, occupied a large building on First Avenue in New York City, and sold a comprehensive line, from syrups to large marble soda fountains. In 1874, the Matthews firm began to manufacture steel fountains, which were a vast improvement over the cast-iron and copper fountains then dominating the market. These new steel fountains were stronger and safer, reducing the likelihood of explosions, leaks, and metallic contamination.[7]

The Matthews firm prospered first under the founder and then under his descendants. When Matthews died in 1870, he was interred in Green-Wood Cemetery, one of the first garden cemeteries in the United States. In the early nineteenth century, church graveyards were often overcrowded, stinking quagmires jammed into small spaces. New York City's Board of Health called that city's graveyards "receptacles of putrefying matter and hot-beds of miasma" (the fetid vapors that somehow caused epidemics). Urban reformers envisioned beautifully landscaped, park-like cemeteries where mourners could visit their deceased loved ones without having to hold their noses.[8]

The cemetery reform movement, coupled with periodic yellow fever epidemics, convinced many New Yorkers that new graveyards should be started in sparsely populated areas. Therefore, when Henry E. Pierrepont laid out the street plan for the newly-incorporated city of Brooklyn, he reserved a tract of picturesque, hilly farmland overlooking the Gowanus Canal for Green-Wood Cemetery. Green-Wood's pastoral atmosphere was an appropriate setting for elaborate monuments like the one that marked Matthews' final resting place. Above a recumbent marble likeness of Matthews rose a 36-foot Gothic granite canopy and spire, richly carved with gargoyles, flora, fauna, Matthews' relatives, and bas-reliefs depicting milestones in his life. Not surprisingly, the imposing monument, which was designed and partially constructed in the Matthews factory, resembled an ornate Victorian soda fountain.[9]

John Matthews Jr., who at a young age began working in his father's shop, proved to be very inventive and played an important role in the industry's technical progress. He patented numerous devices, including a soda water cooler, a glass syrup tank, a solid-plunger syrup pump, a holder for tumblers, and a method for filling portable fountains. After the elder Matthews died, his two sons took over the firm, with John Jr. supervising the technical side while George managed the business side. In 1877, the firm held more than 100 patents, employed 300-plus workers, conducted 38 different trades in its factory, and had sold more than 20,000 fountains. When the second Matthews generation died, George's two sons inherited the business because John Jr. had remained a bachelor and had no children.[10]

Around the time that John Matthews had immigrated to New York City, John Lippincott decided to manufacture soda fountains in Philadelphia. Lippincott's first model was a marble column with two silver gooseneck draft arms. Only one of the goosenecks actually worked; the other was merely for symmetry. The working part of the fountain was beneath the counter, and the soda dispenser had to reach underneath to turn the gooseneck on or off. Despite this inconvenience, the model proved to be very reliable, and one of Lippincott's first fountains was in use for more than 60 years.[11]

John Lippincott's younger brother Charles joined the firm in 1865 and managed it for 26 years. Soon after taking over, Charles abandoned the column-style fountain and began manufacturing box-style marble fountains with multiple spigots for dispensing different flavors. He saw great potential for expanding the industry and helped to popularize soda by operating fountains at the 1876 Centennial Exhibition in Philadelphia and the 1893 World's Fair in Chicago. When Charles retired, he was succeeded by his sons, A. H. and F. Hazard Lippincott.[12]

In the early 1840s, Alvin D. Puffer and Andrew J. Morse entered the soda water business in Boston. Morse, who had an excellent reputation as a skilled coppersmith, manufactured vertical copper generators and portable copper tanks for holding and transporting soda water. Puffer, who had been trained in plumbing and machine work, was a mechanical genius who patented many innovative devices. He began by manufacturing bottling equipment and then added the Frigid Draft Apparatus soda fountain to his wares in 1844.[13]

During the Civil War, Puffer invented the Magic Draft Tube, which allowed water and several flavors of syrup to be drawn through the same nozzle. An ingenious valve connection between the Magic Draft Tube and a series of syrup tanks permitted different flavors to pour from the same nozzle, whereas previously a separate faucet had been required for each syrup. After the customer chose the flavor he wanted, the dispenser squirted the syrup in the glass and then turned the faucet to shut off the syrup and allow soda water from a reservoir to pour into the glass. As the soda water moved through the tube, it flushed the line clean of any remaining syrup.[14]

Puffer used his Magic Draft Tube in the octagonal apparatus he built for Hudnut's, which was one of the busiest soda fountains in New York City. Located on the corner of Broadway and Ann Street in the heart of Newspaper Row, Hudnut's was a favorite hang-out for journalists, who spread the word about its excellent soda water. In the wee hours of the morning, after the newspaper had gone to press, Hudnut's was filled with reporters and editors. It was also frequented by the city's financial and political leaders, including John Jacob Astor, Grover Cleveland, Ulysses S. Grant, John Kelly, Elihu Root, Joseph Choate, and assorted Vanderbilts, Goulds, and Van Rensselaers. Befitting Hudnut's location in the business district, the soda fountain was a male hang-out and its only female patrons were stenographers who worked in nearby buildings.[15]

The large thermometer attached to the front of the Hudnut building was as famous as the soda fountain inside. Along Newspaper Row, weather reporters consulted this thermometer three or four times each day and published the results in the next morning's paper. Thus, Hudnut's thermometer on Broadway became known all over the world and was generally considered more accurate than the weather bureau's official temperature readings.[16]

Hudnut's marble soda fountain worked so well that many drugstores wanted an identical one, making the octagonal style a steady seller for decades. Hudnut's apparatus dispensed eight syrups from each spigot, and the dispenser turned a dial above the spigot to choose the syrup he wanted. In the 1880s, when most fountain drinks cost only a dime, Hudnut's sold up to $400 worth of drinks per day. In the 1890s, Hudnut's became a chain and the original location was torn down to make room for a skyscraper. The Hudnut chain's new flagship, which was situated farther north on Broadway, attracted women as well as men. In fact, it became almost mandatory for fashionable couples strolling along Broadway to stop there for ice cream sodas. This new shop was furnished with a Low's art tile soda fountain, and in warm weather up to

7,000 drinks per day were sold. Not surprisingly, Alexander Hudnut retired a millionaire and lived out his sunset years in a villa in France.[17]

Hudnut's notoriety was an important factor in making Puffer a leader in the soda water business. Puffer's company moved to larger facilities at least three times and shipped soda fountains to Europe, India, and Africa as well as throughout the United States. Puffer's numerous patents included a revolving water gauge, a pressure regulator, and two cooling systems. Even after he turned the daily management of his company over to his three sons, he continued to contribute ideas and suggest technical improvements until he died at age 87, after running to catch a train.[18]

Gustavus D. Dows was a pivotal figure in the development of the soda fountain because he built an early marble box fountain—a landmark in both design and technology. In the late 1850s, Dows, who was the youngest of 21 children, was working as a clerk in a drugstore owned by an older brother in Lowell, Massachusetts. Like other clerks, he made shaved ice for drinks by scraping a chunk of ice across the blades of a plane. This was an awkward, tiring, and time-consuming operation that generally left the clerk with cold, cramped hands. Dows decided that there must be a better way and set out to find it.[19]

His solution was a rectangular marble box that housed an ice shaver, a compartment for ice, a soda water draught tube, a container for cream, and eight syrup tanks, each with its own spigot. The metal crank that operated the ice shaver protruded from one end of the box. When the clerk turned this crank, knife blades attached to a revolving cylinder scraped across the block of ice, shaving off slivers, which fell through a slot into a tumbler. For an ice cream soda, the clerk added two ounces of cream, measured precisely by a lever-and-stop device, from the can inside the box. Then syrup was added, followed by the soda water. Dows' ingenious arrangement produced a very cold, highly effervescent treat that was a big hit in his brother's drugstore.[20]

In addition to advancing the technology of soda fountains, Dows' marble box propelled the industry along the road toward the ornate fixtures that would dominate drugstores and confectionaries by the late nineteenth century. He encased the fountain's working parts in white marble purchased at a local tombstone cutter's yard, producing a handsome, eyecatching fixture. To enhance the visual impact, each silver-plated syrup spigot was decorated with an American eagle, wings spread, perched on a globe.[21]

Dows' fountain was so popular in Lowell that he decided to try his luck in nearby Boston. In 1860 he rented a building and opened a drugstore featuring his fountain, which he promoted as Dows' Ice Cream Soda Apparatus. Although several Boston businessmen warned him that he had chosen a bad location for his shop, his first season's sales far exceeded his expectations. The following year, he leased a building across the street from his drugstore and began to manufacture soda fountains. He was soon swamped with orders for his Italian marble Ice Cream Soda Apparatus, which sold for $225. In December 1861, he was issued a patent for his Combined Soda Apparatus and Ice Cutter.[22]

Among the first businessmen to buy a Dows fountain was Z. S. Sampson, who operated one of Boston's biggest drugstores. This enterprising druggist plastered Bean Town with signs declaring that anyone who did not drink a glass of Sampson's soda water "would miss one-half the pleasure of his life!" Sampson's promotional arsenal also included tokens, a tactic popular with many retailers. Tokens were metal coins or paper coupons good for one glass of soda at the store or stores named on the token. Some stores offered a discount if the customer bought tokens in bulk. They were a convenience for both the customer and the clerk, who did not have to make change.[23]

In Dows' advertising, Sampson endorsed the Ice Cream Soda Apparatus, declaring that his annual soda water sales had increased from $500 to $16,000 in only two years. Even though Dows' apparatus was selling briskly, he continued to look for ways to improve it. He invented a simple spoon-like lever that could be attached to the draught tube, which permitted the dispenser to choose a forceful stream of water or a wider stream with less pressure. This double-stream draught tube gave the dispenser more control and reduced the likelihood that the water would spurt out with too much force, drenching bystanders. Dows claimed that it also produced more effervescence and that soda water drawn from his apparatus retained its bubbles for a half-hour while normal soda water lost its fizz immediately.[24]

In 1867, Dows entrusted his drugstore and factory to the care of a relative while he traveled to France to operate a restaurant and a soda fountain at the Exposition Universelle in Paris. He planned to make the restaurant an American showcase by offering American cuisine served by the best waiters from some of the United States' most famous eateries. The restaurant, which he operated with a partner, was furnished exclusively with American-made products, from the piano to the cooking ranges. With two other partners, Dows set up an American soda fountain at the exposition. The American restaurant was a flop because Europeans considered American cuisine to be inferior, but the soda fountain proved to be very popular. In fact, the crowds of people waiting to be served at the fountain were so large that police were needed to keep them in line. Although Dows lost money on the restaurant, he was not disheartened because the soda fountain was so profitable.[25]

In a report to the United States Senate, the American commissioner for the Exposition Universelle stated that Dows' ice cream soda "was an American specialty, interesting to visitors and amply renumerative to the proprietors. It was popular with the mass of the people, and even kings and emperors often partook of the delicious draught." Dows was convinced that there was a large, untapped European market for soda fountains, and he was determined to develop it. In the ensuing years, he spent most of his time in Europe, establishing soda fountains in several cities. An American newspaper reported that Dows' fountain was "a decided hit" in London, where long lines of people queued up for a refreshing drink on hot days.[26]

In 1871, Dows returned to the United States to devote all his time and energy to his Boston businesses, which had declined during his absence. He soon discovered that more firms had begun manufacturing soda fountains, that the industry had become much more competitive, and that his rivals had lured away many of his steady customers. Nevertheless, he optimistically moved his factory into larger quarters. Only three years later, he again moved to a new facility, where he made and bottled ginger ale, in addition to fabricating soda fountains. Many consumers thought that his ginger ale was the best they had ever tasted, but his fountains were not selling. Slowly but surely, he was pushed to the wall financially and was compelled to sell his foreign interests in order to keep his Boston ventures afloat.[27]

The final phase of Dows' financial troubles began in 1875, when a gas explosion destroyed his drugstore. The contents of his store were insured for less than one-third of their actual value, but the insurance companies refused to pay even that small amount and he was forced to file a lawsuit. His lawyer, Gen. Benjamin F. Butler, eventually reached an out-of-court settlement with the insurers and, coincidentally, pushed one of them into bankruptcy by shaking public confidence in the company's management. But the legal struggle took its toll on Dows and he never completely recovered. When he passed away in 1886, the man who had expected to die a millionaire left little for his heirs.[28]

Shortly after Dows began manufacturing his Ice Cream Soda Apparatus, James W. Tufts decided to buy one for his drugstore in Medford, Massachusetts. Accordingly, he paid a visit to Dows' factory but was told that there would be a long wait due to a backlog of orders. Never one to let the grass grow under his feet, Tufts decided to build his own. Within a surprisingly short time, he had designed and fabricated a fountain that resembled Dows' marble box but had several unique features. Tufts called it "The Arctic" because it kept the soda water and syrups very cold. The syrup tanks were situated in the back of the box, surrounded by ice, and connected with the syrup faucets via tubes passing through the ice. Each faucet was decorated with a star and a liberty cap. Tufts probably chose this motif because he was an abolitionist and a liberty cap was traditionally given to a slave at manumission.[29]

Tufts' friends and business associates were so impressed with the Arctic that they urged him to apply for a patent and open a manufacturing plant. In 1863, he heeded their advice and rented a small facility in Boston. The following year, he moved to a larger building and opened an assembly plant where the workers fabricated the fountains from components produced elsewhere—an unusual arrangement at that time. This plant was not immediately profitable and commanded only a small portion of Tufts' attention because he was involved in other, more lucrative businesses. Nevertheless, he added several items to his soda fountain line and issued a trade catalog illustrated by Kilburn, Boston's leading wood-engraver. Sales improved, prompting Tufts to move his fountain operations to bigger quarters at the end of the Civil War.[30]

In 1869, Tufts took soda fountain architecture to the next plateau by adding a sloping roof to the marble box so that it resembled a small cottage. While earlier fountains had been built of white Italian marble, this one had a multi-colored facade of Tennessee, Vermont, and New York marbles. That same year, Tufts began to use block-tin syrup tanks, which were more durable than the ones customarily used. He also decided to expand his operations by opening a showroom in New York City. Later, Tufts moved his New York headquarters to a Park Place building, which subsequently collapsed during a busy workday, "producing the most frightful disaster of modern times," according to one magazine. Despite this setback, his business grew steadily in both Boston and New York. In 1892, he employed 50 salesmen, 65 clerks, and nearly 600 skilled laborers.[31]

Tufts died a multimillionaire in 1902, while staying at the Carolinas, a hotel he owned in the resort community of Pinehurst, North Carolina. Years earlier, Tufts had purchased 5000 acres of land there, reportedly at $1 per acre, and had been the moving force behind the development of Pinehurst as a popular vacation spot.[32]

In 1891, the four largest soda fountain manufacturers—James W. Tufts, A. D. Puffer & Sons, Charles Lippincott & Company, and the John Matthews Apparatus Company—formed an umbrella corporation called the American Soda Fountain Company. Hartt Manufacturing Company of Chicago, the Midwest's largest soda fountain firm, later joined this trust. The partners acted as a unit to dominate the industry and control prices, but each continued to produce and market fountains under its own company name. In 1892, the trust members posted equipment sales totaling more than $3 million.[33]

A handful of small manufacturers—including Otto Zweitusch of Milwaukee, Bennett & Gompper of New York City, the Robert M. Green Company of Philadelphia, and the Iron-clad Can Company of Brooklyn —continued to operate outside the trust. Cut-throat competition was the norm, and the trust's salesmen were not always ethical. But the smaller firms refused to be intimidated by their formidable competition and proudly advertised that they offered better products at lower prices. Litigation was one weapon the trust used against its smaller rivals, but Goliath lost two very important cases against David. In separate suits, the American Soda Fountain Company alleged patent infringement by Zweitusch and Green. In both cases, the defendants lost in the lower courts but won on appeal. After these two costly defeats, the trust's enthusiasm for litigation waned.[34]

Another minor fountain manufacturer was the Low Art Tile Company of Chelsea, Massachusetts, which made decorative tiles for architectural use. J. G. Low became the best-known American producer of art tiles after he was awarded the gold medal at the 1880 Crewe exhibition in the United Kingdom's famous pottery district. Several years later, Low decided that soda fountains could be a venue for him to showcase his artistic talents and increase his profits. Accordingly, he approached the proprietor of the drugstore in New York's posh Fifth Avenue Hotel and made his first sale, persuading the druggist to buy an ornate art tile fountain worthy of such a fashionable establishment.[35]

The facades of Low's fountains featured intricate bas-relief scenes, which were often allegorical or mythological, executed in colored tiles ranging from pale, creamy yellows and delicate grays to deep greens, browns, and blacks. One of his most elaborate fountains was built for the 1893 Chicago World's Fair at a cost of $10,000. On this fountain, the bas-relief was divided into a triptych, with the center panel depicting angels crushing fruits and filling "The Fountain of Thirst," which was surrounded by people and animals waiting to quench their thirst. One of the triptych's side panels was dedicated to "Water" and the other to "Air"—the basic elements of soda water. This massive fountain boasted seven draughts for soda, eight for ginger ale, and 48 for syrups. After the fair, it was moved to an ice cream parlor in Detroit, where 3,000 to 7,000 glasses a day were routinely drawn from it during the summer. On one scorcher, a record 14,000 glasses were filled.[36]

Although Low's art tile creations never seriously threatened the dominance of marble fountains, they found a market among posh drugstores and confectionaries looking for something different. In 1893, business was so brisk that Low's factory was running 18 hours a day and still couldn't fill all its orders. Both Tufts and Matthews imitated Low, to a limited extent, by incorporating art tiles into several of their fountain designs. A few years after the American Soda Fountain Company was formed, it bought Low's company.[37]

From Sea to Shining Sea

As the United States became more densely populated and new cities were established, the soda water habit spread from the Eastern seaboard to other regions. The scattered references to soda fountains in primary sources give a very incomplete record of the industry's geographical progress. Nevertheless, it is obvious that soda fountains remained largely a big-city phenomenon for several decades, even though some small towns boasted fountains—usually a plain gooseneck or urn since the volume of business would not support an expensive, showy apparatus.

Published records indicate that soda fountains were scattered throughout the South before the Civil War. In the 1830s New Orleans had at least one soda fountain, where a picayune would buy a glass of mead or flavored soda water. Just before the Civil War, an Alabama store advertised that it had installed a soda fountain and arranged for a steady supply of ice. The ad proclaimed, "The syrups will be of the richest and most choice variety, consisting of rose, lemon, pineapple and strawberry, vanilla, sarasparilla, sassafras, ginger, almond, and peach." Georgia humorist William Tappan Thompson (writing under the pseudonym Joseph Jones) reported that he had heard of soda water but had never tasted it until he visited Baltimore in 1845. He wrote that it tasted like "a pint of frozen soapsuds" and that his "tongue felt like it was full of needles." He decided that he preferred chewing tobacco.[38]

Early sources rarely mention soda fountains in the Midwest, but there are a few clues about the first fountains in that region. The first soda fountain in Wisconsin probably belonged to Dr. Edward Johnson, who installed one in his drugstore in Watertown circa 1841. Johnson had seen a soda fountain back East but didn't have enough money to purchase one and have it shipped all the way to Wisconsin. So he decided to design and build his own. At first, Johnson's clientele didn't like soda water, but it gradually caught on. Despite Johnson's enthusiasm, it was several decades before soda fountains were commonplace in Wisconsin.[39]

At least two Missouri towns—St. Louis and Palmyra—had soda fountains in 1850. In St. Louis, the first fountains were silver urns with one or two spigots. The first marble apparatus in St. Louis was a Bigelow fountain purchased by Enno Sander for his drugstore in the mid-1850s. Sander found that he could sell $10 worth of soda water on a warm day. One of Sander's major competitors, M. W. Alexander, began serving soda water from a silver urn with one faucet and then purchased a box-shaped marble fountain before the Civil War. This fountain attracted a brisk business, often producing $40 worth of soda water sales in one day. In 1860, S. S. Lippincott was making up to $200 per day from the five silver urns in his St. Louis drugstore.[40]

In 1848, the first soda fountain opened in Chicago, which had a population of slightly more than 20,000 people. A local druggist, Josiah H. Reed, had seen a fountain in the East and thought that he could improve his profits by selling soda water. Reed, who also laid the city's first stone sidewalk, ordered the generating equipment from New York City. The fountain's other components were made to order in Chicago, and the total cost was $600. Reed's soda water was dispensed via a gooseneck spigot protruding from a plain marble box sitting on the counter. The working components and the ice were stashed under this counter. In order to keep all the ingredients as cold as possible, the syrups were stored in cut-glass decanters nestled in chipped ice.[41]

Many Chicagoans came to marvel at Reed's marble box that dispensed frigid, fizzy water. According to a magazine, "For many days it proved a wonder and was a shrine at which many worshipped." Reed's soda water quickly became such a big seller that one fountain could not satisfy the demand. So he decided to install a second apparatus for women only, because some of the more genteel ladies were intimidated by the crowds. This new fountain was strictly reserved for the fair sex, and a man was never served there unless he was accompanied by a woman.[42]

When the temperature soared in the middle of summer, Reed's fountains often dispensed 2,000 glasses of soda water per day, plain or flavored with sarsaparilla, lemon, vanilla, strawberry, or raspberry. Reed's store was a popular rendezvous, especially on sultry evenings when Chicagoans wanted to socialize and enjoy a cool, refreshing drink. At this early stage of the Windy City's development, there was only one public cab, and a magazine quoted one of Reed's employees as saying "a ride in that vehicle, with a drink of soda after was considered quite an event in one's life."[43]

Naturally, Reed's success prompted several other Chicago businesses to purchase soda fountains. One of the first was opened by John Wright, who installed an elegant apparatus in the Chicago Opera House. In the mid-1850s Reed's soda water business was so profitable that he decided to buy two ornate marble fountains manufactured in Boston. The new men's fountain, which was the larger, had eight syrup spigots. Reed generated his own gas, using marble dust and sulphuric acid, and charged his own water. He sold his soda water for a nickel per glass until the Civil War forced him to raise the price to a dime, due to the high cost of the sugar in the syrups. During the war years, business declined and Reed's soda water sales typically totaled less than $40 per day.[44]

Only about 15 soda fountains were open in Chicago during the Civil War, and most of them were small units built by Dows. After the war, the number of fountains multiplied rapidly as Matthews, Tufts, Puffer, and Lippincott targeted the market and competed ferociously for customers. After the South's surrender, Tufts, who had previously sold no equipment in Chicago, quickly sold five large fountains, but this was only the beginning. Five years later, his Chicago business was so brisk that he established a showroom in the Windy City.[45]

At the time of the famous Chicago fire, at least 200 fountains were operating in the city, but only a few survived the inferno. Among the first construction after the disaster was a building housing Buck and Raymer's Pharmacy, where a soda fountain was soon installed. Although soda water sales were sluggish, this store gradually rebuilt its business. However, most druggists were hesitant to invest large sums of money in nonessentials, and soda fountain sales remained stagnant for a decade. Then the soda water business enjoyed a revival as the city's economic climate improved. By 1896, Chicago claimed to have more soda fountains than any other city.[46]

Because frontier towns had few amenities, it is surprising to learn that some had soda fountains at an early date. Mary Burrell, who traveled from Iowa to California in 1854, was happy to discover a store selling ice cream and soda water in Salt Lake City, Utah. In her diary, she noted that this was "quite a rarity" on the frontier. In 1858, Rio Grande City, Texas, boasted a billiard parlor, an eating saloon, a bakery, and a pharmacy "with a most pretentious soda water fountain," according to a settler's account. That same year, the *Nebraska Advertiser* informed its readers that the drugstore in Brownville, a small riverfront town, had just purchased a soda fountain from back East. Other Western river towns also advertised soda fountains, shipped in via riverboats, before the Civil War disrupted commerce.[47]

In his autobiography, newspaperman William Allen White recalled that during his childhood in the 1870s his father had owned a drugstore in El Dorado, Kansas. At the soda fountain, customers could order soda water flavored with lemon, strawberry, banana, raspberry, or "don't care," a mixture of leftovers from several bottles poured into one. This small-town drugstore proved to be so profitable that White's father was able to trade it for a good farm within a few years.[48]

It is uncertain when soda fountains arrived on the West Coast, but San Francisco had several ice cream saloons in the 1850s. Candy-maker

H. L. Winn is credited with opening the first such business in San Francisco, soon after he arrived in 1849. Winn's Fountain Head served ice cream, strawberries, oysters, ginger pop, lemon soda, root beer, and sarsaparilla "for lovers with their sweethearts and husbands with their better-halves," according to a newspaper ad. Winn's first ice cream saloon was so successful that he opened a second and soon had imitators. Los Angeles' first city and county directory, published in 1872, included an ad for the Los Angeles Soda Works, which manufactured soda water and sold syrups and other fountain necessities. Druggist Charles H. Woodard brought the first soda fountain to Portland, Oregon, in 1868. It was shipped from Boston via Cape Horn. After several years, Woodard decided to buy a new fountain and sold his old one to a druggist in Honolulu, Hawaii. In Seattle, Washington, a company advertised in the 1879 city directory that it was selling soda, sarsaparilla, cider, root cider, and soda fountain syrups.[49]

Aphrodite, Irving, and the Queen of Worcester

Industrial designers have long debated the proper relationship between form and function, but soda fountain manufacturers didn't agonize over this issue. At an early stage, they decided that glitz sold soda water. The plain goosenecks, urns, and columns were practical utensils for delivering the beverage to the consumer. They did the job, and they were fine for dispensing medicine. But they weren't eye-catching, seductive forms that promised the customer a hedonistic treat. When soda water moved from medicine into the rarefied realm of luxury, more dramatic, alluring forms were needed. To entice customers into the store, the soda fountain had to be a work of art.

It isn't clear exactly when the first marble box fountain was built, but it was definitely before 1848 because Reed's first Chicago fountain was a marble box resembling one he had seen in the East. Dows patented his marble box fountain in 1861, but he had actually built his first one a few years earlier. Dows' fountain was noteworthy because it was an ingenious combination of form and function that placed cutting-edge technology in an attractive container. But technology did not dictate later changes in form, and design was largely divorced from function as manufacturers vied to produce the most dazzling fountain. At an early stage, the soda fountain industry reached a fork in the road where form veered away from practicality and headed straight toward fancy.

After the Civil War, marble soda fountains steadily became larger and gaudier. Designers borrowed ideas from virtually every known style of art and architecture, combining elements from disparate eras and cultures to create fountains that were sometimes works of art but more often were monstrosities. The Victorian penchant for large, ornate furnishings was reflected in the ostentatious, heavily embellished fountains that dominated America's drugstores and confectionaries.

Dows' flat-top marble box became a cottage when Tufts added a sloping roof. Then Tufts used a gambrel roof, attached a bouquet holder to the peak, and declared that it was a French cottage. Soon, many variations of the marble box—some with flat tops and others with sloping roofs—were on the market. Tufts manufactured the Icefloe, which had a sloping roof topped with a gaslight globe. Another Tufts fountain, appropriately called the Statue, featured figurines of spear-carriers around the base; the top was decorated with a goddess on a pedestal surrounded by four soldiers, each holding a sword and a gaslight globe. Lippincott's marble boxes ran the gamut from imitation log cabins to miniature replicas of elegant Queen Anne-style houses.[50]

Most of Matthews' cottage fountains appear to have been designed by art school dropouts. The France, for example, was a rectangular box with beveled mirrors and sloping sides that supported a gabled roof topped by a large onion-shaped dome reminiscent of a mosque. This jarring visual hodgepodge was compounded by the use of green, yellow, black, and blue marble along with silver, gold, and bronze ornamentation. Matthews also marketed the Japan, which was a flat-top marble box with four bronze columns supporting a mansard roof decorated with faience tile and topped with an onion-shaped dome. The France was a bad-taste bargain at $625, while the equally ugly Japan cost a whopping $1,380.[51]

As fountain manufacturers vied to outdo one another, the rectangular boxes became larger and taller, often resembling towers, castles, or fortresses. As *Pharmaceutical Era* explained, "With the advent of the marble fountain people refused to patronize the urn and gooseneck, imagining that soda from them was not as good as from the marble. . . . they now feel that the soda water from a small apparatus, albeit of marble, is not as good as it is when drawn from a large and handsome one."[52]

Manufacturers decorated their marble fountains with cherubs, knights, kings and queens, soldiers, gods and goddesses, scantily-clad nymphs, and wild animals. In addition to figurines and gaslights, some of Tufts' designs squeezed in bas-reliefs of nature scenes. As a general rule, the fancier the fountain, the higher the price. In 1878, Puffer advertised that a merchant could buy all the necessities for a small soda fountain business for $345, but starting a large business cost $3,260. In Matthews' 1891 trade catalog, prices ranged from $78 for a simple marble box to $4,500 for an eight-foot-long fountain; the generating equipment was additional. That same year, *Harper's Weekly* reported that there were large, custom-built soda fountains in New York City that had cost $40,000.[53]

Because the fountain's appearance was paramount, design was more important than technology in determining the price of a soda fountain. *Carbonated Drinks* explained, "Beyond a certain moderate limit, the money paid for a soda water dispensing apparatus is paid solely for style —for that which has no value except as it strikes the public eye agreeably and gratifies the subtle sense which enables us to take pleasure in beautiful colors, graceful forms, fit proportions, and highly finished workmanship."[54]

The use of expensive marble was an important factor in both appearance and cost. Tufts is credited with starting the colored-marble trend, but other manufacturers quickly jumped on the bandwagon, searching the world over for lustrous, variegated marbles. In a trade catalog, Matthews explained, "The colored marbles are much more beautiful than the white, retain their freshness longer, are unaffected in tint by syrups or beverages, may be oiled to preserve their polish, and can be re-polished after many years' use and thus restored to their full original beauty. As a rule, the white marbles are used only in comparatively cheap work."[55]

Favorite marbles for soda fountains included Genoa (green), Lisbon (red), Saragossa (shaded cream, veined with dark gray), Bardiglio (delicately veined gray), Sarrancolin (shaded pearl gray with flecks of red), Sienna (golden yellow, clouded with white, veined with green and brown), Tennessee (chocolate, frosted with white), Brocatel (mottled yellow, purple, brown, white, and red), French Gryotte (deep red with brown undertones), Gryotte Fleure (purplish red mottled with white), Warwick (brilliant red, veined with white), Belgian (velvety black), African Yellow (yellow with purple veins), Rouge Antique (deep red), Etrurian (pure white), Italian (white, veined, and clouded with bluish gray), and Knoxville (grayish pink with light blue veining). Mexican onyx became extremely popular in the mid-1890s, even though it was very expensive.[56]

Each fountain model was named, with the nomenclature ranging from the sublime to the mundane. Even though the names were primarily for convenience because they were easier to remember than stock numbers, manufacturers searched for names with positive connotations. Some were supposed to conjure up pleasing mental images. Others were intended to convey a sense of class and elegance.

Matthews' line included the Nautilus, Colorado, Opal, Iceland, Snow-drop, Ontario, Vermont, Citadel, Hudson, Danube, Niagara, Nile,

Lurlei, Arno, Iowa, Icicle, Argosy, Arabia, Ianthe, Frost King, Fire-eater, Amazon, Glacial, Helicon, Theseum, Brighton, Rhine, Corinth, Killarney, Iona, Scotland, Jordan, Delaware, Aphrodite, Sabrina, Yale, Rialto, Pilgrim, Eldorado, Calypso, Virginia, Persia, Sultan, Andes, America, Puritan, Rome, Eros, Moorland, Bagdad, Potomac, China, Egeria, Coldspring, Italia, Olympus, Avalanche, Mayflower, Baltic, Florida, Snow Queen, and Drinkjoy.[57]

Tufts sold the Ideal, Acme, Monitor, Advance, Albion, Paragon, Radiant, Brilliant, Zenith, Alaska, Emperor, Delphos, Dominion, Kenosha, Fashion, Irving, Shandon, Pekin, and Queen of Worcester among others. Puffer's line was smaller and the names less pretentious. The Pharmacy, Tower, Lincoln, Eureka, Montana, Transcendent, and Snowflake were typical.[58]

The marble tower architecture reached its apex with Tufts' Centennial Fountain, which was built for the 1876 Centennial Exhibition in Philadelphia. Soda fountain manufacturers saw the exhibition as an unprecedented opportunity to promote soda water and show off their latest models. They were delighted when temperance advocates succeeded in banning the sale of alcoholic drinks, with minor exceptions, at the fair. (German beer gardens sold lager beer, which was not considered to be an intoxicant, and a few first-class restaurants were allowed to serve both beer and wine.)[59]

Seizing the opportunity to tempt thirsty fairgoers, Tufts and Lippincott joined forces to buy the soda water concession, and each installed 14 of his most ornate fountains on the fairgrounds. The *centre d'attraction* was a massive three-story Tufts fountain of variegated marble with silver ornamentation, more than 33 feet high and weighing 30 tons. It boasted 104 spigots—76 for syrups, eight for plain soda, and 20 for mineral waters. Contemporary reports placed the cost in the $25,000 to $30,000 range. This fountain was installed in a large pavilion built expressly for it near the fairground entrance. According to a contemporary description, "The exterior of the edifice is neat and tasteful, and the interior is fitted up very handsomely and adorned with elaborate frescoes. . . . It is the largest fountain in the world and is by far the handsomest."[60]

Although Tufts' and Lippincotts' fountains were the only ones actually selling soda water at the exhibition, several other manufacturers exhibited their soda fountains among the technological marvels of the day, which included the Corliss engine, the typewriter, Edison's Quadruplex Telegraph, a facsimile machine, Bell's Electric Telephone and Multiple Telegraph, the Krupp cannon, the Tabulating Calculating Machine or Difference Engine (a mechanical computer), the world's largest circular saw, and the hen-encourager, a contrivance that purportedly made hens lay eggs faster.[61]

Philadelphia experienced an unusually hot summer, which naturally increased the demand for cold drinks. From mid-June through late July, there was hardly a day when the thermometer fell below 90 degrees. Shade was at a premium, and the parched fairgoer longed for a cold drink as he tramped from one stifling exhibition hall to another. One of the most popular attractions was the Cataract, a display of industrial pumps that sprayed water into the air, providing a cool spot in Machinery Hall. Public water fountains, a novelty promoted by the temperance movement, were a welcome sight. The Catholic church sponsored the Total Abstinence Fountain in Machinery Hall, and the Pennsylvania Sons of Temperance erected a 13-sided Greek temple housing a large fountain that dispensed free water.[62]

Despite the competition from the free water fountains, the soda fountains attracted many customers. A contemporary writer reported that a glass of soda sold for ten cents and all the fountains were busy. A British newspaperman, who evidently believed that cold foods were dangerous, reported, "One is compelled at considerable risk to be continually eating iced creams and drinking 'arctic waters.'" Another Englishman wrote, "the numerous soda water stands in all the buildings did a roaring trade, and so did the German lager beer sellers."[63]

Despite the brisk business at the soda fountains, Tufts claimed that his huge Centennial fountain had failed to turn a profit. Nevertheless, he felt that it had been a wise investment because it had generated a great deal of publicity for his company. Lippincott stated that his fountains had made "a handsome profit," but other concessionaires joined Tufts in complaining about their poor receipts. When the final balance sheets were published, it was obvious that the Centennial Exhibition stockholders had suffered heavy losses because attendance had been lower than predicted.[64]

After the exhibition closed, Tufts' Centennial soda fountain proved to be a white elephant because no buyer could be found. After being warehoused for a time, it was leased to a Coney Island firm until 1885, when it was purchased by the Famous Clothing Company, a department store in St. Louis. Although the naysayers warned that it was a risky investment, it proved to be a bonanza for the store and paid for itself several times over, attracting many customers who wanted to drink from the world's largest, costliest soda fountain. Sadly, the splendid fountain was lost forever on November 17, 1891, when fire destroyed the Famous Clothing Company.[65]

One-Upmanship

Although a few cottage and tower fountains were hexagonal or octagonal, most were four-sided apparatuses that sat on a counter and were single-faced (spigots on one side only) or double-faced (spigots on two sides). Wall fountains were introduced around 1870 and gradually became the industry norm. These fountains had spigots only on the front side and the back side was flat, in order to stand flush against a wall. A typical wall fountain included a marble base with several spigots, a wooden or marble canopy, one or more plate glass mirrors, and gaslights. The wooden canopy or superstructure sometimes featured Victorian gingerbread or rattan wickerwork. Ornamental statuary, clocks, cornices, balustrades, pillars, and pedestals of many styles were combined to produce design nightmares that nevertheless appealed to popular taste.

A druggist or confectioner who wished to do a booming soda water business knew that a fancy fountain was essential because customers wanted to drink their soda in attractive surroundings. As *The Pharmaceutical Era* explained, "The customer comes in from the hot, dusty life of the street and the sight of the beautiful marble, the shining fixtures and ornaments, the polite and obliging dispenser, all in the purity of perfect cleanliness, gives him a feeling of rest and luxury." Naturally, he wanted to pause for awhile and sip a cool drink.[66]

Because a showy fountain lured customers into the store, it was a permanent, potent advertisement for soda water. An enticing fountain reminded the drugstore customer who came to buy castor oil that he also wanted a cold, fizzy drink. Trade journals told druggists that an up-to-date, attractive fountain paid for itself. A typical article in *The Pharmaceutical Era* said, "People nowadays do not imagine that soda water is as good out of a small fountain or old-fashioned gooseneck as out of a more elegant and improved one." Therefore, the smart businessman regularly discarded his old fountain for the latest, most fashionable model, which created a stir and brought people into his shop to marvel. Naturally, one-upmanship was rampant as drugstores and confectionaries competed to have the most lavish fountain.[67]

Trade papers were filled with testimonials from businessmen who bought new fountains and immediately experienced a dramatic increase in trade. For example, William M. Dale of Chicago reported that he had replaced "a very ordinary fountain, of well-known and stereotyped pattern" with the largest fountain ever seen in the Windy City. "The new fountain was a great curiosity, it was talked about all over the city and out of the city, and many were tempted to drink from the new affair out of curiosity to see how it worked." Soon Dale's cash drawer was over-flowing. Thus, it was "the grossest error imaginable" to assume that operating an old fountain was more economical than buying a new model.[68]

Carbonated Drinks likened buying an up-to-date soda fountain to purchasing a good horse and warned that choosing the wrong fountain was even worse than buying a bad horse "for the one may be improved with training" while the other has no prospects for improvement. Soda fountain salesmen were fond of noting the relationship between sight and taste. "To please the palate you must appeal to the eye" was axiomatic in the fountain industry because lovely surroundings enhanced the sensual pleasure of sipping a luscious drink.[69]

Owning the latest model of fountain was also important because it gave the appearance of prosperity and progress. In the late nineteenth century, Americans believed that bigger was better and that newness was a virtue. They had enormous faith in growth, progress, and prosperity. There was a marked trend toward conspicuous consumption as American industry mass produced items that promised an easier life. Americans believed in the work ethic, and materialism was not a dirty word. Respectable middle-class citizens worked hard and reveled in the luxuries earned by honest labor. The wise businessman realized that a prosperous appearance was important if he wanted to attract these people into his shop. According to a popular Victorian cliché, only a beggar can make a living by looking poor.

While Victorian fountains may not suit modern tastes, they were generally regarded as works of art at the time. In an era when social reformers sought to elevate the masses and refine popular taste, fountains were often seen as a positive influence. *Harper's Weekly* declared, "There are hundreds of thousands of people to whom the soda-water fountain has given their first realizing sense of the beauties of art and the glories of architecture. There are thousands of arid little villages. . . out of whose dull materialism it rises like the fountain in the desert to refresh the weary eye and soul."[70]

The Other Half

Since soda water was a luxury that cost ten cents per glass in upscale shops, soda from a showy fountain was beyond the reach of the lower class. However, there were businesses that catered to customers on the lower end of the socioeconomic spectrum. High-volume fountains in department stores often sold a glass of soda water for five cents or even less, but the cheapest soda was found at the sidewalk stands in big cities.

Street vendors, usually operating out of a cart or a sidewalk stall, were common in the tenement districts of America's large cities. New York City had the greatest assortment of street peddlers, drawn from virtually every ethnic group. These vendors sold anything and everything, including balloons, toys, watches, sponges, canes, whips, flowers, fruit, candy, hokey-pokey (ice cream), vanilla beans, nuts, hot chick peas, corn on the cob, roasted sweet potatoes, pickled tomatoes, cigars and cigarettes, knives, toothpicks and tooth powder, neckties, jewelry, magazines, and photographs of celebrities. Some of the street peddlers were penny-ante con men, but most were desperately poor people trying to eke out a miserable living.

The sidewalk vendors with dilapidated soda fountains were the poor relations of the prosperous druggists and confectioners who proudly showed off their latest marble marvels. The street stands were furnished with old fountains that reminded one writer of "decayed gentility," and they dispensed soda water "suggestive of warm flat-irons." Many sidewalk soda fountains were operated by married couples who kept their stands open around the clock. Typically, the wife ran the fountain during the day and her husband took over at night. Although most street vendors operated independently, there was a chain of sidewalk soda-water stands controlled by one man in New York City. These stands were outfitted with old cottage fountains rented from manufacturers, who took used fountains as trade-ins, reconditioned them, and then leased them. This chain was profitable for a time but eventually failed.[71]

Sidewalk soda water stands were so common on New York's East Side that they forced some neighborhood drugstores to close their fancy fountains. *The Pharmaceutical Era* reported that druggists could not compete with "the street fakirs" selling soda water with cream for three cents per glass or two cents without cream. The reporter wrote, "The principal patrons of the curbstone soda vendor are women and children. Often a woman comes to a stand on a hot day with a child in her arms and with the expenditure of two cents she gets enough of the cooling beverage to cheer both herself and her baby."[72]

Sidewalk soda water was very popular with street urchins, even though social critics complained that the children were spending their money foolishly. A New York newspaper wrote, "A puzzling circumstance to the outsider is that these forlorn, ragged, dirty, pasty-complexioned, bony youngsters seem almost without exception to have an abundance of pocket money. As early as seven o'clock in the morning they are seen crowded around the hokey-pokey cart or the soda water stand." The newspaper scolded poor parents for wasting their money on treats rather than saving up to buy shoes for their children.[73]

Newspaper editor Harry Golden, who grew up on New York's Lower East Side in the early 1900s, remembered that there had been a soda-water stand on nearly every corner in his neighborhood. The typical stand sold candy and cigarettes as well as plain and flavored soda water. The standard flavors were cherry, raspberry, and mulberry. A small glass of plain soda water cost a penny and a large glass was two cents. For an extra penny, the operator would ladle a spoonful of one of the flavorings into the glass. Most of the stands had a handcranked machine for mixing malted milk, which was very popular with immigrants who had never tasted anything quite like it before.[74]

Soda water was popular in all sorts of neighborhoods among all ages and classes of people. The affluent classes enjoyed luscious treats at grandiose marble soda fountains in their neighborhoods. The lower class enjoyed a pale imitation of those treats at shabby, outmoded fountains in sidewalk stands. In this respect, the soda fountain closely mirrored the stratification of American society. Although Americans liked to talk about equality, there was a vast gap between the prosperous classes and the urban poor living in the tenement districts. For all classes, the soda fountain was an inviting place to gather and enjoy a refreshing drink. Perhaps even more than the upper classes, the poor needed little treats, like cold soda water, to brighten their lives.

At the mid-point of the nineteenth century, soda water's new status as a treat seemed to make it more appealing to all classes. Form had become more important than function in the dispensing apparatus, accentuating soda water's role as a luxury rather than a nostrum. Soda fountain owners competed for the consumers' coins, both among themselves and with other businesses, by providing an attractive, inviting environment for socializing over a fizzy drink. Technological advances brought major improvements in the quality of the service, but ambiance was more important than efficiency in attracting customers to the soda fountain. The neighborhood fountain had become a prominent public space that nurtured community life, simply by being a popular gathering place.

THE NATIONAL DRINK

In the last half of the nineteenth century, soda water progressed from a novelty to an institution, becoming the foundation for an entire business sector. Around the world, it was recognized as America's national drink. "Soda water is an American drink. It is as essentially American as porter, Rhine wine, and claret are distinctly English, German, and French," wrote *Harper's Weekly.* "The millionaire may drink champagne while the poor man drinks beer, but they both drink soda water."[1]

From coast to coast, Americans socialized at soda fountains, ranging from old-fashioned goosenecks in the backwoods and the tenement districts to the latest models in posh confectionaries in affluent neighborhoods. They had their choice of more flavors than ever before, and they demanded better service. They could also choose delectable new treats, including ice cream sodas and sundaes. More than 50,000 soda fountains were in service in 1895, and the industry was growing at a breakneck pace.[2]

Citropole, Lemonilla, and Cherry Phosphate

Before the Civil War, fountains generally offered only a handful of flavors. After the war, the variety of flavors mushroomed as fountain technology improved and retailers sought to satisfy the public's more sophisticated tastebuds. Soda fountain menus expanded from a handful of drinks to 100 or more. Consumers suddenly had a penchant for strange combinations with stranger names. Dispensers feverishly concocted new treats, and retailers stretched their collective imagination to coin fanciful names. *The Pharmaceutical Era* noted, "The public is a fickle public, always wanting something new, and the Poet's Dream of last year must give place this summer to other fancifully named concoctions."[3]

The menu at a large fountain might include almond, anise, apple, apricot, banana, birch beer, blackberry, blood orange, catawba, celery, champagne cider, cherry, chocolate, cinnamon, cognac, Concord grape, coriander, crabapple, cranberry, cream soda, crushed violets, currant, egg chocolate, egg cream, egg phosphate, ginger, ginger ale, gooseberry, grape, green gage, grenadine, hoarhound, java, lemon, lime, maple, mead, mint julep, mocha, mulberry, nutmeg, orange, orris root, peach,

peach almond, peach cider, pear, pear cider, peppermint, pineapple, pistachio, plum, quince, raspberry, raspberry cider, raspberry vinegar, root beer, rose, sarsaparilla, strawberry, valencia orange, vanilla, walnut cream, wild cherry, and wintergreen.[4]

A typical large-fountain menu could be found at Riker's, which served 123 flavors as well as a variety of unflavored mineral waters at its 45-foot-long fountain, custom-built by Matthews, in New York City. Riker's signature drinks included Pineapple Smash, Blueberry Tadi, Poet's Dream, Boston Deception, Rosebud, and New York Flip. Like other fashionable fountains, Riker's charged up to 25 cents per glass for its fancy drinks and found plenty of buyers. Since it was located in the heart of the shopping district, its clientele was mainly women, who were the primary market for fancy fad drinks. Although new drinks created a stir, Riker's customers always eventually returned to the standards; strawberry, raspberry, vanilla, and chocolate ice cream sodas were its biggest sellers year in and year out.[5]

Novel names were an important factor in the allure of fad drinks. Fountains freshened up their menus by featuring such drinks as Cream Zoo, Choctow Sling, Cream To-to, Orange Puff, Ginger Ciz, Cream Shamrock, White Cap, Silver Float, Q Shake, White City Dew, Suburban Featheredge, Delmonico's Rose, 400 Mist, Smile Shake, Gardner's Nightcap, Vanilla Warble, and Foam Fun. These fad drinks with unusual monikers attracted customers simply because they were new and "in"— at least for a brief time.[6]

Enterprising fountain owners also attempted to cash in on fads by borrowing names from the latest craze. Take the bicycling craze, for example. The bicycle was invented in the 1830s, but it did not really catch on until the 1880s when the safety bike was introduced. This improved vehicle had pneumatic tires, adjustable handlebars, a cushioned seat, coaster brakes, and chain linkage. Unlike earlier bikes, which had been called "bone shakers," the safety bike was actually fun to ride. A few years after the safety bike appeared, bike manufacturers introduced another fun innovation: the bicycle built-for-two.[7]

Cycling became a national obsession. Even though bikes were expensive, young men and women generally felt that owning one was imperative. During the week, they pedaled to school or work. On weekends, they cycled through the park or took long excursions in the country. Bikes gave youngsters more mobility and freedom than they had known before, causing their elders to worry about America's moral fiber. Young couples could easily escape the watchful eyes of their parents simply by biking to the park or a shady grove. The clergy warned that no good could come of this, and parents feared the worst.

Georgia Journal of Medicine and Surgery stated that biking was dangerous for girls, especially at high speeds when "the body is thrown forward, causing the clothing to press against the clitoris, thereby eliciting and arousing feelings hitherto unknown and unrealized by the young maiden." A noted doctor cautioned female cyclists, "Do not think of sitting down to table until you have changed your underclothing." The Women's Rescue League feared that bicycles would facilitate promiscuity. For modest maidens, shops sold small screens that could be attached to the bike to keep feminine ankles out of sight.[8]

Meanwhile, businessmen warned of dire economic consequences. Because young people were spending their money on bikes, they weren't buying other products. Piano manufacturers claimed that their sales had plummeted because girls were biking instead of studying music. Shoemakers complained because bikers didn't wear out their shoes as fast as walkers. Railroads, steamboats, trolleys, and streetcars had fewer passengers. Riding academies and livery stables were hit hard. Watchmakers and jewelers were suffering because their customers were saving up to buy bikes. It seemed like everybody was jumping on the anti-bike bandwagon. Even a plumbers' union passed a resolution condemning them. "The tailor, the hatter, the bookseller, the shoemaker, the horse dealer, and the riding master all tell similar tales of woe," reported *Scientific American*. The plight of the hat maker was particularly alarming because cyclists were wearing sporty, rakish caps instead of traditional headgear. But there was hope for the poor hatters. In Washington, D.C., a sympathetic Congressman introduced a bill requiring every male bike rider to buy two hats a year, whether he wore them or not![9]

While many businessmen cursed the bike, soda fountain operators tried to exploit the fad by introducing special drinks for cyclists. Clever dispensers concocted Sprocket Foam, Cycle Tonic, Wheelman's Bracer, Cycla-Phate, Pedal Pusher, and similar drinks. Ads touted fountain drinks as remedies for fatigue and depicted smiling cyclists enjoying an invigorating break at the soda fountain. Some druggists installed bike racks in front of their stores and stocked bicycle repair kits. Others gave away local maps and offered advice on the best cycling routes. *The Pharmaceutical Era* said, "Wheelmen may curtail many of their expenses for the sake of wheeling, but they cannot escape the thirst, which follows exertion on a hot day, and the expense of quenching that thirst."[10]

Of course, most of the special drinks for bikers, like other fad drinks, were simply old formulas spruced up with new nomenclature. *The Pharmaceutical Era* commented, "What's in a name? This is an old question and the answer is an old one. An old soda flavor under a new name tastes just the same, but it is a good idea to have a new name occasionally." Renaming an old favorite sparked the customer's curiosity and tempted him to try the "new" treat. Even if Citropole or Frigid Lemonilla tasted somewhat familiar, he felt smug because he was among the first to buy a glass.[11]

The trend toward new taste sensations with exotic names was even noted in the august *Scientific American*, which said, "The largest fountains, where the trade in soda water on a hot day amounts to a thousand or more glasses, have to carry in stock from 50 to 100 different flavors." The journal noted that many new drinks enjoyed a fleeting popularity but few became fountain staples. A dispenser's "knowledge of syrups, waters, and chemicals enables him to mix different ingredients together which will produce a flavor peculiar to itself. It may have no other virtue. But if it is properly named and skillfully advertised, it may have a 'run' or a season that will pay big profits."[12]

Promotion was crucial in creating demand for a new drink. "Enterprising druggists and department stores in the shopping districts get out these special drinks, which can be obtained nowhere else, and publish them in a little pamphlet to distribute among customers or on the street. It is remarkable what this little advertising will do on some hot days. The wording of the advertisement must, of course, be unique and attractive, and the name given to the drinks appropriate to the season and location," explained *Scientific American*.[13]

The demand for new flavors at the soda fountain created a bigger, more discriminating market for bottled syrups. In the fountain's infancy, flavor extracts were produced by distilling herbs or by soaking natural roots and herbs in alcohol. These methods produced recognizable flavors, but they were often harsh and medicinal-tasting. In fact, the same syrups used at the soda fountain were employed in flavoring elixirs and cough syrups. Appetizing fruit syrups were harder to make than herbal extracts because a jelly-like substance formed when alcohol was used and sediment appeared when fruit syrup sat for a period of time. Consequently, many soda fountain operators preferred to prepare their own fresh fruit syrups each day rather than buy them from a wholesaler.[14]

The adoption of new production methods in the last half of the nineteenth century enabled manufacturers to market subtler, fresher-tasting flavorings with little or no chemical aftertaste. These were welcomed at upscale soda fountains catering to the carriage trade. As a rule, the best shops used these more expensive, purer syrups while the cheaper, artificial-tasting extracts and essences were relegated to second-rate fountains, barrooms, and circuses. Of course, the most fastidious fountain owners still made their own in order to insure freshness.

In keeping with the trend toward exotic new drinks, flavoring wholesalers offered syrups that combined flavors. For example, Tufts' catalog listed ambrosia (raspberry, vanilla, and hock), amycose (raspberry and orange), clarique (claret and lemon), goldenade (lemon and egg), jacqueminot (rose syrup and egg), Juliet (ginger, pineapple, and grape), Moorish sherbet (strawberry, pineapple, vanilla, and milk), Persian sherbet (strawberry, lemon, and orange), queen's favorite (pineapple, raspberry, and vanilla), Siberian flip (orange, pineapple, and angostura bitters), and spa fizz (lemon, strawberry, and orange).[15]

While Tufts and other fountain manufacturers bottled syrups as a sideline, some firms counted on flavorings for a major portion of their profits. Two of the best-known were Hance Brothers and White of Philadelphia and J. Hungerford Smith of Rochester, New York. In 1860 Edward and Joseph Hance and Clarkson Griffith opened a wholesale drug business in Philadelphia. When Griffith retired in 1869, Dr. James White joined the firm. In addition to being pioneers in the fruit flavorings business, Hance Brothers and White manufactured nitrous oxide gas, medicated cotton, the Hance percolating and filtering apparatus, quinine pills, podophyllin, phenol sodique, and the Hance drug mill. In the 1880s, its factory was equipped with up-to-date power fruit presses, rollers, and other equipment that extracted and bottled the juice from fresh fruit within hours of its arrival at the plant.[16]

In 1877, after completing a degree in pharmaceutical chemistry at the University of Michigan, J. Hungerford Smith opened a pharmacy in Au Sable Forks, New York, and later moved it to Plattsburg. Smith experimented with flavorings and soon gained a reputation for having the best, freshest-tasting syrups in the area. At that time, Paul Smith operated a popular health resort in the Adironack Mountains, which attracted many wealthy guests from New York City. Some of these tourists visited J. Hungerford Smith's soda fountain and talked about his scrumptious treats after they returned home. Grover Cleveland, P. T. Barnum, and Whitelaw Reid were among the wealthy New Yorkers who spread the word about Smith's fantastic drinks.[17]

As a result of this word-of-mouth advertising, other drugstores began to order Smith's flavorings. Soon, he found it necessary to build a small plant to manufacture his True Fruit Syrups. In 1891, he moved his business to Rochester, New York, where he opened a larger plant. By 1910, Smith dominated the flavorings market, although he had several smaller rivals, including the Cleveland Fruit Juice Company, the House of Middleby, and Cincinnati Extract Works. In 1920, the J. Hungerford Smith Company claimed that it was selling its syrups to 50,000 soda fountains.[18]

Something for Everyone

Location was very important for a soda fountain because, to a large extent, it determined the clientele. Soda fountains in the shopping district, especially in department stores and confectionaries, were likely to be known as ladies' fountains while those in the business district usually catered to men. In 1884, *The New York Daily Tribune* described three representative fountains on Broadway: a men's fountain downtown, a ladies' fountain on upper Broadway, and a family fountain near Madison Square Garden. Each "has its well-marked differences, and one comprehends without difficulty that the drinkers belong to different worlds. The downtown places would frighten the patrons of upper Broadway," said the newspaper.[19]

Upper Broadway was "accustomed to the most delicious mingling of confectionery and soda water" at ladies' fountains, where shoppers lingered over frothy, sweet drinks and dainty confections. Fruit-, chocolate-, and coffee-flavored cream soda were perennial favorites. The ladies rested and chatted while they sipped and nibbled. Such fountains were so emphatically feminine that the occasional male patron seemed like an interloper. Even when accompanied by a woman, a man was apt to feel like a bull in a china shop. At the family fountain, both sexes and all ages were welcome. The women and children generally ordered fancy drinks while the men chose something more robust, such as unflavored mineral water or a mildy alcoholic beverage.[20]

At downtown fountains, businessmen ordered bracing, stimulating drinks. Instead of sacchariny flavors, they often mixed drugs or patent medicines into their soda water to combat indigestion and other minor ailments. One of the most popular men's drinks was a bitter tonic made by mixing chartreuse, quinine, phosphorus, and strychnine. This chartreuse concoction could be stirred into a glass of soda or drunk from a small liqueur glass and then washed down with a soda-water chaser. The men's fountains on lower Broadway served lithiated phosphate, which was supposed to stimulate the kidneys and provide relief from gout and rheumatism. They also served Manhattan punch (a mixture of green tea and lemon juice) and elixir of coca, which imparted "great powers of endurance," according to *The New York Daily Tribune*.[21]

Since fountains had originated in drugstores, it was logical that they continued to sell patent medicines and drinks reputed to have curative powers. A typical fountain sold such remedies as bicarbonate of soda, seidlitz powders, bromo-seltzer, bromo-caffeine, castor oil, aromatic spirits ammonia, pepsin, celery-caffeine bromide, cod liver oil, tincture ginger, quinine, antipyrine, and phenacetine. Morphine, hashish, opium, and cocaine were readily available at drugstores until 1914, when the

Harrison Narcotic Act was passed. Hangover cures were a specialty at some soda fountains, especially in the business district.[22]

Victorians who frowned on frivolity might rationalize a trip to the soda fountain by saying that a cold drink could counteract the blood's tendency to overheat, that an egg drink had high nutritional value, or that mixing drugs with soda water helped them stay down. Weak or nervous individuals were advised to drink chocolate, milk punch, or eggnog, as were persons predisposed to illness in hot weather. Lemon syrup, lime juice, acid phosphate, raspberry vinegar, soda lemonade, claret, Rhine wine, and catawba were recommended for the obese. Dyspeptics could find relief by adding a pinch of magnesia, pepsin, ingluvin, or diastased malt to soda water. Beef-tea soda, wine of cocoa, and wine fortified with iron were recommended for calming the nerves. Grape milk and grape blood, two unfermented drinks made in California vineyards, were supposed to be good for the blood and were quite popular with temperance advocates. Pepsoline was a favorite tonic for stimulating the appetite. Calisaya, another appetite stimulant, was a pulverized tree bark that was often mixed with soda water, tea, ginger ale, chartreuse, or russet cider.[23]

More Than Cold Water

In the late nineteenth century, the quest for new taste treats at the soda fountain was reflected in the popularity of egg drinks, milk-based drinks, and ice cream sodas. None of these drinks were popular before the Civil War. In fact, most of them were invented after the war to satisfy the changing market, as customers demanded novel drinks that were more flavorful and filling than plain soda water.

The origin of raw egg drinks is unknown, but the demand for them grew steadily after the war until they were among the biggest sellers in the 1890s, especially at men's fountains. The most popular was the egg phosphate—a mixture of raw egg, soda water, phosphate (phosphoric acid), and orange, claret, lemon, or chocolate syrup. (A tiny amount of phosphoric acid was the distinguishing characteristic of all the phosphate drinks.) Other favorites were eggnog, egg chocolate, sherbet de egg, egg lemonade, coca egg phosphate, egg flip, vichy egg shake, egg calisaya, and orgeat a la egg. Large fountains bought dozens of eggs each day, making farmers happy. In Chicago, for example, confectioner J. Berry used as many as 360 eggs per day in mixing drinks. In New York City, the Astor House fountain daily bought 300 raw eggs, which were stacked in piles on the fountain, "apparently one for every man, woman, and child of the population. But they do not remain long enough to outlive their usefulness, as they are turned into phosphate in a surprisingly short time," reported *The Pharmaceutical Era*.[24]

Mixing egg drinks was an art that turned many dispensers into local celebrities, because it was a show worth watching when it was done with a little panache. The dispenser began by breaking the egg with a flourish, pouring all the ingredients into a silver-plated cocktail shaker, covering the shaker with a glass tumbler, and thoroughly shaking the mixture. When he judged that it had been adequately mixed, he removed the tumbler, held the shaker with his right hand at arm's length above his shoulder, and poured the beverage into the tumbler, which he held several feet away in his left hand. An alternative method was to pour the liquid back and forth, several times, holding the shaker and the glass farther apart each time. A real showman could do this quickly without spilling a drop. Then, for the finishing touch, he sprinkled grated nutmeg on top, with a showy flourish.[25]

"A first-class soda man throws the drink from shaker to glass, but does not pour it," advised *Saxe's New Guide, or Hints to Soda Dispensers*. Thus, the dispenser acquired a new nickname, "thrower," and a thrower with finesse commanded good wages. Of course, the customer paid a premium price for an egg drink because it was time-consuming to make. "The contortions of a professional thrower please the average patron, who likes to see a good deal of fuss made over his order," explained *The Pharmaceutical Era*. However, the thrower had his critics. Some staid establishments refused to hire throwers, because the managers did not want their shops to have a circus atmosphere. Others argued that throwing a drink allowed all the air to escape, depriving the liquid of its fizz.[26]

Like egg drinks, milk-based drinks were in vogue after the Civil War. Koumyss was an ancient beverage with Asian origins that enjoyed surprising popularity in England and the United States during the late Victorian period. In fact, the British were so smitten with it that the koumyss cure became the rage at fashionable spas. The ancestors of koumyss were kumiss, a fermented drink made from mare's milk in Mongolia, and kefir, a camel's milk beverage drunk in the Caucasus Mountains. Marco Polo described a process for making kumiss and wrote that Genghis Khan kept a stable of 10,000 white horses to insure a steady supply of it. In the United States, koumyss was prepared by allowing cow's milk to sour and then adding fresh milk and sugar. Both fermented and unfermented versions were sold at American soda fountains. The Victorians drank koumyss, which looked a lot like buttermilk, as both a treat and a treatment for anemia, catarrh, and phthisis (consumption).[27]

Malted milk was a trade name registered by William Horlick of Racine, Wisconsin. Horlick supposedly coined the name "malted milk," but his formula resembled one already being marketed in England. He promoted his mixture of dried milk and extracts of malted barley and wheat as a food supplement for infants and invalids. As such, it was widely available in drugstores, both as a powder and as a tablet. Enterprising druggists soon discovered that they could use powdered malted milk to make a cheap syrup to flavor drinks. When ice cream was added, a malted was both tasty and filling, since the dried milk and the ice cream had a high fat content. Druggists promoted the drink as a complete meal and charged a premium price.[28]

Horlick's malted milk was the first in the United States, but it was widely imitated by other manufacturers, including Carnation and Borden's. Although Horlick protested that these other companies were infringing on his rights, his competitors cited legal precedents in their favor. Horlick persuaded some state associations of drugstore owners to boycott his rivals' products, and there was much animosity among the malted milk manufacturers. The controversy continued for years, marked by cutthroat competition and bitter confrontations between the companies' executives.[29]

Malted milk sold steadily for decades and then became a fad in the 1920's, largely due to an electric blender invented by Fred Osseus. Osseus, who lived in Racine, perfected a mixer that blended a smooth, thick drink. At first, he tried to interest Horlick in his invention, but the malted milk magnate ridiculed him. In 1910, Osseus made a trip to New York City, trying to find investors but was unsuccessful and ran out of money. In order to pay his way back to Wisconsin, he persuaded the owner of the Caswell-Massey store on Broadway to take a blender as collateral for a loan. This blender was a big hit with Caswell-Massey's customers, who were fascinated by the way it worked. The sales manager for a leading manufacturer of milk products saw this blender at Caswell-Massey and immediately grasped its potential. Subsequently, his company arranged to buy blenders from Osseus and give them to soda fountain operators who bought 100 pounds of its malted milk. Bulk malted milk sales increased from less than one million pounds annually in 1910 to more than 35 million in 1926. The drinks were so popular that several chains of malted milk shops sprang up on the West Coast in the 1920s.[30]

It is not known exactly when milkshakes were introduced at soda fountains, but they were popular by the mid-1880s. Tufts patented his Lightning Shaker for mixing milkshakes in 1884, and trade publications printed numerous ads for shakers in the 1890s. These handcranked machines agitated glasses filled with liquid, producing smooth, thick drinks. During a heat wave in Centreville, Michigan, in 1888, the local newspaper reported that the most popular spot in town was Jack Hampson's shop, where the rattle of the milkshake machine could be heard all day long. Funk and Wagnall's dictionary, copyright 1890, defined "milkshake" as follows:

An iced drink made of sweetened and flavored milk, carbonated water, and sometimes raw egg, mixed by being violently shaken by a machine specially invented for the purpose.[31]

Tufts' 1890 trade catalog said that the milkshake "has sprung into great popularity in the South in a surprisingly short time. Wherever it has been properly introduced, it has immediately become extremely popular. It can be made of any flavor, but vanilla and chocolate are the most desirable flavors." This catalog included a milkshake recipe, which instructed the dispenser to fill a tumbler half-full of shaved ice, add 1.5 ounces of syrup, finish filling the glass with milk, and shake well. For a little extra punch, the recipe said to add port wine.[32]

In order to make a richer shake, upscale fountains used a combination of heavy cream or ice cream and milk. While most milkshakes sold for a nickel, these creamier shakes cost 10 or 15 cents. *Saxe's New Guide, or Hints to Soda Dispensers* warned against giving the customer a wide choice of milkshake flavors because it slowed down service while the dispenser waited for the patron to decide. The book advised that it was more profitable for a store to promote one or two flavors as house specialties.[33]

By far the most popular, and controversial, drink in the late nineteenth century was the new ice cream soda, or flavored soda water with ice cream. (The old ice cream soda, which had been served before the Civil War, was a mixture of sweet cream and soda water over shaved ice.) By the 1890s, the new ice cream soda was being served at virtually every soda fountain in the country. Not surprisingly, several individuals stepped forward to claim the honor of having created the sensation. Among them, three emerged as the top contenders: Fred Sanders, Philip Mohr, and Robert McCay Green, Sr.

Because there is no unimpeachable evidence, the question of who invented the ice cream soda will probably never be answered. If all the stories about the origin of the ice cream soda prove anything, it's that the human memory is imperfect. Some historians have suggested that different individuals, living in different parts of the United States, may have invented the ice cream soda independently of one another. While this sounds plausible since communications were slow and a media blitz for a new product was unheard of, it is unlikely in the case of Mohr and

Green since their hometowns were relatively close. It's hard to believe that word of a fantastic new treat would not have spread quickly from soda fountains in Philadelphia, Pennsylvania, to Elizabeth, New Jersey —or vice versa.

Fred Sanders was a very successful Detroit druggist who gave a series of interviews that were published in *The Soda Fountain* and *Confectioners' and Bakers' Gazette*. In all the interviews, he was consistent in claiming that he had invented the ice cream soda. But his consistency ended there, and his inconsistency on the details raises doubt about his veracity. In 1906, he was quoted as saying that he had invented the ice cream soda in 1875. He had a steady demand for traditional ice cream sodas at his fountain, but he had trouble keeping the sweet cream from turning sour on hot days. One sweltering summer day his store was crowded with patrons seeking relief from the heat and he had a constant stream of customers ordering traditional ice cream sodas, but the cream became so sour that it couldn't be used. Unwilling to turn paying customers away, he decided to substitute ice cream for the sweet cream and shaved ice. The new drink was an immediate sensation, and before long other Detroit soda fountains were serving it.[34]

Only one year after the first interview was published, Sanders told a reporter a different version of how he had invented the ice cream soda. According to his second version, one night in 1891 he was preparing to close his shop when a newlywed couple stopped in for a cream soda. All the cream had turned sour, but he had a sudden inspiration. He used ice cream in lieu of the sweet cream, and the newlyweds loved it. In fact, they ordered another. Sanders was relieved that they didn't ask him what the drink was called because he didn't have a name for it. The following morning, a fresh supply of cream was delivered, and he sold the usual cream sodas all day.

Then, that night, the young couple returned and asked him to duplicate the previous evening's treat. The following night, they came once again and brought some friends with them. Sensing that he had a real money-maker, Sanders began to promote the ice cream soda. Soon his fountain was attracting a more affluent clientele, and it seemed as if everyone in Detroit wanted to sample the new treat. Then Detroiters began to order ice cream sodas when they were traveling, and soda fountain owners from distant cities wrote Sanders asking for his recipe. "It wasn't many years before ice cream soda was as commonly known as milk all over the country," Sanders was quoted as saying.[35]

Philip Mohr, a German immigrant, owned a soda water and ice cream saloon in Elizabeth, New Jersey. His regular customers included several prominent bankers who commuted from Elizabeth to their New

York offices via the steamers *Wyoming* and *Redjacket*. Banker J. Harvey Fisk, who was one of Mohr's regular customers, often complained that the soda water wasn't cold enough. One day in 1858, when Mohr was experimenting, for no particular reason he added a spoonful of ice cream to a glass of sarsaparilla soda and found it to be both very cold and tasty. He liked it so much that he insisted that all his employees taste it. That evening when Fisk's steamer arrived and the banker dropped in for his usual, Mohr substituted one of the new concoctions. According to Mohr's recollection, Fisk "drank it and actually stood as one transfixed." In fact, Fisk liked the new treat so much that he advised Mohr to open a shop on Wall Street, where the ice cream soda would make Mohr a millionaire. However, the immigrant had more modest dreams and chose to remain in Elizabeth.

Fisk brought his wealthy friends to taste the new sensation, and Mohr's business more than doubled. Mohr decided to advertise the drink by hanging a large sign saying "ICE CREAM SODA" in front of his store. A confectioner from Newark noticed it and helpfully pointed out that the sign painter had omitted the "and" between the words. Mohr explained that this was no mistake and treated his colleague to one of the new drinks. The confectioner loved it, and Mohr gave him permission to sell ice cream sodas in Newark. Soon fountain owners across the land were serving Mohr's creation.

Mohr credited the popularity of his ice cream sodas to the high quality of his ice cream, which he made himself, using fresh cream, sugar, and pure flavorings. He always made his own vanilla and lemon extracts and preserved his own raspberries and strawberries. In addition, he stored his ice cream in porcelain jars, rather than the tin cans that were commonly used, in order to avoid a metallic taste. His ice cream attracted so much favorable attention that he decided to wholesale it. For years, he supplied ice cream to many drugstores and confectionaries in neighboring towns.[36]

Only two years after Philip Mohr's account was published, his son Edward gave an interview that basically confirmed his father's recollections but differed on some of the details. According to Edward, his father had served ice cream sodas to family and friends for many years before he recognized the commercial potential. In 1872, the elder Mohr installed a new soda fountain and had problems because it wasn't keeping the soda water cold. When Fisk complained that his drink was warm, Mohr gave the banker an ice cream soda, saying, "I guess that'll make it cold enough for you." Fisk raved over the treat, and Mohr decided to add it to the soda fountain menu. Edward, who was handy at lettering even though he was only nine-years-old, was recruited to paint a sign advertising the new treat. A few days later, a Newark confectioner asked for the recipe, and the ice cream soda was on its way to becoming a fountain staple.[37]

Robert McCay Green, Sr., has most often been cited as the inventor of the ice cream soda, and he actually had some documentation that gave him more credibility than his rivals. As with Sanders and Mohr, two versions of Green's story have been published. Surprisingly, the better-known version seems less plausible than the obscure one.

In the better-known version, Green was a concessionaire at the exhibition celebrating the semi-centennial of the Franklin Institute in Philadelphia in 1874. This exhibition was held near city hall on a site that would later be occupied by John Wanamaker's department store. Green had planned to exhibit a very elaborate soda fountain built by a New York manufacturer but, for unknown reasons, was forced to settle for a small box fountain. He began serving sweet cream sodas but ran out of cream. Unable to purchase any more—again, for unknown reasons—he bought two small pitchers from a neighboring crockery exhibitor and rushed to Henry Snyder's confectionary to buy ice cream. He had planned to allow the ice cream to melt, but some customers were waiting at his fountain when he returned. Casting caution to the winds, he added ice cream to soda water and the ice cream soda was born! By the time the exhibition closed, Green was making $400 per day selling the new treat. Inspired by his unexpected good fortune, he immediately opened a plant to manufacture soda fountains.

This account, which was published in a New York newspaper, was supposedly based on Green's diary and archival materials from the Franklin Institute. It belongs to the "ah-ha!" or "eureka!" genre of invention stories, where great inventors stumble onto revolutionary ideas more or less by accident—rather than by methodical experimentation and dogged persistence. It has a certain excitement and drama to it, suggesting that the reporter might have found the truth a tad boring and decided to jazz it up.[38]

Green's first-person account published in *The Soda Fountain*, which is the lesser-known version, is not very dramatic but seems more probable. In the spring of 1874, Green began manufacturing small, plain soda fountains and acting as the Philadelphia agent for John Matthews' company. In June, Green learned that the Franklin Institute was planning to hold a major exhibition in City Hall Square. Matthews, who had also heard about the upcoming fair, informed Green that he wanted to display one of his newest, most ornate soda fountains and asked the Philadelphian to apply for space as his agent.

Green arranged for the space, but when he informed Matthews that he had done so, the New Yorker said that he had changed his mind.

Green, who was very disappointed because he was looking forward to the fair, went to the exhibit committee and asked to withdraw. The committee sensed his disappointment and, not wanting to lose an exhibitor, asked if Green could procure another soda fountain. Green informed the committee that he had a used apparatus that was in working order, but it might not be appropriate because it wasn't a showy, up-to-date model. The committee decided to send a member to Green's shop to inspect this fountain and subsequently gave him permission to operate it at the exhibition.

But Green's joy was short-lived. He soon learned that another Philadelphia manufacturer had secured exhibit space and would operate a magnificent, 25-foot-tall soda fountain at the fair. As he watched this handsome fountain being assembled in the exhibition hall, he realized that it would completely eclipse his second-hand apparatus. Rather than be embarrassed, he again decided to withdraw. This time, friends convinced him that he had a duty to honor his contract with the exhibit committee.

Green knew that his fountain would be unfavorably compared to his rival's, unless he could create some new attraction that would excite the public and make his humble fountain noteworthy. Days of worry and nights of insomnia followed as he pondered his options. One afternoon, he stopped at a confectionary for a dish of ice cream. As was the custom, the waitress served a glass of uncarbonated water with the ice cream. As Green looked around at the other customers enjoying their water and ice cream, he wondered why soda water and ice cream, which were so obviously complimentary, weren't served together. He mulled this over until he hit upon the idea of combining the two and serving them in a glass.

In the short time remaining before the fair opened, he experimented with different flavors of ice cream and soda water. After many taste tests, he decided to sell vanilla ice cream with 16 different flavors of soda water: lemon, vanilla, pineapple, strawberry, raspberry, ginger, sarsaparilla, nectar, orange, sherbet, coffee, chocolate, cocoanut, blackberry, orgeat, and hock. He also went to a local printer and ordered flyers, headed "SOMETHING NEW! GREEN'S ICE CREAM SODA," to distribute at the exhibition. These flyers listed the flavors and said "TRY IT AND TELL YOUR FRIENDS." (Decades after the exhibition, Green produced copies of this flyer and his exhibition contract to document his story.)

On opening day, Green was anxious to see how the public liked his new concoction. So he personally served the first glass and watched the customer drink it. This guinea pig definitely liked it, but other people were reluctant to try it. Although an occasional adventuresome customer ordered an ice cream soda, his first day's receipts totaled only $8.

Obviously, more promotion was needed. So Green offered free ice cream sodas to several young people strolling around the exhibition hall and arranged for them to come to his fountain when he signaled for them. Then he made a show of preparing the sodas for them, arousing the curiosity of passersby. Grateful for the free drinks, the young people spread the word about Green's novelty. As more people talked about the new treat, crowd psychology took over and everybody had to try one.

Another of Green's promotional tactics was giving uncirculated money as change. Well-worn shinplasters (paper money worth three to 50 cents) were commonly used for making change, but Green obtained uncirculated currency from the U.S. Treasury Department and made a show of handing out the pristine money. He also used silver quarters and half-dollars, which attracted attention because silver had virtually gone out of circulation since the Civil War. This generated more talk about Green's fountain and gave the fairgoer another reason to patronize it. Customers lined up three or four deep in front of the fountain, and receipts climbed to $200 per day before the exhibition closed.

The splash created by the ice cream soda at the Franklin Institute's exhibition was repeated two years later at the Centennial Exhibition in Philadelphia. Fountains on the fairgrounds and at other sites around town gave many tourists their first taste of the drink that would become the rage everywhere. In *The Soda Fountain* interview, Green stated that he did not want "undue credit" for inventing the ice cream soda. "My self-satisfaction in having contributed in this way to giving wonderful impetus to the manufacture of fountains and to the sale of temperance beverages is a sufficient reward," he said.[39]

After the exhibition, Green continued to build soda fountains and to make significant contributions to the industry, even though his firm was never one of the largest manufacturers. He pioneered the use of porcelain syrup jars, rather than the customary metal syrup cans, eliminating corrosion and reducing the danger of contamination. He also invented a fountain cooling system that collected and recycled waste water from the melting ice, thereby reducing operating expenses. After he was injured in a railroad accident, the Civil War veteran suffered serious health problems and was forced to curtail his activities. He brought his three sons into the firm, and they continued to operate it after his death.[40]

Whoever invented the ice cream soda, the new confection created both opportunities and problems for soda fountain owners. While it attracted customers, it also slowed service. Soda fountain dispensers complained that preparing and serving an ice cream soda took three times longer than a glass of soda water. Therefore, merchants who had formerly employed one dispenser had to hire two or three to wait on the same number of customers. In addition, the merchant had to buy more ice and install an ice cream cabinet.

In 1891, soda fountains could make substantial profits on drinks because the costs of ingredients were so low: one-tenth of one cent for a glass of plain soda water, one-and-one-half cents for a glass of flavored soda water, one cent for a glass of mineral water or root beer, and one-and-one-quarter cents for a glass of ginger ale. In contrast, preparing an ice cream soda with the best ingredients cost five cents. Yet, in many locations, the retail price of a plain soda water or an ice cream soda was the same—a dime. Obviously, the fountain owner preferred to sell a glass of plain soda. The alternative was charging a higher price for ice cream sodas, but the stiff competition among fountains prevented shop-keepers from doing this in most localities.[41]

Another drawback to the ice cream soda was the amount of time required to consume one. "Time is everything to the soda water man on a hot day," explained *The Pharmaceutical Era*. "With new customers crowding and jostling each other to reach the counter, it is money in his pocket to get rid of consumers as quickly as possible." But it took time to savor an ice cream soda. Often the customer dallied over it, using it as an excuse to rest for 10 or 15 minutes. In that same time at least a dozen glasses of soda water could be dispensed. Hence, ice cream sodas were not popular with fountain operators, and some absolutely refused to serve them, except on slow days when there were empty stools at the fountain.[42]

While trade publications debated the wisdom of selling ice cream sodas, customers were oblivious to the controversy. Many agreed with cowboy-philosopher Will Rogers, who called the ice cream soda "the finest thing that you ever tasted in all your life." It became especially popular at ladies' fountains and among the so-called "summer girls" who frequented the posh fountains in big cities. In 1892, *The Pharmaceutical Era* published the following description of the youthful female habitues of Huyler's in New York City:

The sun is bright, the parks are green, the birds are mating. It is now that the sweetly erudite Vassar girl drops her book to her lap and, with hands clasped in ecstasy, looks forward to a glass of ice cream soda. The fountain at Huyler's is the shrine before which the Vassar girl bows down in worship. The gently sparkling liquid, with its soft lumps of frozen delight, has a peculiarly soothing effect upon the membrane of the Vassar girl's graceful throat, and there is no more inspiring sight these days than is afforded by a group of these fair young creatures seated before a fountain.[43]

The ice cream soda was the biggest seller at many department store fountains, but they didn't mind if their patrons dallied since they wanted to keep the customer in the store. A weary shopper could rest her feet and look over her purchases while she consumed her treat. The chances were good that she would spot a friend at the fountain and spend a few minutes gossiping or showing off her purchases. Reinvigorated by her ice cream soda, she then had the energy to spend more money. Department store fountains also attracted working women on their coffee or lunch breaks. In New York City and Chicago, fountain operators noticed a new trend: shop girls and stenographers often ordered ice cream sodas for lunch rather than going to a restaurant for a full meal.[44]

As a general rule, soda fountains operated only during warm weather because there wasn't much demand for cold drinks in the winter. But many drugstores and confectionaries missed the fountain profits in the off-season. As a result, manufacturers introduced hot soda machines and trade publications urged merchants to sell hot drinks, such as tea and hot chocolate. Matthews put his first hot soda apparatus on the market in 1859, and Dows introduced one three years later. Tufts, Lippincott, and several smaller manufacturers subsequently jumped on the bandwagon. By 1873, a variety of hot soda equipment was being marketed, and hot drinks were becoming popular in many locations.[45]

Hot soda produced a reasonable profit, even if sales were slow, because the equipment cost as low as $10, took up little space, and did not require a full-time dispenser. One manufacturer advertised that the cost of operating his hot soda apparatus was only two to five cents per day. Although sales of hot soda never rivaled those of cold drinks, some merchants built up a respectable trade during the winter. This was undoubtedly an important factor in the evolution of soda fountains into a year-round business and later into the quick lunch counter.

Although some major newspapers printed sarcastic articles poking fun at the idea of hot soda, selling it required such a small initial investment that many merchants were willing to try it. After all, people were thirsty in the winter as well as the summer, and many were in the habit of stopping by the fountain for a quick drink. "The public, in too great a hurry to take a seat at a restaurant and wait for a hot drink to be served, are attracted into a drugstore by a showy hot soda apparatus, knowing they will be served without delay," said *The Pharmceutical Era.* "The businessman will not wait. You must let him know that he can be instantly served."[46]

Although fountain owners advertised hot soda, as a rule, the water was not carbonated. In fact, it usually came straight from the municipal water supply. The first hot soda apparatuses were unattractive metal urns or kettles that sat on top of small, equally unattractive burners. They were decidedly industrial-looking, as if they belonged in a boiler room. As the demand for hot soda grew, manufacturers paid more attention to the design of the apparatus, producing handsome, shiny metal samovars appropriate for an upscale store. Dean, Foster, and Company's Aetna No. 1 was a very popular model featuring a nickel-plated exterior and a copper water tank lined with block tin. This unit came complete with an oil or gas heater, six china mugs, and four syrup bottles for $35. Low Art Tile's elegant ceramic urns, which came in a wide range of colors, were also popular.[47]

Like its cold counterpart, hot soda was a luxury item that tasted best in pleasant surroundings. Tufts' trade catalog emphasized this, saying, "The passerby . . . will always be tempted to stop by the sight of a handsome apparatus from which he knows a delicious drink can be instantly served." This catalog urged merchants to serve hot soda in china or silver mugs, to furnish silver spoons and dainty napkins, to store flavorings in cut-glass decanters, and to top off hot drinks with a dollop of whipped cream. The popularity of hot beverages "depends largely upon luxurious surroundings," advised the catalog.[48]

The Pharmaceutical Era agreed with Tufts that presentation was crucial in selling hot drinks. It recommended serving hot soda in pretty china cups, because silver heated up quickly and could burn the lips. "A nice spoon" and "a delicate napkin" were necessities, and the enterprising merchant could promote hot soda as a light lunch simply by serving it with fancy crackers, olives, pickles, salted nuts, cookies, or lady fingers. Thus, hot soda, like the ice cream soda, was a precursor of the light lunches that would become the mainstay of many soda fountains in the twentieth century.[49]

The variety of hot beverages was rather limited, and most shops offered only a handful of choices. A typical menu included coffee, chocolate, ginger tonic, clam bouillon, lemonade, and beef tea (made with beef extract). Hot malted milk, egg phosphate, root beer, tomato bouillon, red wine, and wine punch were also available in some shops. Coffee Royal (coffee spiked with brandy) was a favorite at men's fountains, as were spiked hot eggnog and Brown Velvet (hot chocolate with a dash of whiskey). Tea Punch, Slumber Punch, Hot Tom, and Columbus Cup were hot toddies made with brandy or liqueur. *The Pharmaceutical Era* noted, "The range of syrups and flavorings is small, though if one possesses a little ingenuity and skill in the concoction of formulas, he may prepare a fairly extended and various list."[50]

Not surprisingly, the demand for hot soda was greater in cold climates than in mild ones. In Boston, for example, the market for hot soda grew rapidly during the 1880s and early 1890s until all the large fountains were compelled to serve it or be labeled old-fashioned. Coffee and chocolate were the perennial bestsellers, and a dispenser with a superb hot chocolate recipe guarded it carefully. In Boston, a Mr. Sears had the reputation of making the best hot chocolate in town and refused to sell his recipe to a rival who offered the very tempting sum of $3,000.[51]

Never on Sundae

One tasty by-product of hot soda was the hot fudge sundae. An enterprising soda dispenser who kept his chocolate warm in a chafing dish discovered that pouring a ladleful of the thick, hot sauce over ice cream made a sumptious sundae. Garnishing it with whipped cream and a cherry made it even more delightful. Other hot-and-cold combinations followed, but the hot fudge sundae remained the big seller.[52]

Of course, before hot fudge could be used to make a sundae, someone had to invent the sundae. Little is known with certainty about the sundae's birth: it originated in the late 1880s or early 1890s; one of the first published sundae recipes appeared in *Modern Guide for Soda Dispensers* in 1897; and sundaes were very popular by 1900. Many accounts of the sundae's invention have been published, but there is no definitive evidence about it. The best-known explanation for the sundae is that it was created to circumvent Blue Laws banning the sale of ice cream sodas on Sunday.[53]

Beginning in the colonial era, Blue Laws were promulgated to prohibit certain activities on the Sabbath. In 1610, the Virginia colony required every resident to attend Sunday worship services, and the penalty for breaking this law three times was death! In 1623, the Virginia law was softened considerably: the fine for failing to attend Sunday service once was a pound of tobacco; for a month's absence from church, the fine was 50 pounds of tobacco. In Massachusetts in 1650, the penalty for working on the Sabbath or otherwise profaning the Lord's Day was ten shillings or a public whipping. In 1656 in Connecticut, profaning the Sabbath "proudly, presumptuously, and with a high hand" carried the death penalty. The lesser crime of "rude and unlawful behavior on the Lord's Day"—which included shouting, hollering, screaming, running, riding, dancing, jumping, and sounding horns—carried a fine of 40 shillings.[54]

Over the years, Blue Laws banned many activities, but enforcement was very lax and sporadic. A survey of state Blue Laws in 1890 reveals a wide variety of proscriptions and penalties. For example, Colorado law forbade attending public amusements, such as theaters and circuses, on Sunday. It also outlawed "the encouragement of idleness, gaming, drinking, fornication, or other misbehavior" on Sunday. In a similar vein, Georgia's law forbade "indecent bathing" on the Sabbath. (These laws were strangely silent as to whether idleness, fornication, and indecent bathing were permissible on other days of the week.)[55]

Vermont's Blue Laws forbade visiting another person's house on Sunday except for charitable works or "for moral or religious edification." If this law had been strictly enforced, a person could have been arrested for attending a friend's birthday party on Sunday! In Connecticut, there was a fine for attending a music or dance concert or "other public diversion on Sunday." Delaware law expressly prohibited fishing, fowling, horse racing, cockfighting, and hunting on Sunday. In the District of Columbia, serving "any strong liquor on Sunday (except in cases of absolute necessity)" carried a fine of 2,000 pounds of tobacco. No doubt, more than one toper felt the absolute necessity of imbibing on the Sabbath.[56]

In 1890, only a few Blue Laws expressly mentioned confectionery or soda water. Maryland banned Sunday sales of soda and mineral waters along with tobacco, candy, and alcoholic beverages. Louisiana specifically permitted Sunday sales at drugstores, apothecary shops, bakeries, restaurants, theaters, and other places of amusement as long as no intoxicating drinks were sold. Minnesota allowed the sale of confectionery, drugs, and medicines "in a quiet and orderly manner." Texas law permitted drugstores to open on Sunday and specified ice cream among the articles that could be sold on the Sabbath. Utah's Blue Laws banned a long list of activities on Sunday, but they permitted many businesses, including drugstores and restaurants, to open.[57]

Given the number and scope of the Blue Laws, it is not surprising that the invention of the sundae is often attributed to a druggist trying to circumvent the law against serving soda on Sunday. In one version, President Theodore Roosevelt was responsible for the sundae because he banned ice cream sodas on Sunday and fountain operators responded by creating the new soda-less treat. This tale probably originated because Roosevelt, while serving as head of New York City's Police Board, made well-publicized attempts to enforce the Sunday closing law for saloons. However, it is unlikely that Roosevelt was the father of the ice cream sundae because the New York State legal code specifically permitted the sale of confectionery and drugs on Sunday.[58]

The best-known Blue Laws story concerns Evanston, Illinois, which was nicknamed "Heavenston" because it was closely identifed with the Methodist Church and the Women's Christian Temperance Union. Evanston's pious town fathers passed an ordinance prohibiting the sale of ice cream sodas on the Sabbath. Some ingenious druggist decided to serve ice cream with syrup but no soda, thereby complying with the letter of the law if not the spirit. Evanston's local historians have identified this clever druggist as either William C. "Deacon" Garwood or Newton P. Williams. Regardless of who created it, Evanston's new treat proved to be very popular and soon was a favorite in nearby Chicago.[59]

In a variation on this theme, Cleveland, Ohio, also claimed to be the birthplace of the sundae. After local religious leaders dug up some old Blue Laws and tagged on a new ordinance prohibiting the sale of soda on Sundays, one druggist with a flourishing Sunday trade started serving ice cream topped with fruit. He advertised this treat as a "fruit Sunday," but his regular customers started ordering it on weekdays, too. So he changed the spelling to "sundae." News of the popular dessert soon spread to Chicago, where trendy soda fountains started serving the new sensation.[60]

In another version of the sundae's origin, necessity was the mother of invention. A New Orleans druggist had a brisk soda water trade, but one hot day he discovered that his fountain wasn't working properly and he was unable to draw any soda. However, he had plenty of syrups and ice cream on hand. After hastily conferring with his clerks, he decided to serve ice cream with syrup on top. His customers loved the new treat, and it was quickly named for the druggist, Mr. Sundae.[61]

A similar tale of necessity places the birth of the ice cream sundae at Stoddard Brothers drugstore in Buffalo, New York. The Stoddard family claimed that their fountain ran out of soda water one Sunday. In the face of adversity, Charles Stoddard had a sudden inspiration and instructed the soda fountain clerks to serve two scoops of ice cream with syrup on top. It quickly caught on with Stoddard's clientele and spread to other drugstores.[62]

Buffalo wasn't the only New York city that claimed to be the sundae's hometown. Ithaca also claimed that distinction, and there are two accounts of the birth. The Red Cross Pharmacy was located directly across the street from the barroom of the Ithaca Hotel. Because the bar was closed on the Sabbath, the druggist decided to offer a special Sunday treat to attract the bar's displaced clientele to his fountain. Hence, he created the ice cream sundae.[63]

The second Ithaca legend involves a young clergyman who regularly stopped at the Christiance and Dofflemyer Drugstore for a dish of ice cream after his Sunday morning sermon. One hot Sunday, neither ice cream nor soda water appealed to him because he was in the mood for something different. So he asked the fountain operator to pour cherry syrup over a dish of ice cream. He was delighted with the new treat and named it "Sunday."[64]

Another legend about the sundae's birth recognizes George Hallauer as the father and E. C. Berners as the midwife. Hallauer, a small-town bon vivant, frequented an ice cream parlor operated by Berners in Two Rivers, Wisconsin. One night, Hallauer ordered a dish of ice cream. As Berners was serving it, Hallauer noticed a bottle of chocolate syrup on the back bar and asked Berners to pour some on the ice cream. Berners protested that the syrup would ruin the flavor of the ice cream, but dare-devil Hallauer said, "I'll try anything once." So Berners poured chocolate syrup over the ice cream, and Hallauer liked it so much that he ordered a second dish. Other customers tried it, too, and word of the fabulous new treat spread like wild fire, soon reaching Manitowoc, six miles away.

When Manitowoc confectioner Charles W. Giffey heard about the treat, he was skeptical. Being a level-headed businessman, he knew that it was unprofitable to serve ice cream with syrup for a nickel, but most of his customers couldn't afford a dime. So he rode over to Two Rivers to taste the new dish and confront Berners, who could ruin everybody's business by creating demand for an unprofitable item. After a few bites of the delectable new dish, Giffey knew it would be a big hit, but he was still concerned about the price. He and Berners discussed the matter and decided that they would sell the treat only on Sundays, as a loss leader to lure customers to their fountains.

This plan worked until a little girl came into Giffey's shop on a weekday and ordered the new treat. Giffey patiently explained that it was served only on Sunday and suggested that she order something else. But, with a child's logic, she insisted that it must be Sunday because she had come in to buy one of the special treats. Sensing that the pouting child would sit at the fountain all day or, even worse, start crying, Giffey served her a sundae. From then on, it was available every day of the week. When Berners died in 1939, the *Chicago Tribune* printed his obituary on the front page, headlined "Man Who Made the First Ice-Cream Sundae Is Dead."[65]

Since there is no definitive answer as to who invented the sundae, it's not surprising that the spelling is also a mystery. However, it is certain that the spelling was not standardized for several decades. Early spellings included sunday, sondie, sundi, sundhi, sundae, and sundaye. Linguists have suggested that sundae ultimately became the standard spelling because religious leaders felt that the word Sunday was sacred and should not be commercialized. They also have theorized that the name was chosen because the dessert was only sold on Sunday or because the Sabbath required a special dessert, whereas ordinary ice cream was good enough for weekdays. According to *The Washington*

Star, the treat was originally called Friday but was changed to Sunday because Friday was thought to be unlucky. Whatever the rationale for the name and the spelling, the sundae's phenomenal success inspired a few fountain operators to create mondaes and tuesdaes, but these treats never became staples.[66]

In some locations, especially college towns, soda fountains served college ices, which were sundaes by another name. Timothy A. Brosnan claimed to have invented the college ice while he was working at Easton's Drugstore in downtown Worcester, Massachusetts. During the summer, many college girls on vacation from the Seven Sisters, especially Smith College, frequented Easton's. The Smith girls begged Brosnan to create a classy new treat that they could name after their college.

Brosnan noticed that the college women had a tremendous appetite for ice cream and could eat more than one dish at a sitting. So he began experimenting with new ways of serving ice cream. One day he spooned vanilla ice cream onto a plate and poured a gill of his richest, sweetest chocolate syrup over it. He served it to a Smith sophomore, who devoured it and begged for more. This time, he scooped up a handful of walnuts, sprinkled them over the ice cream, and then topped both with the chocolate syrup. She liked the second dish even more than the first! Next day, she returned with a group of her friends, who were eager to taste the novelty. In Worcester, the new sensation was called a "Smith College ice," but in other locations it was simply a college ice.[67]

So the college ice joined the soda fountain's new, longer menu. As the nineteenth century drew to a close, fountain patrons could order fancy new treats—sundaes, milkshakes, and ice cream sodas—as well as an amazing variety of traditional and exotic drinks. The soda fountain was becoming a year-round business, and industry executives foresaw an unlimited future for the marble mecca. Around the world, soda water was recognized as America's national drink, and the soda fountain was an American institution.

LIQUOR OR LEMONADE?

In the last quarter of the nineteenth century, brand-name drinks proliferated and were added to the soda fountain menu. Many of these new
beverages were formulated by druggists hoping to invent a top-selling
patent medicine or a popular temperance drink. In the Golden Age of
Quackery, a savvy patent medicine man could quickly become a millionaire selling cure-alls to rubes and city slickers alike. Hence, the inventors
of such drinks as Moxie and Dr Pepper hawked secret formulas guaranteed to cure a variety of ills. Other innovators, like Charles Hires and
Thomas Welch, were more altruistic: they wanted to save families by
luring topers away from demon rum.

The vast majority of the new brand-name beverages were local or
regional, but some were distributed nationally and a few are still sold
today. Although most of them were available in bottles, the lion's share
was sold as syrup to be mixed with carbonated water at the soda fountain. A few pessimistic fountain operators worried about competition
from bottled soft drinks, but most foresaw no problem. After all, in 1850,
the average per capita consumption of bottled soft drinks was a paltry
1.5 bottles annually; in 1900, that number had only risen to 12 bottles.[1]

Secret Formulas and Miracle Ingredients

The brand-name bonanza of the late 1800s included Moxie, Hires
Root Beer, Imperial Inca Coca, Coca-Cola, Passaro's Famous Manhattan
Special, Vernor's Ginger Ale, Orcherade, Bean's Great American Root
Beer, Welch's Grape Juice, Wina Vina, Cold Blast, Clicquot Club Ginger
Ale, Snap, Melorama, Golden Key Mint Soda, Centennial Root Beer,
Cherriett, Silver Rock Ginger Ale, Phosferone, Sanga, and Y. T. Mat-
zoon. Most of these drinks faded away after a few years, but a few sur-
vived to become national brands.

Moxie, the brainchild of Dr. Augustin Thompson, was in many
ways typical of the new brand-name beverages. Thompson, a native of
Maine, fought for the North in the Civil War, studied medicine in
Philadelphia, and settled in Lowell, Massachusetts. Circa 1876, Thompson developed a formula for an elixir containing sugar, chinchona, sassafras, caramel, and other flavorings, but the principal ingredient was

gentian, a flowering plant from the Pyrenees Mountains. According to legend, it was named for Gentius, an Illyrian king who was defeated by the Romans in 161 B.C. and hid in a cave in the mountains. There, he ate the roots of a flowering plant that he found to be healthful and invigorating. Thompson called his concoction Moxie Nerve Food and claimed that it was a treatment for almost everything—nervous exhaustion, locomotor ataxia, paralysis, insanity, impotence, imbecility, and "softening of the brain." It was also an appetite stimulant, strength builder, and energy booster![2]

Thompson, who knew a great story when he heard one, declared that he had named the potion in honor of Lieutenant Moxie, who had been his classmate at West Point and had accidently discovered Moxie's rare secret ingredient, a simple sugarcane-like plant grown near the equator and farther south. However, Thompson had never attended West Point, and skeptics were convinced that Lieutenant Moxie was a figment of the doctor's imagination. Moreover, Thompson couldn't make up his mind about the secret ingredient; sometimes he said that it resembled asparagus or milkweed, rather than sugarcane, and sometimes it tasted like a turnip. Interestingly, Thompson's hometown in Maine was located near Moxie Falls, Moxie Cove, and Moxie Pond. In addition, the Moxie Indians lived in his home state. Thompson's Statement and Declaration to the United States Patent Office stated that Moxie was an "arbitrary word," meaning that he had coined it or picked it at random.[3]

After a few years, Thompson added soda water to his formula and changed the name to Beverage Moxie Nerve Food. By 1884, he was selling Moxie both in bottles and in bulk as a soda fountain syrup. His new marketing strategy touted Moxie as "a delicious blend of the bitter and the sweet, a drink to satisfy everyone's tastes." In the 1890s newspaper ads extolled Moxie's medical benefits, under the headline "The Doctor Says." Because Moxie's unusual flavor was an acquired taste, advertisements urged consumers to "learn to drink Moxie" and turned its bitterness into a virtue by boasting that it was "never sticky sweet." Moxie-flavored lollipops were given to children to help them learn to like it. In the 1920s Moxie used an awkward and forgettable slogan: It's the Drink for Those Who Are At All Particular. But Moxie advertising also produced one of the best commercial slogans of all time: What This Country Needs Is Plenty of Moxie![4]

Moxie's promotional strategy wasn't limited to traditional print advertisements. In addition to putting its logo on everything from cardboard fans to Tiffany lamps, it utilized horse-drawn wagons, each carrying an eight-foot-tall Moxie bottle. The wagon drivers dispensed Moxie at county fairs and other community events until the wagons were replaced by the Moxie horsemobiles, patented in 1917. The horse-mobiles were open touring cars with the seats removed and replaced by a horse dummy, usually purchased from a harness maker whose business was dying, thanks to the automobile. The steering column extended through the horse's chest, and the steering wheel protruded from his neck. The brake and accelerator pedals were attached to the dummy's sides, and the driver sat on the horse to steer the car. The first horses were made of wood, papier mache, or reinforced plaster. Because the car's vibrations caused the plaster to crack, the drivers carried a supply of tape to patch up cracks. In 1928, the company began to have the horses fabricated from aluminum, which eliminated the cracking problem. The company also had at least one pony cycle, which featured a dummy pony mounted on the sidecar of a motorcycle. This vehicle, driven by a man, carried two women dressed up as cowgirls.

In 1920, Moxie outsold Coca-Cola, and in 1925 Moxie reached its peak sales of 25 million cases in 35 states. Due to the soaring price of sugar in the early 1920s, Moxie decided to reduce its advertising budget and use the savings to buy sugar. As Moxie's advertising decreased, its sales declined. After World War II, high sugar prices nearly bankrupted the Moxie company and distribution was limited to the Northeast. In 1968, Moxie bought the National NuGrape Company and became the Moxie-Monarch-NuGrape Company, with headquarters in Doraville, Georgia.[5]

Like Moxie, Dr Pepper began life as a medicament. In 1880, John W. Castles opened a drugstore in Waco, Texas—a dusty frontier town with the usual hodgepodge of homes and businesses, churches and saloons, townsfolk and ranchers. Castles' store, like other small-town pharmacies, was a popular place for residents to loiter and chew the fat. Although Waco was small, it was lively. Cowboys and outlaws often rode into town to gamble and drink at the saloons. By 1890, Waco had another attraction for cowboys—Texas' first licensed reservation for prostitutes. For only $10 per year for each bedroom plus $10 for each "bawd or inmate," anyone could open a brothel. Given the nature of the entertainment in Waco, it's not surprising that brawls, gunfights, and accidental shootings kept the local gossips busy.[6]

In 1882, Castles took pharmacist Wade B. Morrison as his partner, but Morrison soon bought Castles out and became the sole proprietor of the Old Corner Drug Store. One of Morrison's employees was Charles C. Alderton, a young pharmacist who also helped out at the soda fountain. Alderton was unusually cosmopolitan for Waco. Born in New York, he had attended college in England and had earned a medical degree at the University of Texas. Since mixing potions was a major part of his work, it's not surprising that he began to experiment with various ingredients and flavorings. His efforts paid off when he concocted an unusual blend that the locals loved. Since he had no name for it, the fountain regulars would order a Waco or simply say, "Shoot a Waco." Although Alderton couldn't remember the exact date when he invented the drink, an affidavit filed with the United States Patent Office designated December 1, 1885, as the date of origin.[7]

Exactly how Alderton's creation came to be called Dr Pepper is unknown. It might have been chosen by Morrison, who had once worked at a drugstore owned by Dr. Charles T. Pepper in Rural Retreat, Virginia. According to legend, Pepper had fired Morrison because the young man had courted the doctor's daughter and had been deemed an unsuitable beau. As a result, the disheartened fellow had pulled up stakes and moved to Texas. Morrison either chose the name Dr Pepper because he still carried a torch for the young lady or because his Waco friends had heard the story of his ill-fated romance and called the drink Dr Pepper. One version of this legend states that Morrison eventually returned to Virginia and won Miss Pepper's hand in marriage.[8]

While this tale has a certain sentimental appeal, the facts indicate either that it was false or Morrison had an unhealthy fixation on a young girl. Pepper had only two daughters; one girl died as a toddler and the other was only eight years old when Morrison moved to Texas. In an unpublished memoir, Texas businessman William H. McCullough wrote that Morrison once told a group of stockholders that he had selected the name because he had been in love with Pepper's daughter. But this could have been an attempt to improve upon history since the truth wasn't particularly interesting. It is certain that Morrison never wed Miss Pepper; instead, he married a Texan named Carrie Jeffress.[9]

The name Dr Pepper may have been chosen because popular nostrums often carried the name of a physician—real or imaginary—to give them legitimacy. Typical patent medicines included Dr. Chandler's Hemlock Plaster, Dr. King's New Discovery, Dr. Bell's Never-failing Wonderful Mixture for Chills and Fevers, Dr. Worden's Female Pills, Dr. Simmons' Liver Regulator, Dr. John Bull's Worm Destroyer, Dr. Ayer's Sarsaparilla, Dr. Church's Anti-Scrofulous Panacea, and Dr. Townsend's Remedy for Catarrh.

Whatever the exact details of Dr Pepper's birth, it is well-established that the beverage was popularized in Waco and that Morrison played a major role. In the beginning, Morrison and Alderton worked in a backroom at the Old Corner Drug Store, mixing up batches of the syrup for sale at their fountain and a few others. When demand increased, they decided to expand and rented a building for that purpose.

They also hired Robert S. Lazenby, a chemist from Fort Worth. In 1891, Lazenby and Morrison formed the Artesian Manufacturing and Bottling Company, which subsequently marketed several soft drinks, including Dr Pepper. In 1894, Alderton left Artesian to work for a drug company.[10]

In 1921, Artesian went bankrupt because it was fleeced of its assets in a complicated stock deal. It was soon reorganized as the Circle A Ginger Ale Company, but the ginger ale sold poorly because it had strong competition from other ginger ales and lemon-lime drinks. Therefore, management decided to focus on marketing Dr Pepper. At this point, Jack O'Hara, Lazenby's son-in-law, took control. O'Hara decided to expand gradually, and by 1936 Dr Pepper's market included the entire South and Southwest. During World War II, Dr Pepper sales nearly doubled. After the war, the company went public and management decided to expand into all 48 states. In 1988, Dr Pepper merged with 7-Up to form the Dr Pepper/Seven-Up Companies, the world's largest non-cola soft drink producer. In 1995, Cadbury Beverages, a division of Cadbury Schweppes, purchased the Dr Pepper/Seven-Up Companies for $1.7 billion.[11]

Although chemists fine-tuned the Dr Pepper formula from time to time, it remained essentially the drink that Alderton had created. Over the years, the company guarded the secret formula closely but stated that cherry, cola, and prune juice were not among the 23 ingredients. One official description of the formula said that the flavor came from blending "pure fruit flavors (gathered from throughout the world) with mystic spices from far-off Madagascar and clean, clear, distilled, sparkling water." In the beginning, Dr Pepper had no caffeine. Then in 1917, Lazenby decided to add caffeine. In 1939, company executives removed the caffeine and the preservative benzoic acid and added vitamin B-1, to make the drink healthier. Unfortunately, the new formula tasted strange, fermented easily, and had a short shelf-life. When sales plummeted, the caffeine was reinstated.[12]

Early advertisements for Dr Pepper's Phos-Ferrates, as it was then called, stressed that it contained no caffeine or cocaine. One ad bragged, "Dr Pepper stands alone on the bridge defending your children against an army of caffeine-doped beverages, as the great Horatius defended Rome." Another promoted Dr Pepper as "the finest tonic beverage . . . a brain food and exhilarant." Consumers were advised to drink it whenever they needed a cool head or had important business to transact. "The public can rest assured that Dr Pepper is non-alcoholic and that it contains nothing detrimental or injurious to the most delicate system," proclaimed another early ad.[13]

One promotional piece listed "One Dozen Peppery Pointers" suggesting that Dr Pepper was a remedy for many health problems, including impotence. The 12 pointers included the following advice:

* If you have that "tired feeling," drink Dr Pepper. It is bracing and invigorating.
* If nervous, sleepless, and restless, drink Dr Pepper. It is a tonic for nerve, brain, and blood.
* If you feel old, weary, and worn, drink Dr Pepper. It makes old men young and restores vim, vigor, and vitality.
* If suffering from indigestion and loss of appetite, drink Dr Pepper. It corrects the stomach and will make you hungry.
* If you have smoked excessively, drink Dr Pepper. It is an antidote for nicotine.
* If you have overindulged in alcoholic stimulants, drink Dr Pepper. It will straighten you out.[14]

In the early years, Dr Pepper experimented with various advertising slogans. "It leaves a pleasant farewell and a gracious call back" soon disappeared, presumably because it was awkward and silly. Other catchphrases included "Dr Pepper for that Dry Feeling," "Equal to the Finest Champagne," and "Dr Pepper the Year Round." A slogan that proved to be very effective was "Dr Pepper—King of Beverages." Early posters with this slogan featured a monarch in all his regal garb, but he was soon replaced by a lion, the majestic king of beasts. A cartoon character named "Old Doc" was introduced in 1926 but was dropped after a few years because the company didn't want customers to associate Dr Pepper with patent medicines.[15]

Dr Pepper's most famous slogan—"Drink a bite to eat at ten, two, and four o'clock!"—was not adopted until the mid-1920s. Eventually it became so well known that it was reduced to a clock with hands pointing to 10, 2, and 4. Because O'Hara believed that Dr Pepper was an energy booster, he asked Dr. Walter H. Eddy, a Columbia University professor, to study human fatigue. Eddy determined that human energy drops to low points at 10:30 a.m., 2:30 p.m., and 4:30 p.m. each day. When O'Hara asked Dr Pepper's advertising agency to use this research in an ad campaign, the agency ran a contest among its employees to find a new slogan. A copywriter named Earle Racey suggested the 10, 2, and 4 motto. He was rewarded with a $75 prize.[16]

The similarities between Dr Pepper and Coca-Cola are striking, but over the years the differences have proved to be more important. Both originally claimed to have medicinal benefits, both were invented by pharmacists, and both companies have fanatically guarded their formulas. But Coca-Cola moved much more rapidly from regional favorite to national brand. As early as 1895, Coca-Cola was being sold in every U.S. state and territory, while Dr Pepper did not become a national brand until after World War II. More recently, Coke has vied with Pepsi in the Cola Wars while Dr Pepper has capitalized on its identity as a non-cola drink with an unusual flavor.

In 1886, Dr. John Smith Pemberton was a well-known patent medicine manufacturer in Atlanta. He was also a broken man, both financially and physically, needing frequent doses of morphine to get through the day. His chronic health problems included rheumatism, war wounds, and a mysterious stomach ailment. A Confederate veteran, he had studied medicine at the Southern Botanico Medical College of Georgia, where he had learned the methods of Samuel Thomson, an herbal practitioner who had written *New Guide to Health; or Botanic Family Physician, Containing a Complete System of Practice, on a Plan Entirely New.*[17]

Thomson railed against traditional physicians who relied on such techniques as bleeding, dosing with calomel, or raising and then popping large blisters. He accused these doctors of murdering their patients with "their instruments of death—mercury, opium, ratsbane, nitre, and the lancet." The enlightened Thomson preferred steam baths because the absence of heat caused obstruction of the glands, thereby producing illness. His therapy also utilized what he called the "six master herbs," including massive doses of lobelia, an herb inducing violent vomiting and commonly called "screw auger" or "hell-scraper." He combined such as rare botanicals as puccoon, cohosh, and unicorn root in potions with intriguing names, such as "liquid flames" and "bread of heaven." Thomson attracted a considerable following, including William Rockefeller, who was a botanic quack as well as the father of John D. Rockefeller. Even though Thomson did not believe in formal education, several colleges were founded to disseminate his theories. At Southern Botanico, Pemberton studied Thomson's methods, other herbal therapies, and a smattering of traditional medicine.[18]

At age 19, Pemberton paid $5 for a temporary physician's license and practiced hydrotherapy for a while. Then he decided to go to Philadelphia to study pharmacy. When he returned to Georgia, he became a druggist, first in Oglethorpe and then in Columbus. Since the division between the medical and pharmaceutical professions was not well defined, he also practiced general medicine and sometimes performed eye surgery. He settled into a peaceful home life with his young wife until the Civil War broke out. In 1862, he enlisted as an officer in the Third Georgia Calvary but soon resigned and organized a home guard. When the Yankees attacked Columbus a week after Lee's surrender at Appomattox, Pemberton suffered bullet and sabre wounds in one of the last skirmishes of the war. He later attributed his survival to wearing a money belt, which had deflected potentially fatal injuries.[19]

After the war, Pemberton returned to pharmacy in partnership with Dr. Austin Walker, a wealthy physician. This business appeared to prosper, but Pemberton's personal finances were always in disarray. In search of greater profits, he began to formulate and market his own creations, including Globe Flower Cough Syrup, Extract of Stillingia blood purifier, and Sweet Southern Bouquet perfume. He subsequently left Columbus and moved to bustling, booming Atlanta to make his fortune.[20]

Reconstruction was in full swing in the city, offering virtually unlimited opportunities for ambitious businessmen. With new partners, Pemberton soon established the largest drug trade in Atlanta, with headquarters in the elegant Kimball House, a luxury hotel with all the latest conveniences, including elevators and central heating. However, in only three years, he was bankrupt. Despite admirable tenacity and repeated comebacks, he never quite recovered from this reversal of fortune. It took him seven years to pay off all his debts and acquire enough capital to begin manufacturing new products. Then, in the next few years, he developed and marketed Indian Queen Hair Dye, Triplex Liver Pills, Gingerine, Lemon & Orange Elixir, and Prescription 47-11.[21]

Although Pemberton was in many ways a typical medical quack, his peers generally regarded him as a respectable businessman. In the context of his time, he was seen as a progressive pharmacist with commendable motives, eager to experiment with new drugs that might relieve human suffering while making himself rich. His professional knowledge was extensive because he read voraciously, including both American and foreign pharmaceutical journals. He served as a charter member of Georgia's examining and licensing board for pharmacists. He spent long hours and a great deal of money on laboratory research and seems to have sincerely believed in the efficacy of his products.[22]

In his quest for a product that would make him a millionaire, Pemberton did not limit his research to local flora but experimented with some of the more exotic plants described in the scholarly journals. Like many of his progressive colleagues, he was excited about experiments with coca, a South American plant with wondrous potential for curing many ills. Although this plant was new to North America, South Americans had long used it as a stimulant, an aphrodisiac, and a longevity drug. The Incas, who had called it the "divine plant," had used it extensively in their religious and commercial activities.[23]

As the nineteenth century wound down, American and European medical journals were filled with articles about the benefits of coca and its principal alkaloid, cocaine. Sir Robert Christison, president of the British Medical Association, reported that he had been wonderfully energized after chewing coca. Dr. Sigmund Freud tried cocaine and found it to be a sexual stimulant as well as an antidote to depression and lethargy. Czech surgeon Carl Koller determined that cocaine could be used as an anesthetic in eye surgery. Former President Ulysses S. Grant used cocaine to relieve the savage pain caused by his throat cancer. Although a few cautious scientists warned that cocaine might be dangerous, its proponents were far more vocal than the doubters.[24]

Naturally, drug manufacturers hastened to market coca tablets, ointments, sprays, liquids, and powders. Entrepreneurs anxious to cash in on the wonder drug produced coca-fortified wines, liqueurs, soft drinks, cigarettes, cheroots, and masticatories. The best known of these products was Vin Mariani, which was Bordeaux wine infused with coca leaf. It is not surprising that Vin Mariani gathered a large following of repeat customers since it contained 0.12 grain cocaine per fluid ounce and the recommended adult dosage was three full wineglasses daily. The child's dosage was one-half of the adult's.[25]

The brainchild of Corsican Angelo Mariani, Vin Mariani was successfully marketed throughout Europe and the United States for decades. Celebrity endorsements were a major component of Mariani's sales strategy, and he proved to be remarkably adept at collecting them. Among Vin Mariani's eminent endorsers were Thomas Edison, William McKinley, Emile Zola, John Philip Sousa, Frederic-Auguste Bartholdi, Lillian Russell, Buffalo Bill Cody, Sarah Bernardt, and Pope Leo XIII. In addition, Mariani boasted that more than 7,000 prominent physicians had written endorsements for the miracle potion.[26]

Of course, Mariani's phenomenal success inspired imitators, and Vin Mariani ads warned consumers against buying cheap counterfeits, such as Coca Cordial, Coca-Malta, Burgundia Coca, and Peruvian Wine of Coca. Another imitation was French Wine Coca, manufactured by Pemberton, who naturally claimed that his formula was an improvement upon Mariani's. Pemberton advertised that his wine coca contained erythroxylon coca from Peru, kola nuts from Africa, grape wine, and damiana (dried leaves of the tropical plant *Turnera aphrodisiaca*).[27]

The African kola nut, which contained the alkaloid caffeine and was grown primarily in Ghana, had its champions in the medical profession but was not as fashionable as coca. For centuries African natives had used kola nuts (which are really seeds) as an energy booster and aphrodisiac. According to the popular press, Henry Stanley was able to find

Dr. Livingstone because his native bearers had chewed kola nuts to keep going. No less an authority than the Surgeon General of the United States Army had conducted tests on soldiers and concluded that troops chewing kola nuts outperformed their comrades on forced marches.[28]

Pemberton promoted French Wine Coca as a treatment for nervous disorders, dyspepsia, mental and physical exhaustion, chronic and wasting diseases, gastric irritability, constipation, headaches, neuralgia, bowel and kidney irregularities, impotency, seminal weakness, alcoholism, and morphine and opium addiction. His ads boasted that French Wine Coca was simply "the most remarkable invigorator that ever sustained a wasting and sinking system." Since Pemberton was dependent on morphine, he may have seen his own salvation in the new cocaine-fortified products, even though he knew that a few doctors believed that addicts using cocaine as a cure were merely trading one form of enslavement for another.[29]

Although French Wine Cola sold briskly, Pemberton was aware that America's respectable middle class was increasingly anti-alcohol. The temperance movement was gaining momentum, both locally and nationally. In 1885, Atlanta voted to experiment with prohibition for two years by closing all saloons, beginning on July 1, 1886. Sensing that the market for temperance drinks would grow dramatically, Pemberton began to tinker with the French Wine Coca formula to develop a new product. He eliminated the wine and blended an assortment of essential oils, primarily distilled fruit flavors, with coca and kola. Due to the bitterness of the kola nuts, all his early attempts were too tart, but adding enough sugar to mask the tartness made the liquid sticky sweet. To counteract the cloying aftertaste, he added citric acid. He continued his experiments for several months, occasionally sending his latest effort for informal market testing at Willis Venable's soda fountain in Jacobs' Pharmacy. During this period, Pemberton and three partners formed the Pemberton Chemical Company.[30]

Pemberton had planned to attend the annual convention of the Georgia Pharmaceutical Society in April 1886 to report on his work but decided to send his paper to be read aloud by one of his colleagues. This paper, which was based on his research and personal observations, extolled the virtues of both caffeine and cocaine. He was particularly enthusiastic about the benefits of coca and noted that the Peruvians, who had vast experience with the plant, did not prefer the coca leaf with the largest amount of cocaine but valued milder leaves with a better blend of alkaloids.[31]

Almost simultaneously with the presentation of his paper, Pemberton decided that he was satisfied with his new soft drink formula, but he couldn't think of a suitable name for the beverage. Frank Robinson, one of his new partners in the Pemberton Chemical Company, suggested Coca-Cola because it captured the essence of the ingredients and because it was alliterative. Such euphonious names were popular for patent medicines, including Botanic Blood Balm, Goff's Giant Globules, Pink Pills for Pale People, Radway's Ready Relief, Dr. Pierce's Pleasant Purgative Pellets, and PPP (prickly ash, poke root, and potassium).[32]

Since Pemberton was burned out and needed a rest, Robinson took control of production and marketing for the new product. He decided on a two-pronged promotional strategy: Coca-Cola was a treatment for headaches and depression; it was also a refreshing soda fountain drink with a unique flavor. Given the close association between the soda fountain and the pharmaceutical counter, such an approach was logical. Moreover, it was already being used for other drinks. Therefore, the label for Coca-Cola syrup claimed that it was an exhilarating fountain drink as well as a cure for nervous disorders, including sick headaches, neuralgia, hysteria, and melancholy. This label also boasted that Coca-Cola was an "intellectual beverage and temperance drink" containing the beneficial properties of both the coca plant and the kola nut.[33]

What is believed to be the very first ad for Coke appeared in the *Atlanta Journal* on May 19, 1886, describing the beverage as delicious, refreshing, exhilarating, and invigorating. It also called Coca-Cola a "new and popular soda fountain drink containing the properties of the wonderful Coca plant and the famous Cola nut." In this ad, Coca-Cola was printed in block letters. Over the next few months, Robinson played around with the logo and eventually decided on the Spencerian script version that would become famous around the world.[34]

Pemberton's frail health continued to decline, and his financial affairs became even more muddled than usual. On June 28, 1887, he registered the trademark Coca-Cola Syrup and Extract with the United States Patent Office in his own name, rather than in the name of the Pemberton Chemical Company. Apparently believing that he alone, rather than the company, owned the formula, he sold two-thirds of his rights and reserved the remainder for his son. A few months later, without informing any of his current business associates, he took in three new partners. By Christmas 1887, at least nine people believed that they owned all or part of the rights to Coca-Cola.[35]

Upon hearing about Pemberton's new partners, Robinson, who had been working hard to launch Coca-Cola, consulted an attorney because he felt that he was being swindled. But the lawyer advised him that it would be a waste of time to sue because Pemberton, who seemed to be genetically incapable of holding onto money, had no significant assets. However, Robinson was not completely without recourse since he knew the Coca-Cola formula. Believing that his chances of successfully marketing Coca-Cola were much better than Pemberton's, he approached Asa Candler, a prominent Atlanta druggist, for capital.[36]

At first, Candler showed no interest because his own drugstore had no soda fountain and he already owned the rights to three products that he believed would make him rich: Botanic Blood Balm, De-Lec-Ta-Lave Dentifrice, and Everlasting Cologne. However, Robinson was persistent and Candler eventually changed his mind. Some accounts state that Joe Jacobs, owner of Jacobs' Pharmacy, persuaded Candler to take over Coca-Cola. Others say that, one day when Candler had a terrible headache, he drank a dose of Coke and was cured. He told his brother that Coca-Cola had cured his headaches and also used his own testimonial in early advertisements, but it's not clear whether he actually discovered these curative powers before or after he had acquired the rights.[37]

Once Coca-Cola captured Candler's attention, he tackled the business with hard-nosed, no-nonsense zeal. Through a series of buyouts— and perhaps a little forgery by someone eager to make a quick buck —Candler gained complete control of the rights to Coca-Cola. When Pemberton died on August 16, 1888, Candler was ready to proceed full-speed ahead. He began manufacturing the syrup and worked closely with Robinson on marketing it. Their aggressive promotion included serving free glasses of Coca-Cola at soda fountains, because they believed that anyone who tasted it would want more. In the summer of 1890, sales of Coca-Cola syrup reached 8,855 gallons, and the new product was on its way. In 1892 in the First Annual Stockholders Report, Candler stated that they had done "very considerable advertising" that had not yet paid off, but he was confident that it would in the future. He was right.[38]

While Candler was busy promoting Coca-Cola, another Southerner was experimenting with the drink that would eventually become Coke's chief rival. Like many other soft drinks, Pepsi-Cola was invented in a drugstore. After Caleb Bradham was forced to leave medical school because his father's business had failed, he opened a pharmacy in New Bern, North Carolina. A gregarious young man, Bradham enjoyed working at the soda fountain and chatting with his customers. He also experimented with drugs, redirecting his thwarted medical ambitions into formulating new remedies.[39]

One of his concoctions, which was intended to relieve dyspepsia and peptic ulcers, became popular with the fountain regulars, who called it "Brad's drink." Realizing that this formula had great potential, Bradham decided that a catchy name was needed. Most sources state that he chose Pepsi-Cola because the formula contained pepsin and cola-nut. However, at least one writer believes that neither was in the formula. He argues that Bradham chose the name because the drink had a refreshing, cola-like taste and, like pepsin, aided digestion. Bradham began serving his drink in the 1890s, but he did not apply for a trademark until 1902. Around the same time, he incorporated the Pepsi-Cola Company, closed his drugstore, and started a manufacturing operation. In 1904, he initiated a franchise system to market Pepsi as both a fountain syrup and a bottled drink.[40]

Virtually all new companies have their ups and downs, but Pepsi had more than most. Bradham had good luck for the first few years and even expanded his manufacturing facilities. Sales growth continued until World War I, when sugar was rationed, forcing soft drink manufacturers to reduce their output. Immediately after the war, sugar prices went on a roller-coaster ride. Bradham bought a large quantity of sugar at a very high price, which drove up the price of Pepsi-Cola syrup. But he could not pass that increase along to the consumer and soon went broke. With the help of Wall Street financier Roy Megargel, Bradham reorganized and sought new investors. Nevertheless, his company was certified bankrupt in 1923. Bradham went back to dispensing drugs and died 11 years later.

The bankrupt company's assets were purchased by the Craven Holding Corporation and the Old Dominion Beverage Company, which established a new Pepsi-Cola Corporation. Megargel was the majority stockholder in this new company and served on the board of directors. By 1928, this company had serious financial problems and became part of yet another new entity, the National Pepsi-Cola Corporation. Three years later, Pepsi-Cola was bankrupt again. This time, Megargel bought the formula and trademark. Then he reached an agreement with Charles Guth, who incorporated the Pepsi-Cola Company of New York and paid an annual fee for using the formula and trademark.[41]

Guth, who was president of Loft, Inc., a chain of soda fountains and candy stores, had been embroiled in a battle with Coca-Cola over the price of its fountain syrup. When Coke had refused to give Guth a substantial discount on its syrup, he decided to make his own. He used Loft's capital to buy Pepsi, but he and Megargel were listed as the sole stockholders of the new Pepsi-Cola company. Guth canceled his contract with Coca-Cola and started serving Pepsi at Loft soda fountains. Sales to other outlets were slow, and Pepsi's financial prospects were poor.[42]

Megargel decided that he had made a bad deal and sued Guth for money he had been promised. To settle the matter, Guth bought out Megargel, using Loft's funds. Moreover, Guth routinely used Loft's resources to promote Pepsi-Cola. After a stockholder revolt in 1935, the Loft corporation chose a new president and sued Guth. The suit claimed that Guth had misused corporate assets and that his Pepsi stock should be handed over to Loft. During the litigation, Guth continued to run Pepsi. After nearly three years of legal procedures, the court ruled that Guth's Pepsi-Cola holdings belonged to Loft. The price of Loft's stock soared, and Pepsi became a Loft subsidiary. Walter Mack was chosen to be Pepsi's new president, with Guth continuing as general manager while he appealed the court's decision. Shortly before Guth's appeal was denied, he finally left Pepsi.[43]

Mack, who had been vice president of Phoenix Securities, was chosen to lead Pepsi because he had a reputation for saving shaky companies. He began by setting up a new bottling franchise system for Pepsi-Cola. Due to Coke's dominance, he had trouble recruiting bottlers, and many of those who signed on had limited capital. To reduce their costs, Mack decided to sell Pepsi in used 12-ounce beer bottles, which were plentiful and cheap because breweries didn't reuse bottles. He went to three large secondhand-bottle dealers, bought their entire stocks, and sold them to his franchisees, 400 bottles for a dollar. These large bottles of Pepsi sold for a nickel—the same price as a six-ounce Coke. After two years, Mack hired designer J. Gordon Carr to create a new 12-ounce bottle with a baked-in label. Since consumers considered Pepsi to be a bargain, Mack decided to continue selling it for five cents.

Mack knew that he had to advertise in order to compete with Coca-Cola, but he didn't have much money to spend. Before he had taken over, Pepsi had signed a contract with a man named Sid Pike, who had a patent on a skywriting system. Since skywriting was a new gimmick, Mack felt that this was a unique opportunity to promote Pepsi. Pike flew over crowded areas, like beaches, and spelled out Pepsi-Cola. Each time the name remained readable for three minutes, he earned $50. On windy days, his pay was meager, but skywriting was so novel that it attracted a lot of attention for Pepsi.

Mack felt that Pepsi needed an ad agency and asked two agencies to compete for the account. After he had chosen one, an executive from the losing agency called because he had a snappy radio jingle that he wanted Mack to hear. He sent the jingle writers, Alan Bradley Kent and Austen Herbert Croom-Johnson, over to Mack's office to sing it:

> Pepsi-Cola hits the spot.
> Twelve full ounces, that's a lot.
> Twice as much for a nickel, too.
> Pepsi-Cola is the drink for you.

Mack thought that radio advertising was a waste of time, but he liked the jingle because it was catchy and decided to give it a try. He wanted to use it as a 15-second radio commercial, even though longer ads were the norm. Because the network radio stations refused to air the short commercial, the jingle initially ran over a small station in Newark, New Jersey, and a handful of independent stations in New York City. After the little ditty caught on, it was aired about six million times.[44]

A cartoon format was often used for Pepsi's magazine ads, which were custom-tailored for each magazine's readership. Mack wanted to use a comic strip for newspaper advertising and tried to buy the Popeye strip, but the price was too high. So, Pepsi's advertising agency developed the Pepsi-Cola Cops, a strip starring two policemen named Pepsi and Pete. Pepsi calendars featured contemporary American art, in order to distinguish them from typical advertising calendars with cheesecake or sentimental artwork. Pepsi staged an annual national competition for its calendar art, with substantial prize money for the winning artists. Under Mack's management, Pepsi was an innovator in community relations, sponsoring college scholarships, business internships for students, square dances in city parks, and Pepsi-Cola Junior Clubs for children.[45]

During World War II, sugar rationing was again a problem for soft-drink manufacturers. Mack arranged to buy large amounts of sugar in Mexico, but Mexican law prohibited the export of sugar. So, Mack built a syrup plant in Monterrey, Mexico, and shipped the syrup across the border, until a change in U.S. law stopped him. Mack also used Louisiana cane juice (the raw fluid from the first pressing of sugar cane) to make Pepsi until the U.S. government intervened, because the cane juice was needed for essential products. The scarcity of sugar forced Pepsi's price up, first to six cents and then to seven. The familiar jingle was changed from "twice as much for a nickel, too" to "twice as much and better, too." After the war, Pepsi adopted a succinct corporate goal: Beat Coke. Both soft drink companies spent enormous sums on advertising, and the competition blossomed into the well-publicized Cola Wars.[46]

From Rum Ruin to Sada Sobriety

During the nineteenth century, American attitudes toward alcohol underwent a gradual but marked change that benefited the soda fountain. Beginning in the colonial era, Americans drank large quantities of fermented beverages, especially fruit-based liquids with low alcoholic content, such as wines and ciders, due to limited preservation options and the widespread fear of water. Most of this liquor was made at home for household use because all family members, even children as young as seven or eight years old, drank alcoholic beverages with all their meals, including breakfast. But tippling was not confined to mealtime. In many New England villages, a bell was sounded at mid-morning to remind workers to cease their labors and take a swig. Weddings, funerals, church dedications, ordinations, and barn raisings were also occasions for drinking. Since taverns often doubled as courtrooms, liquor was usually close at hand during legal proceedings. It was commonly used for sealing a legal transaction, such as transferring a deed, or consoling the losing party in a lawsuit.

Survival was the most compelling reason for making alcoholic beverages. Fermenting fruits and vegetables was a simple means of preserving summer's bounty for winter consumption. Moreover, fermentation could provide nourishment from materials that were plentiful but not especially tasty. The colonists showed their resourcefulness by making alcoholic beverages from almost all available raw materials, including fruits, vegetables, flowers, weeds, and roots. In addition to making potent potables with traditional ingredients, such as grapes and berries, they used parsnips, potatoes, beets, spinach, tomatoes, turnips, dandelions, and tree sap. They brewed their own beer using corn, molasses, tree bark, and roots. Seeds, nuts, fruit kernels, leaves, flower petals, and spices were used to flavor cordials.

Beverage-making began in the colonies soon after the first permanent settlers arrived. Captain John Smith recorded that Jamestown residents produced nearly 20 gallons of wine from hedge grapes in their first attempt at wine-making. The Pilgrims brought apple seeds and cuttings with them to America and began to make cider when the trees matured. But they apparently fermented fruit juice at an even earlier date, since an account of the first Thanksgiving mentions wine made from wild grapes. The Pilgrims also imported malt and learned to make beer from Indian corn. Although the Puritans sternly disapproved of most worldly pleasures, they regarded liquor as one of God's blessings.[47]

In all the colonies, brewing was a routine household chore for the settlers. On farms and plantations, outbuildings housed the press, vats, casks, and other equipment needed for fermentation and maceration. Many farm families also owned a distillation apparatus. In urban areas, most alcoholic beverages were concocted in the family kitchen, although there were a few commercial breweries in the largest cities. As a general rule, the female head of the household was in charge of beverage-making. An English colonist named John Hammond wrote that he had observed "negligent and idle . . . slothful and careless" women who neglected this duty. "They will be adjudged by their drinks, what kind of housewives they are," he warned.[48]

Despite the colonists' daily consumption of alcohol, overindulgence was frowned upon and there were legal penalties for public and/or chronic drunkenness. The Massachusetts Bay Colony, for example, forbade drinking more than one half-pint at a sitting. Connecticut limited tippling to one-half hour per sitting, and New Jersey banned drinking after nine p.m. The punishment for excessive drinking varied from place to place, typically ranging from a fine for the first offense to hard labor, disenfranchisement, or flogging for chronic drunkenness. In New York, the penalty for public intoxication was drinking three quarts of salted water laced with lamp oil. In some towns, a list of known drunkards was posted at taverns and the Supervisor of Drinking regularly visited the pubs to be sure that drunks were not being served. In a few jurisdictions, drunkards were sentenced to wearing a red "D" on their chests, just as adulterers were marked with the scarlet "A." There are even records of a few instances when the "D" was branded into the toper's skin![49]

Moral leaders began to worry about alcohol consumption when Americans started to prefer stronger beverages, such as rum, over the traditional homemade beverages with low alcoholic content. By 1673, liquor was luring so many individuals down the primrose path that evangelist Increase Mather wrote *Wo to Drunkards*, warning that drunks were not only hastening their own personal doom but were inviting God's wrath against society as a whole. Mather declared, "Drink is itself a good creature of God, . . . but the abuse of drink is from Satan . . . the Drunkard is from the Devil." He warned that multitudes of people, young and old, were being debauched by overindulgence in wine, cider, and especially rum.[50]

One of the first major temperance tracts appeared shortly after the Revolutionary War, when Dr. Benjamin Rush, a signer of the Declaration of Independence, published "An Inquiry into the Effects of Spiritous Liquors on the Human Body and Mind." Unlike the preachers who railed against sin, the respected Philadelphia doctor was most concerned with the medical effects of inebriants, giving him credibility with nonbelievers as well as the faithful. As physician-general of the Continental Army, he had had ample opportunity to observe the effects of drinking on soldiers. He refuted the popular notion that drinking alcohol was a source of energy and protected the body against cold. In addition, he argued that consuming strong spirits, even in moderate amounts, over an extended period weakened both the body and the mind. He warned that strong spirits, such as rum, increased susceptibility to yellow fever, jaundice, consumption, diabetes, rashes, flatulence, epilepsy, gout, colic, palsy, apoplexy, gangrene, insanity, and "dropsy of the belly." However, he did not disparage the use of mildly-alcoholic beverages, such as beers and light wines, which he believed could be beneficial if taken in moderation.[51]

Rush's concern was shared by other early temperance activists, including the Reverend Lyman Beecher, father of Henry Ward Beecher and Harriet Beecher Stowe. During his college days, Beecher was shocked by the drinking habits of his fellow students at Yale. After he became a minister, he was appalled by the large quantities of liquor consumed by both his parishioners and his fellow clergymen. His concern prompted him to outline a series of sermons on intemperance, but he didn't deliver them right away because he was waiting for a signal from God. In the fall of 1825, that signal came.[52]

Beecher, a stern man who marched resolutely along the straight-and-narrow, preached six sermons covering the nature of intemperance, the symptoms, the consequences, and the remedies. He stated that intemperance was "a disease as well as a crime" and a major cause of poverty. He argued that daily drinking was harmful, even if one never got drunk, and that mild beverages, like wine, were a prelude to strong spirits. His temperance sermons were published and widely distributed in pamphlet form as *Six Sermons on the Nature, Occasions, Signs, Evils, and Remedy of Intemperance*. In addition, Beecher was instrumental in forming one of the first temperance organizations, the Connecticut Society for the Reformation of Morals, which condemned "Sabbath-breakers, rum-selling, tippling folk, infidels, and rugg-scruff."[53]

Another early temperance society was founded in Millbury, Massachusetts. This group met every Saturday night at the schoolhouse, with each member giving an account of what and how much he had imbibed during the week. If the majority felt that a member had imbibed too much, the group then decided how much it would be proper for him to drink during the coming week. One Saturday night a member reported that he had abstained entirely for seven days, but the group was skeptical, since drinking was such an important part of village life. He further declared that he had decided never to take another drink! His skeptical neighbors kept a close watch on him, but they never caught him drinking.[54]

In many other New England communities, leaders attempted to start their own temperance societies, but they were not always successful. For example, Dr. William Andrus Alcott met with chilling indifference when he tried to organize a group in his hometown. The Massachusetts physician believed that alcohol aggravated his chronic health problems, even though he was only a moderate drinker, and swore off liquor entirely. Convinced that others could also benefit from abstinence, he decided to start a temperance society. Accordingly, he wrote a preamble, declaration, and pledge for his new club. After signing his own name, he confidently marched forth to sign up his neighbors. However, the elder deacon of the town's most important church refused to join because he suffered from a chronic disease that required a daily dose of gin! Because the esteemed deacon would not join, everyone else refused. For 30 years, Alcott remained the president, vice president, secretary, treasurer, and only member of his temperance society.[55]

Another New Englander—the Reverend Justin Edwards of Andover, Massachusetts—was more successful in starting a temperance group. In 1826, after meeting informally for nearly a year, Edwards and a dozen colleagues founded the American Society for the Promotion of Temperance. This group, later called the American Temperance Society, became the first national organization of its kind. The members advocated total abstinence, and their ultimate goal was the passage of state and national laws forbidding the sale and consumption of hard liquor.[56]

Although early temperance activists encountered much apathy, they gradually increased public awareness. Their work began to pay big dividends in the 1830s, a decade that witnessed remarkable growth in temperance societies. By 1833, state and local temperance societies claimed an estimated 1,250,000 members. That same year, representatives from 23 state temperance organizations formed the United States Temperance Union (later renamed the American Temperance Union). Three years later, Thomas Poage Hunt, a Presbyterian minister who called himself "the Drunkard's Friend," founded the Cold Water Army (CWA) to indoctrinate children against alcohol. The dwarfish pastor warned impressionable tots that "a great army of drunkards" was polluting American society. At temperance rallies, thousands of young CWA recruits paraded around, carrying banners and wearing badges with the CWA slogan: HERE WE PLEDGE PERPETUAL HATE TO ALL THAT CAN INTOXICATE.[57]

As the temperance movement attracted a larger, more diverse following, its effectiveness was hampered by internal disunity over its goals and tactics. For some leaders, temperance meant moderation; for others, it meant complete abstinence and/or legal prohibition. There was also dissension over strategy: should the temperance movement rely solely on moral suasion or should it enter the realm of politics, in order to pass laws that would promote and/or enforce sobriety? Inside and outside the movement, these fundamental questions were debated for decades.

In the 1840s, a new element came to the forefront of the temperance crusade—reformed alcoholics. With the zeal characteristic of converted sinners, six chronic drunkards in Baltimore sobered up and started a new organization, the Washington Temperance Society. The so-called "Washington revival" spread across the country, using methods vaguely resembling those that would later be used by Alcoholics Anonymous. In 1842, a group of Washingtonians broke away to form the Sons of Temperance, which relied heavily on the trappings of fraternal orders—ritual, regalia, and secrecy. That same year, the Independent Order of Rechabites of North America was founded. Like the Sons of Temperance, it worked hard to create an atmosphere of brotherhood and camaraderie to replace the conviviality and solace drinkers found in taverns. Both organizations created numerous divisions or auxiliaries for women, teens, and children.[58]

A number of recovering alcoholics proved to be eloquent speakers and/or writers who recruited a multitude of new foot soldiers for the crusade. Among the most popular reformed drunks were John Henry Willis Hawkins, whose binge drinking had impoverished his family, and John Bartholomew Gough, an emotional speaker capable of swaying large audiences. Hawkins, an untrained but natural actor, packed auditoriums with his heart-rending account of his own sordid degradation and remarkable redemption, which had begun when his young daughter begged, "Papa, please don't send me for whiskey today." Gough, a professional actor who often played drunks, starred onstage in *Departed Spirits or a Temperance Hoax*, a satire on Lyman Beecher. After his wife and infant daughter died, the grieving thespian met a Washingtonian who took him to a meeting. When Gough was asked to share his experiences, he mounted the platform and held the audience spellbound for an hour. Washingtonian leaders, recognizing a great proselytizer when they heard one, persuaded Gough to join the temperance lecture circuit. Although the bombastic Gough fell off the wagon more than once, his melodramatic performances convinced many drinkers to sign the pledge.[59]

Despite the high visibility of temperance leaders and the growing numbers who joined the crusade, there was evidence that the movement was ineffective. Saloons prospered despite the temperance pamphlets, meetings, lectures, sermons, and prayers. Total alcohol consumption rose each year, and families were still ravaged by drunkenness. At highly charged meetings led by speakers like Gough, crowd psychology motivated hundreds, sometimes even thousands, to sign sobriety pledges, promising either moderation or total abstinence. But many fell off the wagon almost immediately. According to a common joke, some people were so excited about taking the pledge that they just had to celebrate with a drink.[60]

As temperance leaders tallied their victories and failures, more and more of them became convinced that stricter laws were necessary. Moral suasion simply wasn't enough. Legal prohibition was needed. Moreover, laws must be passed at the state level, since dry towns and counties might be surrounded by wet ones, allowing a person to buy liquor simply by crossing the city or county line. One of the earliest temperance leaders to believe that statewide prohibition was an absolute necessity was Neal Dow, a wealthy Maine tanner and timberman who endorsed total abstinence with a vengeance. Dow, an excommunicated Quaker who practiced a kind of muscular Christianity in which right and might were intrinsically linked, set his sights on drying up Maine. Over the years, his dedication to the cause earned him several colorful sobriquets, including the Sublime Fanatic, the Napoleon of Temperance, and the Moral Columbus.[61]

With the help of Brigadier General James Appleton, Dow formed the Maine Temperance Union, dedicated to total abstinence. The union shunned political partisanship, supporting any candidate who favored prohibition, regardless of party affiliation. After years of organizing, mobilizing, and lobbying, Dow won a surprising victory in 1846 when the Maine legislature enacted a prohibitory law. However, this law proved to be a sham riddled with loopholes and void of any enforcement mechanism.[62]

Discouraged but far from defeated, Dow renewed his political activities and was elected mayor of Portland in 1851. That same year, he cashed in his political IOU's in the state legislature, and Maine passed a new law prohibiting the sale and manufacture of any intoxicating liquor except for medicinal and industrial use by officially appointed agents. Although everyone, including Dow, admitted that this new law was virtually impossible to enforce, it was an inspiration to temperance forces across the country. In the next four years, 11 states and two territories enacted similar laws. However, within a few years, most of these laws were overturned by the legislature or the courts.[63]

From the late 1850s until the end of the Civil War, the temperance movement simmered on the back burner while more urgent issues commanded the public's attention. Compared to the momentous questions of states' rights, secession, and slavery, prohibition seemed almost trivial. After the Civil War, temperance leaders slowly began to regroup. Perhaps the most significant new development was the high-profile involvement of women activists. In terms of numbers, women had always been vital to the temperance movement, but men had commanded the vanguard and chosen the tactics. In fact, women seeking leadership positions in the 1850s had been firmly rebuked by the men. After the war, ladies marched down Main Street and held vigils in front of saloons— praying, reading the Bible, singing hymns, and demanding that the grogshops be closed. Taunts and threats did not frighten these women, even when a saloonkeeper in Cincinnati aimed a cannon at a group of them, who bravely prayed on.[64]

The praying bands forced local governments to close many illegal taverns, convinced thousands of topers to sign the pledge, and even persuaded a few saloonkeepers to close their bars and pour their booze down the gutter. Some of the ladies, bouyed by their success in the battle against the Poisoned Cup, formed the Women's Christian Temperance Union in 1874. The WCTU, nicknamed "Organized Mother Love" and "the Conscience of the Nation," became the largest, most powerful temperance organization in the United States and a potent force for social reform. The WCTU's ultimate, paramount goal was the passage of a constitutional amendment that would make prohibition the law of the land. In addition, the Christian ladies endorsed an eight-hour work day, prison reform, preschool education, world peace, equal rights for women, harsher penalties for crimes against women, and the abolition of the double moral standard. [65]

Under the leadership of educator Frances Willard, one of the WCTU's primary objectives was to teach youngsters to hate booze. To that end, the WCTU published horripilating propaganda to endoctrinate young minds. Children were warned that alcohol in any form was toxic and that regular drinking was responsible for many serious disabilities, including mental retardation, deafness, and nervous disorders. The Christian ladies told children that a toper's body could become so saturated with alcohol that it could spontaneously ignite and burn! They also explained that a drunkard's breath could catch fire, causing him to explode! Despite these outrageous tales, the WCTU's Department of Scientific Temperance Instruction in Schools and Colleges persuaded the legislatures in every state and territory, except Arizona, to enact laws making temperance education compulsory in the public schools. The United States Congress passed a similar law for schools under federal control.[66]

As part of its educational strategy, the WCTU organized a youth group, the Loyal Temperance Union (LTU), with a militant slogan— TREMBLE, KING ALCOHOL, WE SHALL GROW UP! But alcohol was not the LTU's sole target. The group leveled its guns against a multitude of bad habits, and earnest children worked hard to honor the LTU's pledge:

> I promise not to buy, sell, or give
> Alcoholic liquors while I live;
> From all tobacco I'll abstain
> And never take God's name in vain.[67]

As women became more outspoken, their new activism was the object of both ridicule and praise. While some men made jokes and told the ladies that they should stay at home where they belonged, many observers applauded them. In defense of the women's temperance crusade, *Scribner's Monthly* said, "It is a shame to manhood that it is necessary; it is a glory to womanhood that it is possible." Far too many women had a personal stake in the movement because they suffered abuse at the hands of an alcoholic father, husband, or son. Because few females were financially independent, many had no choice but to submit to verbal or physical abuse from drunken males.[68]

In 1893, the Reverend Howard Hyde Russell and some associates at Oberlin College started the Ohio Anti-Saloon League, which soon became a national organization. Hiram Price, a five-term Republican congressman from Iowa, served as the group's first president. Like other temperance organizations, the new league had a member's pledge:

> I stand for prohibition,
> The utter demolition of all this curse of misery and woe;
> Complete extermination; entire annihilation—
> The saloon must go!

The founders chose the name because the word "saloon" conjured up negative images of dark dives infested by riffraff—drunks, fallen women, brawlers, gamblers, and shiftless ne'er-do-wells. The crusade to close such joints attracted widespread support, especially among the upper classes, because the cheap saloon was a vile place that bore little resemblance to the polished brass-and-mahogany bars patronized by the carriage trade.[69]

New York Graphic described the typical slum saloon as "unfit for horses or swine." Unscrupulous barkeepers routinely served watered-down drinks and adulterated booze, which occasionally proved to be lethal. Few bartenders hesitated to serve minors or felt a responsibility to cut-off drunks. Cleanliness was not a priority, and topers became accustomed to the foul stench of stale whiskey. The saloon floor was rarely washed but was covered with sawdust to absorb spills and tobacco juice that missed the spittoon. In the lowest dives, tipplers drank directly from the barrel, via a rubber hose. For three cents, the toper put the end of the hose in his mouth and drank as much as he could without breathing. The moment he stopped for breath, the bartender yanked the hose out of his mouth and passed it to another customer. Some gin mills operated brothels on the second floor and allowed prostitutes to solicit openly. As Dr. Ella Boole of the WCTU put it, "The saloon filled the brothel; the brothel filled the saloon." A survey of drinking establishments in Philadelphia confirmed her view. The study found 8,037 drinking places in the City of Brotherly Love and concluded that nearly half of them had direct or indirect connections with "houses of ill fame."[70]

For temperance crusaders, the saloon symbolized all that was abhorrent about drinking. However, to liberal social reformers, the anti-saloon crusade had an undesirable class bias. They argued that the rich man could join an exclusive club and the middle-class man could join a fraternal order, but the poor man had only the saloon. In a blighted tenement district, the neighborhood tavern was an oasis of beer and cheer. At the local gin mill, the working stiff could meet his buddies and steal an hour or so of boozy pleasure, away from his squalid apartment, nagging wife, and crying kids.

Many saloons had an added attraction for workingmen—the free lunch. At noontime, the consumer could buy a nickel beer and help himself to the free buffet. In some cases, the buffet was an elaborate spread with a variety of meats, vegetables, and breads. In other saloons, only snacks were offered. The barkeepers preferred salty or spicy foods that kept the customers thirsty. Favorites were pretzels, salted peanuts, potato chips, peppery sausages, kippers, pickles, smoked herring, rollmops (marinated herring), and sardellen (pickled sardines). The free lunch probably began in Chicago, although some sources state that it started in New Orleans or San Francisco. A German who toured the USA in 1851-52 wrote that he first encountered it in Cincinnati. Wherever it originated, it soon spread across the country. The major breweries became involved in the late 1880s, using their resources to supply saloons with enormous quantities of food at low prices. At first, temperance leaders applauded the free lunch because they felt that eating counteracted the effects of alcohol. However, it soon became obvious that the free food was creating new drinkers because nondrinkers started going to bars just for the cheap lunch.[71]

Whatever the social rationale for saloons, their political importance was undeniable. In many cities, political candidates routinely used booze to buy votes and the most direct route to the city council or the state legislature ran through the barroom. Political machines, like Tammany Hall in New York, relied on barkeepers to keep the regulars faithful to the party. The machine bosses patronized local taverns, especially around election time, handing out small favors and reminding the regulars of past favors. *Frank Leslie's Weekly* bluntly declared, "The saloon is master of every important city." Nevertheless, the Anti-Saloon League set out to challenge the traditional cozy relationship between pubs and politics. The league's aggressive tactics enhanced the political clout that the temperance movement had been cultivating for several decades and helped pave the way for passage of the 18th Amendment. The pragmatic league leaders even supported political candidates who were known tipplers if they promised to vote dry.[72]

In 1880, it was estimated that New York City had one saloon for every 100 male residents. In Chicago, the average was one saloon for every 300 males. These two cities were not unique, because gin mills were plentiful in all large American cities, especially in the tenement districts. In industrial towns, taverns were popular hangouts where workers sought relief from the harsh conditions they endured in sweatshops, mines, and factories. Saloons were also commonplace in frontier settlements, where they were usually the only entertainment available. So-called "whiskey towns" sprang up around frontier saloons and were sometimes named appropriately. Boozeville, Delirium Tremens, Drunkenman, Winesville, Whiskey Springs, Whiskey Diggings, and Whiskey Hole all dotted the map of the Old West.[73]

Not surprisingly, temperance advocates believed that saloons must be eradicated. But even the most zealous teetotaler realized that closing the saloons would leave a void in American social life, especially for the lower classes. If men could no longer hang out at the bar, there must be somewhere else for them to go. Hence, it became fashionable in temperance circles to talk about finding alternatives to the saloon. In New York, temperance crusaders opened the Church Army Tea Saloon, where consumers could enjoy free sandwiches and dessert with the purchase of a nickel cup of tea. Unfortunately, many visitors were turned off by the heavy religious overtones, including a nightly worship service and "tea missionaries" who gave instructions on how to brew and drink tea. New York's Church Army Tea Saloon failed, as did many similar ventures in other cities. Fortunately, one wholesome alternative to the saloon was already well established: the soda fountain.[74]

Although drugstore fountains had traditionally served a few mildly alcoholic drinks, the soda fountain industry as a whole had a sanitary reputation. Industry leaders, sensing that higher profits were in the offing, encouraged fountain owners to ditch the liquor altogether and promote the soda fountain as a pristine alternative to the saloon. Industry trade journals jumped on the bandwagon, and most soda fountain operators embraced abstinence, publicly if not privately. For some fountain operators, the exorbitant price of a liquor license was an added incentive for eliminating booze after the temperance societies persuaded state and local governments to raise the price of permits.[75]

The Pharmaceutical Era bluntly advised druggists, "Don't dispense ardent spirits at your fountain, especially if you cater to good trade, as many a man will get his nip there but will forbid his family to trade with you." The trade journal strongly criticized the few "black sheep" druggists who persisted in serving liquor at the soda fountain with "no regard for the dignity of their profession or their own personal reputation and standing." The editors believed that the entire industry would benefit from the elimination of all fountains where a customer who gave the right signal could buy a cherry wink (a soda fortified with liquor).[76]

Teetotalers were delighted when soda fountains began to take choice business locations away from saloons in the big cities. In the early 1890s, the number of soda fountains surpassed the number of bars in New York City and more men were frequenting fountains in the business district. In the early 1900s, drugstores or confectionaries with soda fountains replaced saloons on many of Chicago's busiest street corners. In 1908, the Windy City boasted more than 3,500 fountains. By 1906, whiskey sales were declining even in New Orleans, a city noted for its bars, and men in unprecedented numbers were patronizing the Crescent City's soda fountains. In 1907, a government official called Atlanta "the city of fountains," noting that the southern metropolis had a soda fountain on almost every street corner.[77]

Industry efforts to promote the soda fountain as an alternative to the saloon were paying off. Even bigger dividends lay ahead.

Marketing Temperance

Like Pepsi and Coke, Hires Root Beer claimed to have medicinal value, but Charles Elmer Hires was more worried about demon rum than disease. After studying at the Philadelphia College of Pharmacy and the Jefferson Medical School, Hires opened a drugstore in the City of Brotherly Love. When his meager savings and a $3,000 loan proved to be insufficient to get his business off the ground, he was discouraged. Then, he noticed that a nearby excavation site was yielding tons of fuller's earth, an absorbent clay used for filtration. He easily persuaded the construction workers to dump the clay behind his store, rather than haul it three miles to a landfill. He formed the clay into small disks, sold them, netted $6000, and was on his way to being a successful entrepreneur.

Root beer was a traditional American beverage, dating back to the Colonial era, and a family with a good recipe usually passed it down from generation to generation. On his honeymoon, Hires tasted one of these superb family recipes, which belonged to the innkeeper's wife at the New Jersey lodge where he had taken his bride. Although Hires felt that the beverage's strong laxative power was a drawback, he asked his hostess for the recipe. She took him into the woods to show him the wild plants used in the drink. When Hires returned to Philadelphia, he asked two college professors to help him develop a powder that could be mixed with water, sugar, and yeast to produce an outstanding root beer like the one he had enjoyed in New Jersey—but without the laxative punch.[78]

After considerable experimentation, Hires chose a combination of 16 roots, herbs, and berries—including juniper, pipsissewa, spikenard, wintergreen, sarsaparilla, vanilla beans, ginger, licorice, birch bark, dog grass, and deer's tongue. A devout Quaker and teetotaler, Hires decided to name his new powder root tea, rather than root beer, to avoid the implication that it might be intoxicating. One market that he hoped to reach was the hard-drinking Pennsylvania miners, because he believed they could benefit from a refreshing temperance drink. But tea was not a favorite with the miners. Uncertain about the name, Hires sought the advice of Russell Conwell, a Philadelphia clergyman and the first president of Temple University.[79]

Conwell was a spellbinding speaker who preached the capitalistic gospel with the zeal of an infomercial pitchman. He encouraged every American to aspire to riches, saying, "To secure wealth is an honorable ambition and is one great test of a person's usefulness to others." He was famous for telling a parable called "Acres of Diamonds," the story of a Persian farmer who searched the world over for riches but died poor because he failed to see the acres of diamonds in his own backyard. Thus, in response to the question of where to look for wealth, Conwell answered, "Right where you are. At home." He was very supportive of Hires' venture and advised the young entrepreneur that miners were more likely to drink a manly beer than a wimpy tea.[80]

By 1876, Hires was marketing 25-cent packets of powder that yielded five gallons of root beer when mixed with water, yeast, and sugar. These packets were sold at drugstores and via direct mail. Consumers liked the robust flavor, which Hires attributed to the fact that the roots were gathered during cold weather when they were most potent because the sap was concentrated at the base of the tree. At Philadelphia's 1876 Centennial Exposition, he cultivated new customers by giving away free glasses of root beer. The following year, George Childs, a Philadelphia newspaper publisher, advised Hires to advertise his root beer. Even though Hires felt that he could not afford advertising, he was persuaded to buy a few small ads in Childs' paper. When sales improved, Hires became convinced of the importance of advertising. For the next ten years, he poured nearly every cent of his company's profits into advertising.[81]

Many of the advertisements featured well-fed, rosy-cheeked children enjoying Hires Root Beer. A typical ad assured mothers that it was fun to mix up a batch. Another claimed that Hires Root Beer "gives children the strength to resist the enervating effects of the heat, bridges the convalescent over the trying part of a hot day, helps even a cynic see the brighter side of life." Although Hires was more interested in promoting his beverage as a temperance drink than a patent medicine, some ads touted its healthy properties, claiming that it was "soothing to the nerves, vitalizing to the blood, refreshing to the brain." In keeping with Hires' personal convictions, the ads often featured religious illustrations and scriptures. The cherubic Hires Boy was closely identified with the product because he was used in much of the point-of-sale advertising.[82]

In 1884, Hires began producing a liquid extract and a concentrate for use at soda fountains. However, there was a problem in dispensing root beer using the traditional fountain method of pouring the concentrate into a glass and then filling it with carbonated water, because this produced too much foam. To remedy this, Hires began shipping his root beer in kegs, which proved to be very popular with soda fountain operators. Later, the company introduced a special fountain dispenser called the Hires Automatic Munimaker. In the 1890s, Hires began packaging root beer in small bottles, which were promoted as a convenience for people on the go.[83]

In 1890, the Charles E. Hires Company was incorporated for the large-scale manufacture and sale of Hires' root beer, cough syrup, and vegetable extracts and compounds. Over the next few years, extensive advertising played a crucial role in the company's expansion. For example, in a three-month period in 1893, Hires spent more than $200,000 on newspaper ads, signs, trade cards, posters, and other forms of advertising—a remarkable expenditure at that time. That same year, he promoted his root beer by renting a booth at the Chicago World's Fair and installing an elaborate soda fountain where visitors could enjoy a free sample.[84]

Unfortunately, Hires' choice of "root beer," rather than "root tea," caused a serious problem. In 1895, his temperance beverage was banned by the vocal and powerful Women's Christian Temperance Union (WCTU). The ladies argued that any sweet fermented beverage was alcoholic and that root beer was no less sinful than any other beer. For three years, the women fought the Root Beer War, as the newspapers called their crusade, and Hires sales plummeted. The WTCU was finally convinced that Hires Root Beer was harmless when an independent chemical laboratory stated that one bottle contained half as much alcohol as a loaf of homemade bread. Charles Hires published the lab's findings in full-page advertisements. After the WCTU called off its boycott, sales improved, eventually making Hires a millionaire. He turned daily operations of the company over to his son in 1923 but continued to serve as chairman of the board until his death from a stroke at age 85.[85]

Like Hires Root Beer, Welch's Grape Juice began life as a temperance drink. Dr. Thomas Bramwell Welch was a dentist, a devoted family man, an ardent prohibitionist, and a former Methodist minister who had left the pulpit because preaching strained his vocal cords. While he was practicing dentistry in New York City, he visited his sister in Vineland, New Jersey, a small town in the rural southern portion of the Garden State. Vineland, one of the earliest planned communities, had been developed by Charles Landis, a Philadelphia banker and lawyer, who had visions of creating a model city. He believed the Vineland area was ideal for growing fruit and wanted to make it a food-processing center. (Appropriately, Vineland resident John L. Mason invented the Mason jar, which was a great boon to food preservation.) Welch was so charmed by the neat, quiet community that he moved his wife and seven children there in 1868.[86]

In Vineland, Welch opened a typical, small-town dental practice and pursued other ventures, in order to support his large family. In the local newspaper, he advertised "painless extraction . . . under gas" and guaranteed that his false teeth were "good chewers, or no sale." He also manufactured a patent stomach remedy, Dr. Welch's Neutralizing Syrup, but the largest portion of his income came from selling Dr. Welch's Dental Alloys to other dentists. His Phosphate of Zinc and Welch's Gold and Platina Alloy sold so well that he eventually closed his dental practice and devoted all his time to marketing the composites. To promote his alloys, he began publishing a dental journal, which soon had a large circulation within the profession.[87]

In the predominantly Protestant Vineland, the former minister found many neighbors who shared his values—strict observance of the Sabbath, generous support for overseas missions, and abolition of demon rum. Welch's antipathy toward liquor apparently sprang from his childhood, when his father had indulged in drinking sprees that upset his mother. The adults' loud arguments over his father's drinking had frightened the young boy and convinced him that alcohol was the cause of many family problems. As he grew older, this conviction deepened and he was increasingly dogmatic about it.[88]

During his early years in New Jersey, Welch intensified his personal crusade against alcoholic beverages. As a founder of the local Temperance League, he was a leader in the drive to make the towns of Vineland, Millville, and Bridgeton totally dry. Of the three, Bridgeton proved to be the greatest challenge for the teetotalers. When local officials brought 12 saloonkeepers to trial, the witnesses were mobbed and three days of rioting ensued. The temperance forces eventually triumphed, closing all the dram shops in Bridgeton.[89]

Shortly after Welch moved to Vineland, he was asked to serve as communion steward at the local Methodist church. He was already troubled by the fact that churches served wine as a sacrament, and his official role as communion steward put him in a quandary because he didn't like serving wine under any circumstances. He was galvanized into action when a visiting minister stayed at the Welch home. The visitor, apparently an undiagnosed alcoholic, so enjoyed the communion wine that he went on a bender. Deeply repulsed by the sight of the drunken minister, Welch vowed to create a non-alcoholic beverage to replace the sacramental wine.[90]

An unfermented grape-based drink was the obvious choice for a wine substitute. Welch, a voracious reader, was familiar with Louis Pasteur's experiments with heating grape juice to kill the wild yeast that contaminated the juice and gave wine an acid flavor. After Pasteur had eradicated the bad yeast, he had innoculated the juice with desirable yeast and produced a better wine. Of course, Welch's goal was not to produce wine at all but to prevent grape juice from fermenting.[91]

Since Welch, like many of his Vineland neighbors, grew grapes in his yard, he had a ready supply for experimentation. He began by cooking the grapes for a few minutes. Then he squeezed the juice through cheesecloth, filtered it, and poured it into bottles, which he sealed with cork and wax. He immersed these bottles in boiling water to kill the yeast and, he hoped, prevent fermentation. When weeks passed without the explosion of a single tightly sealed bottle, Welch was elated.[92]

Ironically, the dentist had created a sugary, purple drink likely to cause cavities and stain dentures. But more importantly, he had created a nonalcoholic wine substitute. In 1869, he made his first attempts to market his oxymoron, Dr. Welch's Unfermented Wine. If he had expected his fellow believers to embrace this revolutionary product, he was mistaken. Serving wine for communion was a sacred tradition that could not be lightly abandoned. The opposition to unfermented juice was so formidable that he could not overcome it even in his own local church. After four years, he was forced to admit that Dr. Welch's Unfermented Wine was a failure.[93]

But he was not the only Welch who saw the need for a temperance drink. Welch's third child was a son, Charles Edgar, whose faith in Dr. Welch's Unfermented Wine proved to be greater than his father's. At age 20, Charles moved to Washington, D.C., to study dentistry, but he didn't forget about the grape juice. While home on vacation, he decided to resurrect his father's juice business. Although the elder Welch didn't strenuously object to the idea, he really wanted his son to be a dentist. So Charles returned to college in Washington, after he had arranged for a local farmer to press the grapes and had convinced his father to supervise the juice-making. Thus, the business was resurrected on a small scale.[94]

Five years later, Charles moved back to Vineland, practiced dentistry, and married a local woman. After another three years passed, the entire Welch family moved to Philadelphia, where father and son started Welch's Dental Supply Company. As a sideline, Charles continued to sell small quantities of Dr. Welch's Unfermented Wine, which was now being produced on a cousin's farm. In Philadelphia, the elder Welch became active in a secret organization, the Law and Order Society, dedicated to ferreting out and informing on saloonkeepers who violated their liquor licenses. Membership entailed a certain amount of danger because angry barkeepers sometimes sought revenge against the informants.[95]

In 1886, Charles, who was now a widower with two young sons, returned to Vineland and built a small juice factory, dividing his time between practicing dentistry and selling grape juice. Five years later, he moved the juice business to a larger building. When having two careers became too demanding, Charles decided that he preferred pressing grapes over extracting teeth. With Charles' full attention and more advertising, juice sales slowly improved and then received a real boost when he operated a concession at the Chicago World's Fair, introducing his product to many new customers. In 1894, he doubled the size of his manufacturing facilities.[96]

That same year, Charles encountered serious supply problems when black rot struck New Jersey's grape vines, forcing him to buy grapes from upstate New York. When the supply problem continued, he decided to move his family, which now included a new wife and five children, to Watkins, New York, where he believed the business would benefit from a more reliable supply of grapes. Located on the southern tip of Seneca Lake, Watkins was a lovely village set amid fertile glens and rolling hills. There, Charles purchased an old flour mill and worked under tremendous pressure to convert it to a grape juice factory before the fall harvest.[97]

Only months after relocating, Charles realized that he had made a serious mistake. The price of local grapes had shot up and was expected to go much higher. He decided that he must move again, even though he was courting financial disaster because he had spent so much money buying and renovating the flour mill. This time he chose Westfield, New York, near Lake Erie in an area called "the Grape Belt." On April 19, 1897, Charles incorporated the Welch Grape Juice Company, in hopes of attracting investors who would provide an infusion of capital. Despite his shaky finances, he managed to buy land in Westfield and complete the move.[98]

Westfield proved to be a wise choice, and the business prospered as never before. Later, Charles wrote that the move to Westfield had been "the turning point toward success." In 1903, the Welch company was rechartered, and three years later it built a second factory in Westfield because its original plant could not meet the demand even though it was producing 350,000 gallons per year. In 1911, the company expanded again, buying a large manufacturing facility in North East, Pennsylvania. Over the years, Welch's expanded its product line to include such items as grape jelly and blended juice cocktails. In 1956, the company was purchased by the National Grape Co-operative Association, a coalition of grape growers, and was renamed Welch Foods. In 1981, the Dr Pepper Company purchased the rights to Welch's Sparkling Grape Soda and its other soft drinks.[99]

A major reason why Charles succeeded where his father had failed was because the younger Welch understood the importance of advertising. He realized that the consumer was not familiar with unfermented grape juice and, therefore, a market had to be created. He began by mailing flyers to churches and placing ads in *The Christian Advocate*, a religious periodical. He also mailed circulars to physicians, telling them that grape juice eased digestion, teemed with nutrition, and hastened convalescence. He sent free samples to all doctors and ministers who requested them. Ads in medical and pharmaceutical journals recommended Welch's grape juice for the treatment of thyphoid fever, stomach problems, pneumonia, pluritus, peritonitis, rheumatism, and all chronic diseases except diabetes. Ads in soda fountain trade journals touted grape juice as a refreshing, wholesome treat.[100]

Charles even started his own magazine, *The Acorn*, serving as typesetter and printer as well as editor-publisher. Bold-face ads promoting Dr. Welch's Unfermented Wine for communion and for medicinal use were a prominent feature of *The Acorn*. Subsequently, Charles began to publish *The Progress*, an unabashedly prohibitionist periodical with the slogan "Strictly Temperance in All Things." In addition to promoting his juice in his own publications, he advertised widely in mainstream magazines, including *Cosmopolitan, Good Housekeeping, Ladies' Home Journal*, and *Youth's Companion*. In advertisements that foreshadowed today's commercials linking sex and soda pop, Welch's most memorable ads featured pictures of lovely, wholesome young ladies with pouty mouths and tiny waistlines saying, "The lips that touch Welch's are all that touch mine."[101]

The Welches must have been especially gratified to see their grape juice replace alcoholic beverages at many official social functions during

President Woodrow Wilson's administration. When Secretary of State William Jennings Bryan, a staunch prohibitionist, began to serve Welch's at diplomatic dinners, the drys applauded him. However, many newspaper editorials and cartoons lampooned his "grape juice diplomacy." At least one cartoonist depicted him with angel wings and a bottle of grape juice strapped to his chest. When Bryan continued his temperance activism after war broke out in Europe, journalists stepped up their criticism, arguing that the secretary had his priorities wrong and should be paying more attention to foreign affairs. Undaunted, Bryan continued his prohibition crusade, speaking to large audiences and convincing thousands to take the pledge.[102]

Wilson's Secretary of the Navy, Josephus Daniels, banned alcoholic beverages from U.S. Navy vessels and naval yards. In doing so, Daniels noted that both the navy's surgeon general and *The Journal of the American Medical Association* had recommended this ban. He also pointed out that the army had long ago replaced its daily liquor ration. However, naval officers were accustomed to their wine mess and there was much grumbling about Daniels' ban. One admiral warned that officers would take to smuggling whiskey and cocaine aboard ship to replace their traditional wine and beer. As a substitute for the officers' liquor ration, the navy began to dispense Welch's Grape Juice. This prompted widespread protest and ridicule, including the following little ditty:

> Josephus Daniels is a goose
> If he thinks he can induce
> Us to drink his damn grape juice.

Despite the protests and dire warnings, Daniels refused to rescind his order regarding alcoholic beverages. Later, one of Daniels' bitter enemies, Admiral William S. Sims, said that banning alcohol "was the best thing that ever happened to the navy."[103]

Although the temperance advocates were the butt of many jokes, their numbers were growing and their greatest success was yet to come. In the bitter battle between wets and drys, the momentum was definitely shifting toward Prohibition. Soda fountain operators were waiting in the wings, ready to serve wholesome non-alcoholic beverages to former topers. The soda fountain was poised to enhance its role as a neighborhood social center by replacing the saloon and other drinking establishments. In addition, fountains were the major distributor of new drinks claiming to have medicinal benefits, like Moxie and Pepsi-Cola. This was a familiar role since the soda fountain had begun as a dispenser of mineral waters believed to have curative powers.

MEET ME AT THE FOUNTAIN

In the early twentieth century, soda fountains continued to thrive. Parched Americans could quench their thirst at an estimated 100,000 soda fountains in drugstores, ice cream parlors, department stores, confectionaries, restaurants, trains and train stations, five- and ten-cent stores, hotels, and sidewalk stands. Even a few grocery stores and packet boats had soda fountains. In 1906, 30 companies manufactured soda fountains and related equipment. In 1910, when most fountain drinks cost a nickel or a dime, Americans spent $500 million on carbonated drinks. This astounding sum was more than twice the United States government's annual budget for the army and navy.[1]

The soda fountain continued to compete with the saloon for business, and its most important asset was respectability. Whether in big cities or small towns, the fountain was a community social center. The big city fountain drew its clientele from the surrounding neighborhood, giving it a clubby feeling. In affluent neighborhoods, well-dressed customers frequented richly appointed, sparkling-clean fountains where drinks were made with the best ingredients, chilled to just the right termperature, and served in crystal-thin glasses by courteous waiters wearing crisp uniforms. The amenities included mahogany tables, electric ceiling fans, and soft gaslights or bright electric chandeliers. In the slums, street urchins and frazzled housewives bought cheap, warm soda at dilapidated street stands. In small towns, sooner or later everyone visited the soda fountain on Main Street, making it the community's second most important social center—the church being the first.

Soda fountains catered to both sexes and all ages. Many youngsters spent part of their allowance at the soda fountain each week or did odd jobs to earn enough money for an ice cream soda. If a boy had just graduated from knickers to his first pair of long trousers, he headed for the drugstore to strut around in his new grown-up duds. If a girl had a brand new hat or dress, a visit to the fountain was in order, to show off her finery. Adults also went to the soda fountain to see and be seen, although they were generally a little subtler about it.

In towns both large and small, promenading couples stopped at the soda fountain to enjoy a treat and to chat, because it was one of the few places where a proper young lady could go alone with a beau, without risking gossip. A courting couple could share a table with friends or seek privacy at their own table in the back of the store. Lovebirds could order one soda with two straws and hold hands underneath the table. Fountain managers sometimes tried to assist Cupid by serving concoctions with romantic names, such as Lovers' Delight, Heart-throb, Kiss Me, or Soul Mate.

In industrial towns, soda fountains were a respectable gathering place for young men and women who had forsaken the farm to work in factories and offices. Since many of these youngsters were away from home for the first time and had no friends in town, they were attracted to the soda fountain as a safe place to meet people their own age. In the evenings, the factory girls dressed in their good clothes, strolled along Main Street, and stopped at the soda fountain, where a girl could safely flirt with a young man and perhaps find an escort for the next evening's promenade.[2]

After a play or musicale, there was sure to be a festive crowd at the soda fountain near the theatre. In the days before jukeboxes, some fountain owners supplied a piano and the latest sheet music or a player piano. Group singing was popular with young people, especially college students. In small-town fountains a few tables were usually set up with games, like dominoes and checkers, which both entertained the customers and kept them in the store, because the longer they stayed, the more money they spent. At least, that was the theory.

In small-town drugstores, the old timers hung around the fountain in the summer and the woodstove in the winter. The term "drugstore loafer" was coined to describe fountain regulars who spent too much time at the drugstore, as far as busier folks were concerned. The small-town druggists and the regulars heard all the gossip. They knew when a woman wasn't happy at home and when a married man had strayed. They knew who got drunk on Saturday night and when a woman had veered off the straight-and-narrow. They knew when a young man was seriously wooing the girl-next-door and who was in a family way. Although women had a reputation for gossiping, the men who hung around the drugstore had their antennae up, just like any female busybody.[3]

As the temperance movement became a full-fledged prohibition movement, the soda fountain flaunted its wholesome image and courted ex-tipplers. Many politicians stopped campaigning in bars and, instead of buying a keg for the boys, treated them to soft drinks. Men everywhere were urged to patronize the grape-juice circuit or the water wagon. In hot weather, temperance groups paid for wagons carrying ice and tanks of water to drive around the slums in New York and other large cities. The idea was to entice men out of saloons, but the topers generally weren't interested. However, the cold water proved to be very popular with children, who ran after the wagon and brought pitchers from home to fill up. Temperance groups also installed public water fountains in Boston and New York City, at a cost of $150 each.[4]

Soda fountain trade papers gleefully reported the prohibitionists' victories and lauded dry leaders, like William Jennings Bryan and Billy "Whiskey Is Hell" Sunday. They also promoted temperance drinks, such as near beer, apple cider, egg lemonade, prohibition punch, iron brew, and ginger ale. They gave hints on how to make soft drinks more palatable to ex-tipplers. For example, to give a fizzy fountain drink a little extra snap, the dispenser added a dash of pepper sauce and a sprinkling of salt; then he stirred it well and added a pinch of cayenne. The doctored drink produced "a rather considerable sting and an after-effect of warmth," according to *The Soda Fountain*. Another technique was to pour a shot of catsup into the bottom of a glass, fill it with carbonated water, and top it off with a generous dash of salt, which produced a reddish foam.[5]

As the industry's efforts to replace the saloon paid off, *The Ice Cream Trade Journal* dubbed the soda fountain "the new American bar." In some cases, fountains literally replaced bars as hotels converted their barrooms into soda fountains. Some saloonkeepers jumped on the bandwagon and added a soda fountain in an attempt to gain respectability and keep customers who had taken the pledge.[6]

The Soda Fountain declared, "The soda fountain of today is an ally of temperance. . . . Ice cream soda is a greater medium for the cause of temperance than all the sermons ever preached on that subject, and in this capacity is doing better and more far-reaching work all the time."[7]

Drug Topics was more succinct: "The bar is dead, the fountain lives, and soda is king!"[8]

Cleaning Up

Around the turn of the century, Americans became more aware of the link between sanitation and disease. Magazines and newspapers published alarming exposés of filthy food processing plants and the harmful ingredients in packaged foods. Under the direction of Dr. Harvey W. Wiley, the Bureau of Chemistry of the United States Department of Agriculture investigated food additives and lobbied for new laws to ensure the purity of processed foods. On June 30, 1906, the United States Congress passed two landmark laws: the Pure Food and Drug Act and the Meat Inspection Act.

The campaign for government regulation was given a tremendous boost by *The Jungle*, a novel by Upton Sinclair. Sinclair's graphic, chilling book describes the bleak life of immigrant Jurgis Rudkus, who works in the Chicago stockyards. Rudkus is abused by his bosses and exploited at every turn by greedy businessmen and corrupt politicians. Gradually, he is beaten down by the relentless brutality of his life. When he cannot find work, he degenerates to a tramp, a petty thief, and then a highwayman. Finally, he realizes that he and his kind can only survive if they band together and demand justice as a group. Therefore, he becomes a socialist and crusades for a fair deal for the working man.[9]

Sinclair intended *The Jungle* as a powerful argument for socialism, but its impact was not exactly what he had hoped for. Ironically, his repulsive yet riveting descriptions of the filthy meat-packing plants were so gripping that readers focused on them and skimmed over the socialist propaganda. (One humorist declared that he was so upset that he couldn't eat anything more nourishing than a cucumber for a whole week.) President Theodore Roosevelt, who invited Sinclair to the White House to discuss pure food legislation, appointed a committee to investigate stockyard conditions. The resulting report confirmed every allegation in Sinclair's novel. When it was released to the public, meat sales dropped dramatically. The meat packers, who had previously opposed Roosevelt's demands for government inspections of their plants, realized that such inspections were necessary to restore public confidence. Hence, they dropped their opposition to inspection legislation, and Congress soon passed it.[10]

The pure food movement had a lasting impact on the fountain industry. As the cleanliness crusade gained momentum, responsible fountain owners strived even harder to serve a pure product in a sanitary environment. Straws and paper cups became commonplace at soda fountains as owners tried to satisfy their fastidious customers. Although the soda fountain had a wholesome image, this did not preclude criticism. Some of this criticism was valid, but much of it was malicious gossip spread by pro-liquor interests who wanted to discredit the fountain.

A serious problem for soda fountain owners was the widespread concern that some soft drinks contained "dope," especially cocaine. Both Wiley and the WCTU took up the crusade against hidden narcotics and alcohol in soda pop. One of their major targets was Coca-Cola, and they were instrumental in getting it banned from U.S. military bases in 1907. Coca-Cola's most vocal critic was probably evangelist George Stuart, who often thundered against the soft drink from his pulpit. In a public letter to a prominent Methodist bishop, Stuart asserted that excessive consumption of Coca-Cola at a girls' school had led to "wild nocturnal freaks, . . . violations of college rules and female proprieties, and even immoralities." But the evil was not confined to girls' schools. According to Stuart, Coca-Cola kept young men awake at night and tempted them to masturbate![11]

In 1908, President Roosevelt appointed the Homes Commission to study the use of alcohol, drugs, and tobacco in the United States. After investigating, the commission published a voluminous, sensational report on its findings. This report stated that the sale of soda fountain beverages containing caffeine and cocaine had "assumed large proportions." It went on to say:

It is well known that some of these products are mixed under the most insanitary conditions. The sugar, water, and drug material will be dumped into a pot standing in the cellar of some low building, or even a stable, where the ceiling is covered with dust, cobwebs, and dirt of all descriptions and the floor littered with filth. The steam from the boiling kettle, condensing on the ceiling, collects the dirt in the drops of water and this soon falls back into the mixture.[12]

Not surprisingly, the Homes report alarmed many Americans. Additional public concern was aroused when the federal government indicted several soft drink companies. Although public officials estimated that up to 100 popular soft drinks contained cocaine, the government successfully prosecuted only a handful, including Koca-Nola and the harmless-sounding Celery Cola. The latter was manufactured by J. C. Mayfield, who had once been Pemberton's business partner and claimed that he was using the original Coca-Cola formula.[13]

In 1909 in a case recorded in legal annals as *The United States v. Forty Barrels and Twenty Kegs of Coca-Cola*, the government accused The Coca-Cola Company of selling an adulterated, misbranded product. Government attorneys argued that Coca-Cola was adulterated because caffeine was a deleterious added ingredient; it was misbranded because it did not contain the whole coca leaf and had only a tiny amount of kola nut. Since cocaine had been removed from Coca-Cola several years earlier, the government focused on proving that caffeine was harmful. But the public was more concerned about the rumors that Coke contained cocaine. The company staged a public-relations blitz, producing a small army of chemists who stated that Coca-Cola did not contain cocaine or dangerous amounts of caffeine. In fact, some of the experts declared that Coca-Cola was a healthy drink. A chemist from the Schaefer Alkaloid Works testified that Coca-Cola was made with coca leaf after the cocaine had been removed. The barrels case dragged on for years and eventually was settled out of court, with the company admitting no wrong but agreeing to reduce Coke's caffeine content.[14]

The Coca-Cola company's crusade to convince the public that its drink was safe convinced most consumers but did not silence its most rabid critics. For example, *The Jeffersonian*, an Atlanta newspaper, warned:

Any man, woman, boy, or girl who tampers with Coca-Cola will form the Coca-Cola habit. Any man, woman, boy, or girl who has become a slave to the Coca-Cola habit is on the road to ruin. . . . It will injure the eyes, wreck the nerves, weaken the brain, loosen the moral structure. It were better that your boy were a drunkard than a Coca-Cola fiend.[15]

The lurid allegations against soft drinks cast a shadow over the soda fountain, which the liquor interests gleefully exploited. The liquor lobby bought full pages in major newspapers to publish what appeared to be news articles about the dangers lurking at soda fountains. In Chicago, an article paid for by breweries stated that fountain drinks were "a combination of bad water and decayed fruit juices," usually fortified with both cocaine and caffeine. A Boston newspaper said that the carbonated water at sidewalk stands was forced through lead pipes, which generated a deadly poison. In New York City, the *Sunday American* reported that some soda fountain drinks contained morphine. It also stated that soft drinks had caused the rapid rise in drug addiction and warned that the cocaine menace in America would soon be as serious as the opium problem in China.[16]

According to a pamphlet published by the United States Beer Association, "Little, if anything, can be said in favor of the various drinks dispensed at the soda fountain. Many of these are manufactured under the most unsanitary conditions, from decayed or unripe fruits." A spokesman for the Liquor Dealers' Benevolent Association warned that the soda fountain was "the kindergarten and the primary school for the young women drunkards of the land." Another liquor spokesman accused fountain owners of hypocrisy because they sold women whiskey-laced medicines but criticized men for going to saloons.[17]

The soda fountain industry fought back by forming a new trade association, the National Pure Soda Water League. The league adopted sanitary standards for soda fountains, and retailers who met those standards were issued certificates, which could be prominently displayed to reassure customers. The league also supported the passage and enforcement of pure food laws, cooperated with the Board of Health and other regulatory agencies, and initiated a public relations campaign.[18]

Although the rumors about illicit drugs in soft drinks were alarming, many consumers were more concerned about germs. Flu epidemics and the rising incidence of both polio and tuberculosis were making Americans more aware of contagious diseases. Public health officials recommended that all glasses and dishes used at soda fountains be sterilized and/or washed with a disinfectant. While fountain owners agreed that glassware must be clean, disinfecting and sterilizing hundreds, or even thousands, of dishes each day greatly increased their overhead. Fortunately, they had an alternative. Manufacturers were beginning to produce disposable paper products, including cups and straws.[19]

Because fastidious customers worried about drinking from a glass used by others, many fountains provided straws so that the customer's lips never touched the glass. "Natural" straws were made by picking rye stalks and cutting them to a uniform length. For farmers, selling rye straws to soda fountains was a profitable sideline, since they planted rye to feed their chickens and cows, anyway. To make top-quality straws, the farmer cut the rye while it was still green and took it to the barn to dry. (If it was allowed to dry in the fields, the stalks split and were worthless.) After the grain head was cut off and set aside for fodder, the farmer peeled off the stalks' outer covering and made uniform bundles, according to length and diameter. He clipped the tops and bottoms obliquely with scissors because this showed that the straws were handmade, rather than machine cut, and therefore brought a higher price. Sometimes making straws was a family activity because even children could do it. Home-grown American straws dominated the market, although an occasional upscale fountain preferred imported straws from European farms.[20]

Natural straws were gradually replaced by "artificial sippers," or paper straws, which were superior in terms of hygiene. The development of new manufacturing equipment meant that machines replaced the manual labor, producing straws untouched by human hands, thereby reducing the spread of germs. Early paper-straw manufacturers attempted to reproduce the appearance of the familiar natural straws. For example, Coe Manufacturing Company advertised that its Fluted Soda Straw was "a delicate translucent reproduction of the natural rye-straw with the same golden gloss and the same fluted straw fibre." In fact, Coe claimed that it was practically impossible to detect the difference between its straws and natural ones.[21]

Some manufacturers coated their paper straws with paraffin and wrapped them in tissue or waxed paper. This further enhanced sanitation because the soda clerk handed the wrapped straw to the customer, who had the satisfaction of knowing that it had not been touched. By 1910, special straw holders and dispensers were being marketed. These rectangular metal boxes, which dispensed a straw when the customer pressed a lever or turned a knob, protected the straws from dust and airborne germs. Shortly after the metal dispensers were introduced, glass jar straw holders were also patented and marketed.[22]

Since paper straws were inexpensive, soda fountain managers adopted them more readily than the paper cup. Within the industry there was a spirited debate over whether glasses or paper cups were more practical. Some fountain managers argued that it was cheaper to hire a dishwasher than to buy paper cups. But others argued that disinfected, sterilized glasses were too expensive because additional sinks and drainboards were required, as well as a dishwasher. If a fountain could not afford to hire a dishwasher, then the soda clerk had to clean the glasses. Since most dishwashing was done in the basement or backroom, cleaning glasses took the clerk away from the fountain and often led to the loss of sales. In addition, fountains had considerable glass breakage— another expense to be figured in. A few fountains gave the customer his choice of a glass or paper cup and charged an extra penny for the paper cup. The fountains in Schrafft's confectionaries and John Wanamaker's department stores were among the first to switch to paper cups.[23]

As early as 1892, the National Automatic Fountain Company of Cincinnati, Ohio, marketed the ancestors of today's vending machines, which were called "slot machines" because the customer dropped his coin into a slot. The company attempted to sell these machines, which dispensed a soft drink in a paper cup, to drugstores as an adjunct to their soda fountains. Chicago and New Orleans had significant numbers of these slot machines, but they were not big sellers in most locations because the machine could dispense only one flavor, compared with the dozens available at the soda fountain. Moreover, the beverage was often warm and watery. In some locations, temperance groups bought slot machines and sold a cup of water or cherry phosphate for a penny. Although some early soft-drink vending machines dispensed paper cups, most required the consumer to drink from a glass that was also used by other customers.[24]

At the turn of the century, Americans routinely drank from public drinking cups, sharing their germs with both friends and strangers— healthy and sickly. In public places, such as schools and train stations, a tin cup or dipper was chained underneath the water faucet. Anyone who was thirsty filled the cup and drank from it. America's growing awareness of good hygiene led some people to question the wisdom of these public drinking vessels. Dr. Samuel Crumbine, a Kansas physician, was one of the first and most vocal critics of the common drinking cup. In

1909, Crumbine became the head of the Kansas State Health Office and Kansas became the first to abolish the public drinking cup. Wisconsin and Massachusetts soon followed the Sunflower State's lead. By 1915, 40 states had outlawed the public cup.[25]

With the common cup banned in so many places, it was imperative to find alternatives. Small, envelope-like paper containers were widely used on trains and in depots. In some buildings, the public water faucets were simply shut off or removed. A few people carried their own tin cups with them wherever they went. The bubble fountain, the ancestor of today's public water fountain, was the substitute chosen for many schools. For example, bubble fountains were installed in all of Boston's public schools at a cost of $17,000—a price widely considered outrageous.[26]

Naturally, alert entrepreneurs saw an opportunity to make money replacing the outlawed common cup. Several businesses, including the Public Service Cup Company of Brooklyn, invested in the most up-to-date automated machinery to produce sanitary paper cups. According to *The Soda Fountain*, the Public Service machines were "almost human." The manufacturing process began when pneumatic fingers deftly picked up the top paper disc from a large stack. These fingers deposited the disc on a pleating machine, and another digit centered it on the pleater. The disc was then pleated, deposited in a heated mould, and stamped by a die. The pleated, stamped cup was given "a sudden smart toss" onto a conveyor belt. As it traveled along, it was showered with hot paraffin and then picked up by a mechanical digit and shaken, to remove any excess paraffin. After this, it was deposited on another conveyor belt, where an electric fan dried the paraffin. When the cup reached the end of this belt, it was ready to be packed. The machines were tended by young women, dressed in white uniforms, who wrapped the finished cups in tissue paper and stacked them in cartons.[27]

Although several companies manufactured paper cups, the Dixie Cup became the best-known trade name. In 1908, an enterprising young man named Hugh Moore dropped out of Harvard University and started a business, the American Water Supply Company of New England, to sell vending machines that dispensed water in paper cups. Moore, a native of Kansas, teamed up with another Kansan, Lawrence W. Luellen, an inventive fellow who held several patents. In 1908, Luellen applied for patents for a paper cup and a coin-operated vending apparatus. The following year, he applied for a patent for a cup-dispensing device. Subsequently, all three patents were approved and became the foundation for the business.[28]

In search of financial backing, the two young men went to New York City and checked into the Waldorf-Astoria Hotel in an attempt to impress potential investors. Time after time, they were rejected by businessmen who didn't foresee big profits in paper cups. Finally, a hypochondriac banker named Edgar Marston, horrified by Moore's description of the dread diseases spread by germ-laden common drinking cups, saw the potential. He put them in touch with the president of the American Can Company, William T. Graham, who invested $200,000 in their venture, which was incorporated as the Public Cup Vendor Company in 1909. The name was soon changed to the Individual Drinking Cup Company, in order to emphasize its opposition to the common drinking cup.[29]

Moore and Luellen peddled a cumbersome porcelain vending machine with a five-gallon water tank, a compartment for ice, a stack of paper cups, a drain for waste water, and a receptacle for used cups. A five-ounce cup of water cost one penny. The young entrepreneurs were excited when the Anti-Saloon League endorsed their slot machine, but sales were sluggish. Then, a representative of a medical supply company told Luellen that hospitals needed small paper cups to collect sputum samples. So, Moore and Luellen decided to abandon the vending machines and concentrate on selling their cups to institutions, such as hospitals, clinics, schools, and railroads. The Lackawanna Railroad, which had a fictional spokeswoman named Phoebe Snow, was the first railway to use Moore and Luellen's cups. The imaginary Phoebe preferred the Lackawanna because its trains used anthracite coal, which burned cleaner than other varieties, leaving no soot on a lady's clothes. A typical Lackawanna advertisement went as follows:

> Says Phoebe Snow, about to go
> Upon a trip to Buffalo,
> "My gown stays white both day and night
> Upon the Road of Anthracite."
>
> Her laundry bill for fluff and frill
> Miss Phoebe finds is nearly nil.
> It's always light, though gowns of white
> Are worn upon the Road of Anthracite.

In another advertisement, the paper cups were promoted with the following tortured ditty that sounds like the writer was scraping the bottom of the barrel for rhymes:

> On railroad trips, no other lips
> Have touched the cup that Phoebe sips.

Each cup of white makes drinking quite
A treat on the Road of Anthracite.
Phoebe dear, you need not fear
To drink from cups that you find here.
With cups of white, no bugs will bite
Upon the Road of Anthracite.[30]

In 1912, Moore decided that a snappier name was needed for the paper cups. With the blessing of a top advertising man, Health Kups was chosen. Unfortunately, this name didn't stir the public's imagination. Then, in 1919, Moore was inspired to change the name again. As he arrived at his office one morning, he stopped to chat with the man who owned the business next door, the Dixie Doll Company. As they talked, Moore glanced at the dollmaker's sign and recalled an anecdote that he had heard as a child.[31]

In the days when each individual bank could issue its own currency, a bank in New Orleans had an excellent reputation among the traders along the Mississippi River. This bank issued notes printed in English on one side and in French on the other. The riverboat men called the ten-dollar notes "dixies" because "dix"—which is ten in French—was printed in large letters on one side. (Some etymologists believe that these bank notes were the origin of the nickname "Dixie" for the South, but others believe the sobriquet was originally a reference to the Mason-Dixon Line.)[32]

As Moore mused about the word "dixie," he decided that it would be the perfect name for his cups. It was short and catchy; it was easy to say and remember; it looked good in print; it even had an interesting history. When Moore asked the dollmaker if he could use the name, the man agreed immediately. (Today, there would probably be lengthy negotiations, involving several lawyers, before an agreement would be reached allowing Moore to use the name in exchange for royalties, a percentage of the gross, or some such.) Finally, Moore had hit upon the right name! Dixie Cups became synonymous with paper cups, and other brands were routinely called Dixie Cups, regardless of the name printed on them. Lexicographers even added "Dixie Cup" to the dictionary.[33]

In the 1920s, the introduction of Dixie Cups filled with ice cream gave a tremendous boost to sales. In 1936, the Individual Drinking Cup Company merged with the Vortex Cup Company to form Dixie-Vortex. In 1943, the name was changed to the Dixie Cup Company. At that time, the corporation was producing a full line of paper containers at plants in Illinois, Pennsylvania, South Carolina, and Canada. In 1957, the Dixie Cup Company was acquired by American Can Company, and in 1982 the brand was sold to the James River Corporation of Virginia. In 1990, the company estimated that 42 million Dixie Cups were used every day.[34]

Everything's Up-to-Date

In the early twentieth century, Americans embraced technology like a child with a shiny new toy. They rushed to make automobiles, electricity, and telephones as common as corsets and Celluloid collars. Although it would be decades before rural areas had all the new-fangled conveniences, big cities vied to be the most up-to-date. Not surprisingly, the soda fountain changed significantly during this era. New fountain technology included iceless fountains and automatic carbonators, which saturated water with carbon dioxide more efficiently than the old-fashioned methods. There were also important non-technical innovations: the counter-service fountain, the luncheonette, and twisted-wire furniture.

At the turn of the century, virtually all soda fountains were wall models—that is, the back of the apparatus sat flush against a wall, the faucets protruded from the front, and the clerk had to turn his back to the customer to dispense the syrup and carbonated water. Even though the customers sat at the counter, the business end of the fountain was against the wall. In 1903, the American Soda Fountain Company introduced the first modern counter-service fountain, called the Innovation. As the company's promotional literature explained, "All operations are reversed. The soda dispenser, instead of turning round with his back to the customer and drawing syrups and soda from an apparatus against the wall, is now enabled to face the music at every stage of the game."[35]

The first Innovation fountain was installed in J. W. Stoever's pharmacy in the Broad Street railway station in Philadelphia. All the syrup pumps and soda drafts were attached to the counter, where the customers sat. In keeping with the new emphasis on cleanliness, this arrangement allowed the consumer to watch his drink being prepared, so he could be absolutely certain that nothing impure went into it. It also improved sanitation by reducing spills, which produced bad smells and attracted water bugs. "Disorder of all sorts are things of the past," boasted the American Soda Fountain Company.[36]

American's rivals ridiculed the idea of the counter-service fountain, but they were forced to change their tune when it proved to be very popular with retailers. Soda dispensers found the new arrangement to be more efficient because it required less walking, reaching, and bending over. They were able to provide faster service, and they also liked the increased eye contact with their customers. Counter fountains had a design advantage because they could easily be customized to fit the needs of each store. Retailers willing to invest in a custom design could have an island (four-sided), peninsula (three-sided), or oval fountain.[37]

Since the counter-service fountain left the back wall bare, most stores added a back bar, which usually featured large mirrors and electric lights. Although the back bar was mostly ornamental, it could also be used as a display space for the clean glassware. Clever clerks devised eyecatching pyramids and other formations to show off the polished dishes. For fountains serving light lunches, special luncheonette back bars were available with drawers and shelves as well as space for the coffee urns.[38]

In the early twentieth century, the trend toward serving light meals at the soda fountain gained momentum. Trade papers encouraged fountain owners to increase their profits by becoming a luncheonette, thereby attracting customers at noonday, which was traditionally a slack time at soda fountains. A trade journal outlined two routes to gaining lunch business. The first was simply to add a number of dainty, cold sandwiches to the regular fountain menu and gradually expand the offerings as the lunch trade grew. The second was to revise the menu completely, install the necessary kitchen equipment, and hire a short-order cook. *The Soda Fountain* assured its readers that the transition from serving saltines with a cup of cocoa to serving sandwiches and then a "combination lunch" was a natural progression. Serving lunch was certainly a logical extension for soda fountains in the business and shopping districts Fountains that built up a steady lunch trade sometimes added breakfast, too.[39]

In order to serve meals, stores usually had to expand their seating capacity. Since it took longer to eat lunch than to drink a soda, seats did not turn over as quickly at noon. Moreover, most women felt that it was not proper to eat lunch on a stool at a counter. Therefore, in order to accommodate the lunch trade, many stores added tables and chairs. Several styles of furniture were manufactured especially for soda fountains and ice cream parlors, but wire furniture was the most popular.

In 1900, the Uhl brothers, who operated a small bicycle shop in Toledo, decided to diversify by making metal tables and chairs. Using cold-rolled steel, they fashioned sturdy tables and distinctive chairs with U-shaped backs. Their business grew quickly because their furniture proved to be durable and economical. Not surprisingly, other firms soon began to produce similar styles. In 1905, J. Silverman, a Chicagoan who made bicycle handlebars, started the Great Northern Plating Works to manufacture twisted-wire furniture. The backs of his chairs featured a heart-shaped design, which became the classic soda-shop style still popular today.[40]

While the counter-service fountain and wire chairs were primarily design innovations, improved carbonators were an important technological advance. In 1884 Roger Scannell patented the first spray carbonator, which was a simple but efficient device for thoroughly saturating water with carbonic acid. Improved spray carbonators were developed by Harry Robertson in 1886 and Henry Carse in 1892. The first spray carbonators were operated manually, but in the early 1900s automatic electric carbonators were introduced to the market.[41]

The iceless fountain was a welcomed technological advance, even though it wasn't actually iceless. Using natural ice to cool soda water, ice cream, and syrups was expensive, time-consuming, and labor-intensive. Icing a fountain involved hauling large blocks of ice from the storeroom or cellar to the fountain, breaking the blocks into small pieces, and arranging the chunks around the pipes inside the apparatus. The soda fountain owner was at the mercy of the ice trust, which controlled prices. The trust always strived to keep prices high, and in bad years, when there was a mild winter and the ice harvest was small, the prices were exorbitant. "Ice is money" was a cliché often heard in drugstores.[42]

The iceless fountain utilized waste brine, created as the salted ice around the ice cream cans melted, to cool the entire fountain, allowing operators to ice only once per day, saving both labor and money. Although using waste coolant sounded very simple, it was tricky because the entire system would freeze up if the brine were too cold. Engineers calculated that there was an eight-degree range where the soda water was cold enough and the equipment was not too cold. Keeping the system within this temperature range was the challenge that had to be overcome before an iceless fountain could be marketed.[43]

The L. A. Becker Company, the Liquid Carbonic Company, and the Bishop & Babcock Company were pioneers in manufacturing iceless fountains. In 1903, Liquid Carbonic began experimenting with an iceless system and subsequently built a prototype that was placed in a Chicago confectionary. In 1904, Becker placed its first prototype in a store and soon built an improved test model in its Chicago factory. In 1906, R. C. Roberts, who operated a fountain in Detroit's Union Station, designed and built his own iceless apparatus. After he obtained a patent, he sold it to Becker, who set about improving Roberts' design. Almost two years later, Becker's first "perfected" model was installed at the Consumers Drug Company in Chicago. In Indianapolis, William H. Wallace invented an iceless soda fountain, obtained a patent, and installed a prototype in a local drugstore in 1908. He sold his patent to Marietta Manufacturing Company, which was soon purchased by the Bishop & Babcock Company of Cleveland.[44]

The fierce competition to be the first to market an iceless fountain was marked by charges and countercharges between Becker and Liquid Carbonic. Each claimed to have had the idea first, and each accused the other of industrial espionage. Both were relatively young companies, headed by dynamic, aggressive presidents. Louis A. Becker was born in Minnesota in 1869, graduated from the Chicago College of Pharmacy, and managed a pharmacy on Chicago's South Side. After a few years, he left the pharmacy to become a salesman for the American Soda Fountain Company, where he broke all the company's sales records and became something of a celebrity in the industry. In 1898, Becker started his own manufacturing firm, in partnership with John S. Nash. This new company manufactured the Twentieth-century Sanitary Soda Fountain, which was designed for easy cleaning. The Twentieth Century was revolutionary because it came complete with a counter, a base, and a workboard. Traditionally, wall fountains had come without these accessories, and the retailer had been forced to hire a local carpenter and a tinsmith to construct them.[45]

Becker's sales expertise and his flair for promotion soon put his company in the vanguard of the industry. Inspired by the efficiency movement popular at that time, Becker and Nash implemented a system designed to expedite every step of the manufacturing process from the arrival of the raw materials until the completed product was shipped. After only five years, the L. A. Becker Company occupied three large buildings and was planning further expansion. In 1905, Becker invented the first non-corrosive metal dripless syrup pump, which was made of almost pure aluminum and was quickly adopted by other fountain manufacturers.[46]

In 1906, Becker's company employed more than 500 workers and produced a soda fountain, ready for shipment, every half-hour. In 1911, Becker opened a new manufacturing plant but soon encountered problems. Within a few months, his company was absorbed by Bishop & Babcock, manufacturers of carbonators, soda fountains, and brass products. The new corporation was known as the Bishop-Babcock-Becker Company, and Becker became a vice president, in charge of the soda fountain division. Nash was a director of the new firm, which operated factories in Chicago, Cleveland, and Indianapolis. In 1918, Becker retired from business to devote himself to volunteer war work in Chicago and Washington. Only a year later, he died due to high blood pressure and heart disease. The Bishop-Babcock company continued to make fountains until the Depression, when it sold its soda fountain division to Liquid Carbonic.[47]

Becker's major competitor was Jacob Baur, president of Liquid Carbonic. Baur was born in Kentucky in 1856, attended public schools in Indiana, and as a teenager clerked in his father's drugstore in Terre Haute. After graduating from the Philadelphia College of Pharmacy, he returned to Terre Haute to manage his father's store. He soon doubled the size of the business and made Baur's Pharmacy the largest drugstore in town. But Baur's ambitions ranged far beyond Terre Haute. He studied all aspects of the retail drug business and decided that there was a large potential market for liquefied carbonic acid gas. Then he set about perfecting a process for making and bottling it.[48]

Baur planned to manufacture carbon dioxide on a large scale and bottle it in metal canisters that could be shipped easily and cheaply. The most obvious use for this new product would be carbonating drinks at the soda fountain and in bottling plants. A few factories in Germany were already manufacturing compressed carbon dioxide, and a German had opened a factory in the United States in 1886, but this venture had quickly failed because he did not understand the American bottling business. Shortly thereafter, the American Carbonate Company of New York began to generate carbonic acid gas by heating marble in a kiln and then cooling and compressing the gas to a liquid.[49]

In 1888, Baur opened a small plant in Chicago, becoming the Midwest's first manufacturer of liquefied carbon dioxide. He soon discovered that manufacturing a new product was easier than selling it, but he persevered and slowly built a successful business. Within ten years, he had expanded his product line to include soda fountains, syrups, extracts, and crushed fruit. At first, he sold fountains manufactured by the Onyx Soda Fountain Company, but he later bought Onyx and built his own fountains.[50]

By 1903, Liquid Carbonic also was manufacturing the Perfection Electric Continuous Automatic Carbonator, a small machine capable of producing 30-40 gallons of carbonated water per hour. This remarkable machine stopped and started automatically, mixing the liquefied gas and water in the correct proportions. It was ideal for use at the soda fountain because it plugged into an ordinary electric light socket and took up little space. Moreover, it was economical, producing carbonated water for one cent per gallon. Subsequently, Liquid Carbonic marketed an entire line of carbonators, including hand-powered, hydraulic, and electric models.[51]

In 1903, Liquid Carbonic built a modern eight-story factory, and three years later it added a new plant that covered a whole city block. In 1910, it employed 3,000 people, celebrated the completion of a million-dollar plant in central Chicago, and claimed to be the largest business of its kind in the world. In addition to its Chicago facilities, it owned several smaller plants and maintained sales offices in major U.S. cities from Boston to San Francisco.[52]

Baur took pride in having state-of-the-art factories with the latest in labor-saving devices. Liquid Carbonic's largest plant was located on the south branch of the Chicago River, so that raw materials and fuel could be brought in by boat. In addition, railroad tracks ran up to the loading docks for easy freight-handling. An overhead electrical traveling crane lifted freight from the boats or rail cars and transferred it to another crane system that carried materials to all sections of the plant. Electrical conveyor belts and elevators were used extensively throughout the factory. Electrical motors almost wholly eliminated the need for old-fashioned overhead belting and shafting. Hydraulic machinery compressed the wood veneer panels used in fountain cabinets and the cork slabs used for insulation. Huge circular saws were used to cut up tons of multicolored marble slabs, which were then polished by honing machines.[53]

The factory had separate brass and bronze foundries along with metalworking rooms for finishing and plating operations. The fruit and syrup department occupied several acres of floor space, and all the food-processing equipment was designed to meet the highest sanitary standards. There was a modern cold storage plant for chilling large quantities of fruits until they could be made into syrups. Due to the tremendous popularity of electrically illuminated art glass in back bars, the design department hired many artists, who painstakingly cut the glass designs and assembled them in metal matrices. For the welfare of the workers, the Liquid Carbonic factory had an emergency clinic, a gymnasium, indoor restrooms, and an overhead sprinkler system. The facility also housed a restaurant and clubrooms for employees.[54]

After Baur died in 1912, Charles Minshall became president of the company, and several members of the Baur family held upper-management posts. In 1926, Liquid Carbonic began to sell solid carbon dioxide, or dry ice. In 1935, the company built a new office building and a manufacturing plant, even though the world economy was still recovering from the Depression. At that time, the company had a total of 23 manufacturing facilities in the USA, Canada, Cuba, and Trinidad. After World War II, its operations were expanded to include frozen food technology and commercial sales of oxygen, nitrogen, and argon. In 1984, Liquid Carbonic became a subsidiary of CBI Industries.[55]

Liquid Carbonic indirectly spawned another leading soda fountain manufacturer, the Bastian-Blessing Company. For many years, Charles Bastian was Liquid Carbonic's chief engineer. When he suddenly lost his eyesight, it seemed that his career was over. But he was determined not to let this handicap ruin his life. So he decided to start his own company and formed a partnership with Lewis Blessing, another Liquid Carbonic employee, in 1908. At first, Bastian-Blessing built carbonators and parts for other soda fountain manufacturers. Then Bastian-Blessing bought the Fountain Specialty Company of Grand Haven, Michigan, and adopted Fountain Specialty's well-known tradename, the Guarantee Iceless Soda Fountain. Bastian retired in 1931, but the company continued to make fountains under Blessing's leadership.[56]

While newer firms prospered, the older soda fountain manufacturers were struggling. In 1901, A. D. Puffer & Sons withdrew from the American Soda Fountain Company and became the Puffer Manufacturing Company, headed by Daniel and Luther Puffer. In 1902, the American Soda Fountain Company's net profits showed a sharp decline from the two preceding years, but company executives assured stockholders that the business was sound and "future prosperity" was expected. Five years later, American announced that it was necessary to consolidate its operations in order to be profitable. Therefore, the company closed all its manufacturing facilities, except the largest one in Boston and one in New York, which supplied parts for the Beantown plant.[57]

The American Soda Fountain Company's retrenchment plan had serious consequences for two of its constituent companies, Lippincott and Matthews. The Lippincott company withdrew from American and then bought American's Philadelphia factory. Operating as A. H. & F. H. Lippincott, the family revived its soda fountain business, bought the largest marble mill in Pennsylvania, and built a new complex of buildings along the Schuylkill River. The revitalized Lippincott company introduced a new model designed to combine the best features of iceless and direct-icing fountains, but competition was fierce. In 1917, Lippincott merged with Puffer, and this new company operated until 1928, when it closed permanently.[58]

The J. Matthews Corporation had serious problems that led to its own retrenchment. In February 1911, it was forced into bankruptcy by a creditor trust company, even though it had enjoyed a large increase in sales the previous year. The court appointed a receiver, who attempted to save the company by tightening the purse strings. However, these efforts proved to be futile and the corporation's entire stock was sold at auction. George and John Matthews, grandsons of the founder, soon secured the capital to start a new business using the name "John Matthews." This company sold soda fountain supplies, including fruit syrups and carbonators. It was also the sales agent for soda fountains manufactured by George Spalt of Albany, New York. But the new, smaller John Matthews firm never attained the stature of its predecessor.[59]

The truncated American Soda Fountain Company, headed by Leonard Tufts, stayed in business until it was purchased by the United Soda Fountain Company. United's president was R. Lee Smith, who had worked for American as a salesman and then as sales manager. When Smith resigned and formed United in 1919, many of American's key employees joined his fledgling company. Ten years later, United purchased all of American's assets, and Smith became president of the new United-American Soda Fountain Company.[60]

Sammie and the Sugar Shortage

Although the United States did not declare war on Germany until April 6, 1917, the impact of World War I was felt in the USA soon after the fighting started in 1914. For the soda fountain industry, the most serious problem was the shortage of certain foodstuffs, generally accompanied by higher prices. The supplies and prices of both sugar and nuts were unpredictable throughout the war. The sugar shortage gradually worsened, until rationing became necessary. However, on the bright side, the war indirectly brought more and cheaper chocolate to the American market, which was good news for fountain owners.

Imports, in general, declined because naval combat made shipping dangerous, commercial vessels were converted for military transport, and consumer goods were left on the docks in order to make room for war materials. International trade was further restricted by developments in the money market, causing European banks to cancel letters of credit and demand cash from American companies. Moreover, changes in the exchange rate were unfavorable to American buyers. Only a few months after the first shot was fired, the French government placed an embargo on the exportation of foodstuffs. The other warring nations also took measures to curtail food exports.[61]

Because American soda fountains used almonds, English walnuts, and filberts in confections, large quantities of these nuts were imported from France, Italy, and Spain. After the fighting started, only tiny, sporadic shipments came through. With European nuts scarce and expensive, Americans looked for alternatives. There was increased demand for black walnuts, butternuts, hickory nuts, hazel nuts, and Brazil nuts. The lowly peanut also became more popular in American confectionery. Before the war, the United States had exported mountains of peanuts to Europe for food and for use in manufacturing soap. When peanut exports to Europe suddenly plummeted to zero, bargain-basement prices were the result.[62]

In the overall scheme of things, sugar was a much more important commodity than nuts. Before the war, nearly 40% of the world's sugar was produced in Germany, Austria, France, Belgium, and Russia. Most of this supply disappeared as armies trampled European crops and farmers were unable to harvest their sugar beets. The sugar situation was especially bleak in Britain, which was dependent on imported sugar. To a large extent, the United States competed with Britain for sugar imports, since sugar cane production had declined in Louisiana and Hawaiian production was at or near capacity. After the war began, Britain and the United States were caught up in a bidding contest for Cuba's raw sugar stocks. Britain also relied heavily on its sugar-growing possessions in the West Indies and bought refined sugar from the United States.[63]

After the war began, sugar consumption declined slowly but steadily in the United States while it plummeted in Europe. In France, sugar was strictly rationed, and the government permitted the use of saccharin, which had been banned for more than a decade. American farmers planted more sugar beets, and new factories were opened to process them, but spot shortages occurred. The federal Food Administration urged all Americans to voluntarily reduce their sugar consumption. As a result, the United States was able to export significant amounts of refined sugar to Europe. Nevertheless, by 1918, the annual household sugar ration was only 13.2 pounds in France and 24 pounds in Britain. By comparison, the average U.S. household consumed 55 pounds.[64]

Washington postponed sugar rationing as long as possible, but in 1918 it could not be avoided any longer. To ensure sufficient supplies of sugar for commercial food processing and home canning, the government decided to restrict manufacturers of less essential items, such as confectionery and soft drinks. Beginning May 15, 1918, the Food Administration allowed manufacturers of candy and soda fountain syrups to purchase 80% of the sugar they had bought during the same time period of the previous year. Six weeks later, this ration was cut to 50%. Serving quick lunches kept many soda fountains solvent while familiar sugary treats had to be taken off the menu. Although the war officially ended on November 11, 1918, the supply and price of sugar did not stabilize until the mid-1920s.[65]

In contrast to sugar, the chocolate situation was rosy as far as American soda fountains were concerned. Because Latin America's trade with Europe was disrupted, the region's cocoa planters shipped their entire output to North America. Before the war, Europe had bought about 65% of Latin America's cocoa beans. Without that market, wholesale prices dropped and the United States was suddenly blessed with abundant, cheap chocolate. Before the war, a substantial portion of the USA's chocolate imports had arrived via Europe, where Latin American crude cocoa was shipped for processing. During the war, Latin America shipped directly to the United States, cutting out the European middleman. Since there was plenty of chocolate, there was no danger of rationing. The only sacrifice chocolate processors had to make was to change their packaging. Instead of using the traditional tin and steel boxes, they were asked to substitute paper or other nonmetallic materials.[66]

When America joined the war effort, it was necessary to recruit and train hordes of new soldiers. The United States War Department opened temporary training camps to augment the permanent military bases and zealously prepared the recruits for fighting in Europe. In keeping with the spirit of the times, Uncle Sam decided that the best soldier was a sober soldier. Accordingly, the government announced that it was unlawful to sell liquor to any man in uniform and banished barrooms from close proximity to military bases. Immediately, soda fountains and ice cream parlors near military facilities reported an upsurge in business.[67]

To safeguard the health of American soldiers, the War Department set up an inspection system for soda fountains and restaurants near military facilities. The requirements included serving pasteurized ice cream, sterilizing all glasses and utensils, and keeping all equipment clean. Each fountain that passed the rigorous inspection was given a certificate to prove that it had been "selected and approved by the government" as a sanitary place for soldiers to eat.[68]

When the USA entered World War I, many army bases had canteens with soda fountains, but ships with fountains were extremely rare. By the end of the war, installing soda fountains on ships had become a trend, which would accelerate in the next decade. Under the navy's policy, the commanding officer of each ship had the authority to permit a soda fountain onboard his vessel. The usual procedure was for the commander to canvas the ship's crew and, if the majority wanted a fountain, to purchase one. The money to buy the fountain was taken from the ship's funds and then reimbursed with income from fountain sales. After fountain expenses were paid, any profits were spent for educational or recreational purposes. Generally, they were used to buy books for the ship's library or athletic equipment for the gym.[69]

When the American soldiers—nicknamed Sammies by the press—arrived in London, they discovered that the Young Men's Christian Association had established a large recreation center, housed in a quonset hut, to make them feel at home. This facility offered billiards, game rooms, reading rooms, an auditorium, a cafe, and a real American soda fountain. The YMCA set up similar, small-scale huts near the frontlines because Sammies longed for soda wherever they went. The American YMCA canteen in France, in one order, requested ten tons of chocolate bars and enough concentrated flavorings for one million ice cream sodas. Clearly, the American soldier overseas yearned for familiar, comforting treats.[70]

When the war ended, American soldiers returned home to find that Main Street's soda fountains were still a vital public space. The fountain industry continued to profit from the temperance movement's momentum, which prompted the liquor interests to attack fountain operators, accusing them of selling adulterated beverages. Fountain owners fought back by upgrading their standards for cleanliness and adopting new hygienic aids, such as straws and paper cups. Technological improvements made the fountain more efficient, but the most important developments were non-technical, including the counter-service fountain and the conversion of many fountains into lunch counters. Once again, the soda fountain was evolving to remain profitable by meeting the demands of American consumers.

MAKE IT QUICK!

For Americans, the defining events of the 1920s-1930s were Prohibition and the Great Depression. In January 1920, the Volstead Act went into effect, making Prohibition the law of the land. The children educated by the WTCU had grown up and were enthusiastic teetotalers, confident that absolute abstinence was a panacea for social ills. The Reverend Billy Sunday triumphantly presided over John Barleycorn's funeral, sending him off in a horse-drawn coffin, shouting, "Good-bye, John. You were God's worst enemy! You were Hell's best friend!" The evangelist confidently predicted a rosy future for dry America. "The slums soon will be only a memory," he promised. "We will turn our prisons into factories and our jails into storehouses and corncribs."

The Dry Era, a grand social experiment that proved to be a colossal failure, lasted until 1933, when it was finally abandoned in the midst of the Great Depression. Prohibition benefited the corner drugstore in two ways: new customers patronized the soda fountain and the prescription counter was the only legal place to buy liquor. The trend toward expanding the soda fountain into a luncheonette proved to be a major asset during the twenties and thirties. Because the soda fountain was an inexpensive place to eat, it weathered the Depression better than most businesses. In 1930, more than 75% of city fountains served lunch, and soda fountain sales reached $1.5 billion as businessmen, working girls, and shoppers flocked to the luncheonette to grab a quick bite.[1]

Quick and Cool

Soda fountain owners eagerly awaited Prohibition, and they were not disappointed. The five industries that benefited most from Prohibition were, in order: savings banks, soft drinks, ice cream, motion pictures, and candy. The leading manufacturers of soft drinks reported that their sales increased an average of nearly 200 percent in the first six months of Prohibition. Men with sandpaper throats and cotton-coated tongues turned to the soda fountain for refreshment, even though many agreed with G. K. Chesterton, who detested "silly drinks that fill you up with gas and self-righteousness." Eager to please their new customers, soda fountain owners promoted tart, hearty drinks with masculine names. Some even had special menus for men, featuring such libations as "John Collins—first cousin of the late lamented Tom." A few, ancestors of the modern sports bar, redecorated with sports themes and posted the latest scores in the window or on a bulletin board.[2]

Prohibition, both directly and indirectly, accelerated the trend toward eating lunch at the soda fountain. Men who were accustomed to the free lunch at the local bar went to the fountain for a cheap lunch. To make them more comfortable, some drugstores reserved several tables just for men during the noon hour. Restaurants that had previously served alcoholic beverages found their receipts drastically reduced, because selling drinks was generally more profitable than serving food. Consequently, they were forced to raise their food prices to recoup their lost liquor income. Since soda fountains didn't have this problem, they were able to keep their prices low.[3]

To attract men to the luncheonette, soda fountain owners expanded their menus, offering more meats and hot dishes. The dainty finger sandwiches were replaced with hearty, man-sized sandwiches. Making strong, freshly-brewed coffee became a high priority as Prohibition increased the demand for a cup of hot java. Whereas soda clerks had once made coffee one cup at a time, large coffee urns became a common sight at fountains. Soda fountain trade journals debated the fate of the nickel cup of coffee. Some fountains raised the price, but many managers believed that it was wise to serve a cup of coffee for five cents, even if that meant losing a penny or two on the sale. They argued that the nickel cup of coffee kept customers coming back to the fountain.[4]

In order to serve quick meals, fountain operators needed the most modern equipment. By the late 1920s, fountain counters held toasters, griddles, waffle irons, hot dog steamers, sandwich grills, mixers, blenders, broilers, deep-fat fryers, hot plates, fruit juicers, automatic egg timers, slicing machines, and conveyor belts for removing dirty dishes. In the 1930's, soda fountains began to buy automatic dishwashers, either compact counter models or freestanding floor models. But by far the most important new equipment was mechanical refrigeration.[5]

In the early 1900s, mechanical refrigeration was becoming more efficient and was widely used in such industries as brewing and meat-packing. Soda fountains, however, were slow to adopt mechanical refrigeration. A few intrepid druggists experimented with it, but most hesitated. In 1905, George Kneuper, who owned a drugstore on Broadway in New York City, had a one-ton ammonia refrigeration system installed in the basement of his store. He was so pleased with it that he soon upgraded to a three-ton machine. That same year, Philadelphia's largest drugstore, owned by George B. Evans, had a one-ton refrigeration unit in its basement. A year later, Hegeman's fountain in the Times Building in New York was operating a six-ton refrigerating plant in its sub-basement. But these pioneers were far ahead of the pack. Most fountain owners were reluctant to invest in mechanical refrigeration because it required a large initial outlay and because they did not understand how it worked.[6]

In 1915, the Henry G. Loeber Company introduced a new model of soda fountain that was designed to use ice but could easily be converted to mechanical refrigeration. That same year, after more than a decade of experimentation, Lippincott marketed a fountain cooled with circulating brine pumped through the pipes by an electric motor. Subsequently, some manufacturers marketed "50% fountains," which used a combination of ice and mechanical refrigeration. Despite these new models, the vast majority of soda fountains were the direct icing type or the "iceless" models that used waste brine but still required a substantial amount of ice.[7]

In the early 1920s, attitudes toward mechanical refrigeration changed dramatically. Fountain owners who had dared to switch spread the good news about ammonia refrigeration. It was clean and efficient, kept food at a constant temperature, and required little maintenance. Moreover, it was economical. For a typical soda fountain in a retail store, mechanical refrigeration cost about 30 cents per day, compared to $2 for natural ice. Suddenly, retailers were rushing to update their fountains and eliminate the ice. In 1933, a national survey of fountain owners found that 56% of soda fountains had mechanical refrigeration.[8]

In addition to purchasing soda fountains with mechanical refrigeration, many retailers bought counter-top ice cream freezers. When ice cream concoctions became popular at the soda fountain, retailers had a simple choice: buy ice cream or make it. Many chose to make their own—which was a tiring, tedious task because the ice cream had to be hand-cranked in an old-fashioned freezer. In the early 1900s, ice cream freezers using circulating brine became available, but they were not suitable for small retail operations. Then, in 1926, Charles Taylor of Buffalo, New York, invented an ice cream freezer that used mechanical refrigeration, made small batches, and was compact enough to fit on a counter in a retail store.[9]

Taylor, whose father and grandfather had been ice cream manufacturers, understood the mechanics of making ice cream. His machine not only eliminated the drudgery of hand-cranking, it produced ice cream with a uniform texture and fresh taste. Circa 1930, a second manufacturer began making counter freezers. Surprisingly, the demand for counter freezers grew during the Depression, even though some state legislatures, after intense lobbying by ice cream manufacturers, passed laws prohibiting their use. Soda fountain operators bought counter freezers because they were both convenient and economical. In only a decade, the price of a counter freezer fell from as high as $5,000 to as little as $800.[10]

After soda fountain owners had cooled their drinks and ice cream, the next step was cooling their customers. In the early twentieth century, public buildings usually were sweltering and stuffy in the summer. A few were cooled by packing a mixture of salt and ice around pipes and circulating the air with electric fans, but this was not very effective. Around 1914, Willis Carrier produced the first commercial air conditioner. In 1919, the first air-conditioned movie theatre opened. By 1930, Americans could watch movies in cool comfort in more than 300 theatres, but air conditioning was rare in other buildings. In big cities, an occasional department store had air conditioning. In rural areas, many people had never been inside an air-conditioned building. Then Westinghouse and other manufacturers began to market cooling systems suitable for small businesses, such as drugstores and restaurants.[11]

Installing air conditioning was expensive, but the pay-off was substantial for businesses that served food. Since heat suppressed the appetite, customers ate more at a fountain in an air-conditioned store. Moreover, customers liked to stay in the cool store, so after eating they looked around and bought cosmetics, patent medicines, and so forth. In the late 1930s, the chain drugstores installed air conditioning in the majority of their units, and independent druggists were beginning to understand that they must cool their stores, too, in order to compete.[12]

Location, Location, Location

Competing with chain stores was a major challenge for independent retailers after World War I. Although small retail chains had existed for a long time, the emergence of large chains with dozens, or even hundreds, of stores was a trend that intensified in the Jazz Age because manufacturers, in the postwar euphoria, produced a large surplus of consumer goods that far exceeded the demand. Unable to dispose of this merchandise through ordinary retail channels, they sold the surplus to chain stores at reduced prices. The chain stores passed the savings along to their customers and established a reputation for quality goods at low prices. During the 1920s, chain stores also benefited from consumer demand for conveniences and luxuries that earlier generations had never dreamed of. In 1914, it was estimated that U.S. chain stores had a total of 8,000 units. By 1927, that estimate had risen to 100,000 units.[13]

During the 1930s, the chain stores' policy of high volume at low margins stood them in good stead. In the first four years of the Depression, chain stores experienced both a smaller loss in total sales and a smaller increase in cost ratios than independent retailers did. Retail drug chains included the Walgreen Company, Economical-Cunningham Drugstores, Louis K. Liggett Company, Read Drug and Chemical Company, Hook Drug, Peoples Drug, and Thrifty Drugstores. In the midst of the Depression, a survey found that more than 64% of chain drugstores had annual sales of at least $50,000, but only 4% of independents were doing that well.[14]

The drugstore chains chose their locations carefully, usually after several weeks of monitoring the traffic flow and checking out the neighborhood. They advertised heavily and often undercut the prices of independent drugstores. They controlled their inventory closely, continually eliminating slow-moving and unprofitable items. They trained their employees in the latest sales techniques, emphasized quick turnover of merchandise, and eliminated waste.[15]

Chains transformed the entire drugstore sector by modernizing store interiors and using the latest display ideas. Whereas traditional drugstores kept merchandise in closed display cases and drawers, chain stores put their goods on open shelves where customers could touch them. The chains also used freestanding gondolas to make merchandise more accessible. Customers bought more because they could browse and pick up impulse items. Another chain innovation was offering a vast variety of goods. For example, each Walgreens unit sold approximately 13,000 different products, including radios, toasters, golf balls, camping equipment, curling irons, lampshades, shoes, and many other items never seen in as old-fashioned drugstore. Because the chains relied on their soda fountains to build traffic, they regularly featured soda fountain specials in their advertising, and fountain sales rose significantly in open display stores.[16]

For many years, the United Drug Company, which manufactured Rexall products, was the single biggest player in the retail drugstore sector. United Drug was the brainchild of Louis K. Liggett, a patent medicine salesman. Liggett, who grew up in Detroit, had limited formal schooling but educated himself at the Detroit Public Library. He had great enthusiasm for business and was a natural, aggressive salesman. Nevertheless, his career had more ups and downs than an elevator. One of his first ventures was marketing a headache cure, PDQ (Pain Destroyed Quickly). At the same time, he operated the Handy Lunch Box, packing box lunches for workers in Detroit's business district. Both businesses were booming when Liggett became gravely ill with typhoid fever and almost died. By the time he recovered, both were bankrupt.

Liggett soon found a job with Chester Kent and Company, selling Vinol, a nostrum of cod liver oil and sherry, to druggists in New England. Before long the company promoted him to general manager. As he traveled around the country and talked with his customers, he found that they had a common complaint—low profit margins. While the druggists felt that higher retail prices were the solution, Liggett decided that it made more sense to approach the problem from the other end—lower wholesale prices. He decided to start Drug Merchants of America, a cooperative that would enable a large group of retailers to bargain with wholesalers for lower prices. In 1900, Drug Merchants was formed and quickly proved to be a success. Two years later, Liggett persuaded 40 retail druggists to band together to take the cooperative idea even further. Each of these druggists invested $4,000 to start a factory to manufacture patent medicines, which drugstores would buy directly from the factory—eliminating the middleman entirely. This new venture became United Drug.[17]

Liggett planned to create a distinctive line of products, with a new brand name, to be marketed by independent, agency drugstores. Each store would be the exclusive agent for the line in a specific geographic area—usually a small town or several blocks in a large city. He asked Walter Jones Willson, his office boy and an amateur linguist, to invent the brand name. It had to be short, distinctive, original, and easy to pronounce; it also had to look good in type and meet the legal requirements for a trademark. Willson submitted a long list of coined words, including "Rexal," to Liggett, who added another "l." Since "rex" was the Latin word for king, the new name supposedly meant "king of all." (According to another explanation, "Rexall" stood for "RX for all.") The first Rexall product was a dyspepsia tablet, which was launched with heavy national advertising. Other early products included cherry cough syrup, an asthma remedy, liver pills, and Saturday Candy, which was advertised all week but was sold only on Saturdays. Eventually, the Rexall trademark was used on thousands of different products.[18]

United Drug grew quickly. In its first four years, more than 1,000 druggists became Rexall agents. Liggett's enthusiasm never faltered as he added new Rexall products, enlarged the manufacturing capacity, raised the money for expansion, and exhorted the agents to sell more. In 1909, the Louis K. Liggett Company was formed to operate retail drugstores in large cities because Liggett wanted to increase the number of Rexall outlets. Small regional drugstore chains had begun to appear, and he wanted to force them out of business. Initially the Liggett chain was limited to a handful of cities, but it reached 706 units by 1930.[19]

United Drug expanded aggressively in Canada and Britain as well in the United States. As the 1920s began, United owned the Rexall manufacturing and warehousing facilities, a chain of cigar stands, a real estate company, two chocolate manufacturers, a rubber company, a food processing company, and several drugstore chains. Although the corporation appeared to be sound, the price of its stock was falling. Liggett decided to stop this decline by using his personal fortune to buy large amounts of United Drug stock. After months of buying, his personal wealth was gone and the stock price was still falling, apparently due to manipulation by a Wall Street financier. During the buying spree, Liggett had borrowed money from 60 different banks, and his short-term loans were starting to come due. If he sold his United Drug shares to raise money, the market would be flooded and the price would fall again, threatening the company's stability. To save both Liggett and United Drug, a group of stockholders formed the Rexall Loyalty Trust Fund, which raised enough money to pay off most of Liggett's debts and prevent financial disaster.[20]

After surviving the near disaster, United Drug continued to expand. In 1928, Liggett was involved in creating a holding company, Drug Inc., that included Sterling Products, Vick Chemical, Bayer, Life Savers, and Bristol-Myers as well as United Drug. Drug Inc.'s brand names included Vick's Vaporub, Vitalis, Ipana Toothpaste, Sal Hepatica, Fletcher's Castoria, Life Savers, Bayer Aspirin, and Phillips Milk of Magnesia as well as Rexall. When the Depression hit, Drug Inc. was basically sound. However, the Liggett drugstore chain had severe financial problems, largely due to high real-estate costs. During the 1920s, the Liggett retail chain had bought expensive land for some stores and had taken long-term leases with high rentals for others. When the Depression hit, sales went down, but the steep rents and mortgages didn't. Consequently, the Louis K. Liggett Company tottered on the brink of bankruptcy. At the last minute, an ad hoc committee representing large creditors prevented the appointment of a receiver, and the Liggett Landlords National Protective Committee negotiated large reductions in the stores' rent payments. The Liggett chain's financial situation was complicated because Drug Inc. both owned the chain and was its largest creditor. Moreover, Liggett was a subsidiary of United Drug, which was in trouble because another of its drugstore chains had gone bankrupt. To shore up United Drug, management decided to sell off a British drugstore chain and sent Liggett to London to arrange the sale. After lengthy negotiations with several potential buyers, Liggett emerged triumphant, with a very profitable deal.[21]

In 1933, Drug Inc.'s management decided to dissolve the giant holding company. Louis K. Liggett emerged with control of United Drug, including Rexall and the Liggett drugstore chain. In 1942, United Drug put Justin Dart in charge of Rexall and the Liggett chain. Although Dart was was only 34 years old, he had considerable experience in the drug business. After several years of Dart's management, Rexall was losing money. The problem was a badly-timed plan to open large, new stores. Many of the old stores were sold at heavy loss, while the costs of the new ones were far higher than projected. In only four years, the number of company-owned Rexall drugstores fell from 540 to 300. Then in 1955, Dart announced that Rexall would sell all its company-owned stores in order to focus on marketing its products through the agency stores.

In 1969, Dart sold Rexall's prescription drug manufacturing facilities. In 1977, the remainder of the company was sold at a bargain-basement price to a small group of investors, who subsequently chose Larry A. Weber to run it. Weber added new Rexall products and dropped many unprofitable old ones. At this time, Rexall manufactured only 10 percent of the products bearing its name, whereas it had once made every item it shipped. In 1986, the Rexall name was sold to a Florida company that marketed suntan products. As Rexall-Sundown, this company expanded its product line to include nutritional supplements, natural remedies, skin-care products, and more.[22]

For decades, United Drug's chief rival was the Walgreen Company, started by Charles Rudolph Walgreen, who was born in Knox County, Illinois, in 1873. In his teens, Walgreen had to have a finger amputated. The doctor who did the surgery took an interest in him and found him a job at the local drugstore, where he rolled pills and ran errands for the pharmacist. After a few years, Walgreen grew restless and moved to Chicago, where he immediately found work at a drugstore. After he became bored with this job, he found another at a drugstore in Chicago's North End. When his new boss scolded him in front a customer, Walgreen's first inclination was to quit. However, after thinking it over, he decided to stay and make himself indispensable before he quit. His hard work prompted his boss to give him repeated raises, so he stayed with this job until the Spanish-American War broke out.[23]

Walgreen enlisted in the hospital corps of the First Illinois Volunteers and was sent to Cuba. There he fell victim to a tropical disease and became so sick that the army doctor said he could not possibly survive. A clerk, who overheard the doctor, entered Walgreen's name on the casualty list and newspapers reported his death. But he amazed everyone by recovering. After the war, he returned to Chicago and went to work in yet another drugstore. When the owner of this store decided to retire, Walgreen borrowed money from his father to buy it.[24]

Walgreen threw himself into retailing, convinced that customer service was the key to success. When he took telephone orders, he repeated each item aloud as the customer gave him the list, so that the delivery boy could hear him and box up the order. Then, while Walgreen chatted with the customer, the delivery boy would hustle off with the box, usually arriving just as the customer hung up the phone. With such prompt service, customers naturally kept calling.

For seven more or less uneventful years, Walgreen operated one store. Then a competitor who owned a nearby drugstore offered to sell out to Walgreen, who bought it with the help of a partner, Arthur C. Thorsen. Although the rent on this new store was high, Walgreen was able to make it profitable. He used bright, eye-catching window displays and attractively showcased his merchandise. Knowing that a soda fountain increased traffic, he rented the vacant building next door, cut an archway in the wall, and opened a fountain, where he sold his own brand of rich ice cream. He also served quick lunches cooked by his wife Myrtle, who arose early every morning to prepare sandwiches, soups, and pies in her kitchen at home. A porter carried the food to the soda fountain in time for lunch, and Myrtle's home cooking was a huge hit.[25]

For seven years beginning in 1909, Walgreen bought an additional store each year. Then he decided to merge his stores, which had been operating independently, into one corporation to facilitate management. By 1920, his small chain had grown to 19 stores, all in Chicago. Nine years later, there were 397 Walgreens stores in 87 cities.[26]

After the Depression hit, Walgreens' acquisition of new stores slowed down and average sales per store dropped. However, the average profits per store rose slightly because the company cut overhead to the bone. While United Drug was forced to sell assets and regroup during the Depression, its major rival was weathering the economic storm with relative ease. In contrast to United Drug, Walgreens had had the foresight to negotiate long-term leases with two-year options that tied rental payments to sales. When profits went down, so did the rent. In 1930, Walgreens had 419 stores, mostly in the Midwest. In the next three years, it opened 50 more stores, despite the dismal economy.[27]

In 1933, Walgreens paid a dividend on its stock for the first time. That same year, Prohibition was repealed and Walgreens stores rushed to apply for liquor licenses because the income from liquor sales had been sorely missed, especially in stores near affluent residential neighborhoods. At the Century of Progress exhibition in Chicago in 1933, Walgreens operated four model stores, which were decorated with the latest fixtures, advanced lighting techniques, and the hottest new colors.[28]

Chain-wide, the most profitable department in a Walgreens drugstore was the soda fountain, which Charles Walgreen described as a magnet, drawing customers into the shop. Walgreens fountains were famous for their "shop girl's lunch," but they also attracted many businessmen. One of the bestselling lunches was the 35-cent cold salad plate: chicken salad, potato salad, tomato, cucumber, and coleslaw on a bed of lettuce, served with toast. In 1934, the average Walgreens fountain used 105,000 slices of bread; 16,425 eggs; 1,100 pounds of ham; 550 pounds of bacon; 3,845 gallons of ice cream; and 455 gallons of chocolate syrup.[29]

In interviews, Walgreen always seemed to be slightly surprised and bemused by his own success. He was proud of being "an ordinary man"—a Methodist, a Republican, a Mason, and an ardent anti-communist. He often said that having courteous salespeople was just as important as having the right merchandise. His "commandments" for his employees included the following:

> Greet each customer with a smile.
> Give each customer your entire attention.
> Always have your customer's interest at heart.
> Never become impatient.
> Never speak discourteously.
> Be honest with the customer, the company, and yourself.
> Give your customers reason to appreciate Walgreens service.

While many retail chains flourished for a time and then disappeared, Walgreens continued to expand. The 1,000th Walgreens store opened in 1984 and there were more than 2,200 stores in 1997.[30]

Streamlining the Fountain

The 1920s to 1930s were years of great innovation in design, and the soda fountain reflected the latest trends. Scientists and engineers invented a plethora of new miracle materials: acetate, vinyl, plexiglas, melmac, styrene, polystyrene, formica, cultured marble, acrylics, noncorrosive metal alloys, and more. Designers used these new materials to create modernistic soda fountains very different from their Victorian predecessors. Streamlining was the buzz word, and gingerbread was history.[31]

Not only were the new materials attractive and colorful, they were durable and easy to clean. The new thermosetting plastics could be molded into virtually any shape, and new manufacturing equipment made traditional materials, like marble, easier to cut and shape. Form followed function as colorful materials were used to create more efficient, hygienic fountains. In keeping with the fountain's role as a luncheonette, new designs featured wider counter tops, rails for holding purses and shopping bags, and padded, swivel stools with back support. To accommodate more diners, many stores lengthened their soda fountains, and 40-foot counters became commonplace in the 1930s.[32]

One of the most popular new materials was formica, a composite available in many attractive colors. It was sturdy, wiped clean, required no polishing, resisted acids, and retained its finish for years. Marsh Tile and Marshmarble were attractive composite materials that simulated marble and ceramic tile. Catalin, a phenolic-resin product with the lustre of glass, came in a rainbow of colors. Carrara, a highly polished glass used for counters and tabletops, was especially stylish in combination with bronze, aluminum, or stainless steel trim. Micarta, a lightweight yet strong synthetic product, was a richly colored material used with metal inlay or moulding to produce decorative patterns. Many soda fountains were surrounded by tiled floors, terrazzo, or a terrazzo look-alike because bare wood floors were no longer acceptable. These new floors were easy to clean, fire resistant, and had fewer cracks to shelter dirt and insects. If fountain sales didn't justify the expense of tile or terrazzo, improved linoleum floor coverings were attractive and affordable.[33]

Porcelain enamel, an older material that had been used in soda fountains for many years, found wider use after it became available in a range of vivid colors. It was sometimes used for countertops and was also popular for decoration, especially when combined with bronze, aluminum, or stainless steel. Porcelain-enameled stools and table bases did not absorb dirt or grease, and they resisted the wear-and-tear caused by wet mopping and sweeping. Vitrolite, which was available in several colors, was promoted as a mar-proof, stain-proof, odor-proof structural glass that was "better than marble." It was used for counters, tabletops, storefronts, and wainscoting. Monelmetal was a noncorrosive, shiny nickel-copper alloy ideal for syrup pumps and similar applications. Sanimetal, made of cast iron coated with white porcelain enamel, was used for stools, bases, tabletops, and table legs.[34]

Soda fountain designers and engineers found numerous applications for stainless steel. Dispensers loved stainless steel because it was durable and required no polishing. In addition to being used for the operating parts of fountains, it was in vogue for counters. Stainless steel sinks, refrigerators, dishwashers, coffee urns, and ice cream cabinets practically shouted cleanliness to customers. Brushed or satin-finish stainless steel could be combined with marble or terrazzo for striking design effects. Marble, the old standby in fountain design, was still popular but was used with more restraint. Richer, heavier-veined marbles were combined with metal trim for eyecatching effects. Fountain designers often preferred the Breche marbles in rose, tawny yellow, or purple.[35]

Contrasting inlaid woods arranged in geometric patterns were stylish for back bars, but wood carving and fussy gingerbread were definitely not chic. In many stores, the fountain back bar disappeared entirely. In some cases, it was replaced by panels with handsome art deco motifs or by a mural painted on the wall. Round or oval mirrors, often etched with a simple geometric border, were also fashionable on the back wall. The newest trend in mirrors was tinted plate-glass in peach, blue, light green, or gold. Subtle, indirect lighting was often used with tinted mirrors to reduce glare and create a subdued, relaxing ambiance. Some fountain owners preferred to replace the back bar with extra storage space. Glass display cases were popular because the sight of a fluffy meringue pie or rich chocolate cake tempted customers to order dessert.[36]

Curb Your Appetite

In the late nineteenth century, a few drugstores began to offer a new outdoor service. A thirsty customer could drive his wagon or carriage up to the front of the store and ring a bell hanging from a tree. If the soda dispenser wasn't busy, he would come outside, take the customer's order, and fill it. Then the customer could enjoy his fountain treat in the comfort of his own vehicle under a shade tree. This unusual service was not widely available, and it didn't have much impact on the soda fountain industry—until the automobile arrived.

Although America's car culture would ultimately be a major factor in the demise of the soda fountain, the fountain industry largely ignored "automobilists" in the beginning. The vast majority of fountain owners went about their daily routine, viewing the automobile as neither threat nor opportunity. Some regarded driving a car as a craze, like dancing the turkey trot, and expected the fad to taper off after a while. A few forward-looking fountain owners thought that drivers were a market waiting to be developed. Some of these fountains were already offering outdoor service for buggy drivers, so serving car drivers was the logical next step.[37]

In the early 1920s trade journals began to advise soda fountain owners to cultivate the trade of motorists because their number was growing rapidly, especially in urban areas. *The Soda Fountain* advised its readers to create special dishes for drivers and give them appropriate names, like Speedway Sundae and Auto Appetizer. According to the journal, it was important to emphasize two points in newspaper advertising aimed at drivers: "quick and efficient service if they remain in their cars . . . and assurance that their cars will not be stolen if they get out of the cars and go into the store." (Early autos did not have door or ignition locks.) Lighting the store's exterior was very important in attracting passing motorists. "Autoists simply will not stop at dull-looking, poorly lighted stores," the journal said.[38]

The Fortune & Ward Drugstore in Memphis, Tennessee, was a pioneer in curb service and advertised itself as "the world's first drive-in." Around the turn of the century, Fortune & Ward's began serving buggy drivers outdoors. This outside service was especially popular during band concerts in the park across the street from the drugstore. Then, as early as 1912, Harold Fortune saw the potential in serving automobile drivers and passengers at the curb. He hired extra waiters and ran ads telling motorists to honk twice for curb service. At first, Fortune's Auto Soda Service attracted only three or four cars each night, but that number grew steadily. When Memphis residents complained about the resulting traffic congestion, the city passed an ordinance banning curb service in the business district.[39]

Undaunted, Fortune moved his store to a new location with more parking space. As more people bought automobiles, the line of cars grew until it stretched a block in either direction from this new store. At this point, Fortune organized a new company, which opened another curb-service store. Two years later, this business had grown so large that the company bought a lot extending the entire length of a block in a residential area and built a new store catering to drivers. The large parking lots and wide cement driveways could easily accommodate 150 automobiles at a time, and as many as 1,500 cars were served on busy days. But even this larger facility could not satisfy Memphis' demand for curb service. So Fortune opened another new store, Fortune & Ward's Soda Tea Room, with Spanish-style architecture, wide driveways, and ample parking space. On a typical night at the tea room, 14 "car boys" stood at the curb, waiting for customers. Although the boys were paid only a nominal salary, tips were good and there was always a waiting list of young men wanting to work.[40]

Fortune was not alone in seeing the potential in curb service, but he was in the minority. Across the United States, a handful of soda fountains worked hard to build curb-service trade and a smattering of others offered it without really promoting it or trying to make it a major drawing card. The lack of parking space was usually a serious problem because most drugstores and confectionaries were located in crowded downtown areas. The seasonal nature of the business was also a draw-back in colder climates because, in the days before cars had heaters, curb service had to be limited to the warm months.

While the soda fountain industry flirted with curb service, some entrepreneurs aggressively pursued motorists. For example, the General Oil Company and the Auto Inn Corporation opened a chain of Go-Zip gas stations and Auto Inns along Alabama's highways in the early 1920s. Like today's interstate service plazas, these stops sold fuel for both the car and the driver. The standard Auto Inn was a wood pavilion with col-orful, stripped awnings. Inside, a large room featured a marble soda fountain, tables, and a dance floor. The pavilion's flat roof was set up for outdoor dining, with tables shaded by stripped umbrellas. For customers who preferred to eat in their cars, a cadre of teen-aged boys offered curb service.[41]

Root beer provided the impetus for another early drive-in chain. The force behind A&W Root Beer was Roy Allen, an entrepreneur who bought old hotels, renovated them, and then sold them. While Allen was working on a hotel deal in Tucson, Arizona, he tasted a refreshing, fla-vorful root beer and decided to buy the recipe from the pharmacist who had concocted it. In June 1919, Allen opened a roadside restaurant, sell-ing hamburgers and root beer, in Lodi, California. He contracted with J. Hungerford Smith Company, which specialized in soda fountain fla-vorings, to make the root beer extract using his recipe. Although the Vol-stead Act would not go into effect until 1920, the United States was already under a wartime prohibition order that restricted liquor sales. So Allen decided to entice thirsty patrons with a nostalgic pub-like décor, complete with a bar and barstools. Consumers, especially soldiers returning from World War I battlefields, found Allen's root-beer pub to be a wholesome substitute for the pre-war tavern.[42]

In 1920 Allen opened another root beer restaurant in Stockton, Cali-fornia, and formed a partnership with one of his employees, Frank Wright. The two partners subsequently opened five root beer stands in the Sacramento area and named their business A&W (for Allen and Wright). In 1922, the partners expanded their small chain, opening out-lets in Houston, Texas. Because cars were becoming more popular, Allen decided that their roadside stands should be transformed into drive-in restaurants with car-hop service, which he envisioned as being similar to bell-hop service in hotels. Hence, he hired "tray boys" to wait on cus-tomers in their cars.[43]

In 1924 Allen bought Wright's share of the business and registered the name "A&W Root Beer" with the United States Patent and Trade-mark Office. He also developed a strategy for expanding his business throughout the United States via franchises. He began by selling the rights to franchises in Oregon, California, Washington, Nevada, and Arizona to H. C. Bell and Lewis Reed, who used Allen's recipe but called their product "Reed & Bell Root Beer." Then Allen relocated his business headquarters to Salt Lake City, Utah, and began to create his own A&W drive-in chain. His franchise agreements were meticulous, specifying the design and floorplan of each outlet, the exact recipe for the root beer, and the design and weight of the serving mugs. By 1930, A&W Root Beer Drive-Ins were familiar sights in several states.[44]

The Depression's impact on A&W's outlets varied from location to location. Some outlets thrived, while others were forced to close. A&W drive-ins were especially hard hit in the South and in the Dust Bowl. Nevertheless, the number of A&W outlets increased from around 170 in 1933 to more than 260 in 1941. World War II brought hard times for A&W due to shortages of labor, sugar, and other ingredients used in making root beer. By the time the war ended, nearly 80 A&W outlets had gone out of business. In 1945 Reed and Bell's franchise agreement expired, terminating all their rights and transferring their outlets to Allen, who was ready for the postwar boom. Soldiers were anxious to return to civilian life, and many wanted to start their own businesses, using GI loans. A&W franchises sold quickly, and more than 450 outlets were in operation by 1950.[45]

During the 1950s, the number of A&W outlets continued to increase. When Allen's wife became seriously ill, he retired and sold the business to Gene Hurtz. Hurtz's management style was much more relaxed than Allen's, and he allowed individual franchisees great latitude. Hurtz's most important decision was to allow franchisees to enlarge their menus and to emphasize the drive-in trade. By 1960, there were 1900 A&W restaurants located throughout the United States. In 1963, Hurtz sold A&W to J. Hungerford Smith Company, which was purchased by the United Fruit Company three years later. In 1970, United Fruit merged with AMK Corporation, becoming United Brands Company. In the early 1970s, United Brands decided to sell A&W root beer in bottles. Subsequently, United Brands divided the business into two wholly owned subsidiaries, A&W Beverages and A&W Restaurants. In the 1980s, United Brands sold both subsidiaries, and A&W Beverages was renamed A&W Brands. Then in 1993, Cadbury Schweppes PLC bought A&W Brands for $334 million. The following year, Sagittarius Acquisitions purchased A&W Restaurants.[46]

Allen and Wright weren't the only men building a chain of drive-ins in the 1920s. Texan Jessie G. Kirby, who sold candy and tobacco in Dallas, was convinced that people were so lazy that they would welcome the opportunity to eat in their cars. He persuaded Dr. Reuben W. Jackson, a local physician, to invest $10,000 to build a prototype drive-in specializing in barbecued pork sandwiches. Called the Pig Stand, it opened on the Dallas-Fort Worth Highway in September 1921. Customers were served by young men wearing a traditional waiters' uniform —white shirt, bow tie, black pants, white apron, and white cap. As the driver pulled off the road, one of the eager waiters would hop onto the car's running board and quickly take the order. According to legend, this was the origin of the term "carhop."[47]

In 1923, the second Pig Stand opened. In a surprisingly short time, the chain grew to 60 units. When Kirby died in 1926, Jackson took over and managed the company for three decades. In the midst of the Depression, there were more than 100 Pig Stands selling "America's Motor Lunch" in Texas, California, Louisiana, Mississippi, New York, Florida, Oklahoma, Arkansas, and Alabama. Jackson obviously grasped many of the fundamentals of building a chain, but he failed to emphasize standardization, which would prove to be crucial to the success of chains. For example, Pig Stands did not have a standardized, immediately recognizable architecture. Some Pig Stands were starkly utilitarian, almost ramshackle, wooden rectangles with windows on three sides. Others were octagonal buildings, while some resembled Oriental pagodas, with tiled roofs. At least one was shaped like a pig. The number of Pig Stands declined dramatically during World War II, but a few survived. In 2000 the chain, headquartered in San Antonio, had seven restaurants.[48]

Take-out Takes Off

While some restaurateurs were experimenting with drive-ins in the 1920s, others were busy building hamburger stands that would prepare the way for the burger giants of the future. White Castle set the pattern for the early burger chains, and it had many imitators—most notably, White Tower. Today the hamburger is ubiquitous, but it wasn't always. For a long time, hamburger meat had an unsavory reputation because consumers couldn't be sure what went into it. Hamburgers were sold at fairs, carnivals, and amusement parks, but they rarely appeared on restaurant menus. White Castle and White Tower elevated the status of the lowly hamburger, standardized their operations to a high degree, and introduced Americans to take-out. They discovered the fundamentals of successful burger chains: inexpensive, predictable food in familiar surroundings. Standardization, high volume, and quick turnover kept prices low and customers happy.

Walter Anderson was an itinerant restaurant worker who had a string of dead-end jobs. When he tired of traveling, he found a wife in

Utah and then settled down in Wichita, Kansas, where he bought a house from real estate broker Edgar Waldo "Billy" Ingram. Because Anderson was very fond of "flat meatball" sandwiches, he experimented with various ways of cooking ground beef until he found exactly the right technique. In 1916, he rented a parked, remodeled streetcar and turned it into a small diner, where he cooked hamburgers his way. He would place a meatball on the griddle, flatten it with a spatula, mash shredded onion into it, quickly cook it on one side, and flip it. He would cover the flat meatball with a bun while it finished cooking, in order to seal in the juices.[49]

Anderson's first diner was profitable, and he decided to open a second. Then a third and a fourth. Despite his success, there were still many people in Wichita who regarded hamburger stands as a risky investment. One of these was a dentist who owned land that Anderson wanted to lease for another restaurant. Fortunately, Ingram, who was helping Anderson negotiate with the dentist, had no such qualms. In fact, he saw great potential in hamburger stands. The realtor cosigned the lease on the dentist's property and borrowed $700 to invest in the new restaurant. It was Ingram's idea to name it White Castle because "white" symbolized purity and cleanliness while "castle" suggested strength and permanence. The new partners built a small cement block building that vaguely resembled a castle, complete with a turret. They served a very limited menu built around nickel hamburgers. Ingram's motto was "he who owes no money cannot go broke." So the partners paid off the $700 loan in three months and did not build another outlet until they could pay cash for it.[50]

To allay the public's fears about hamburger meat, Anderson and Ingram served only U.S. government-inspected beef. In addition, they experimented with grinding up different cuts of meat until they found a combination with just the right proportions. They used a combination of cuts because they felt this improved the flavor and texture and allowed them to control the fat content. In the beginning, the burgers, nicknamed "sliders" or "belly bombers," were made from fresh ground beef. In the 1930s, White Castle switched to frozen patties. Later, five small holes were cut out of each patty before it was frozen because the perforated patties cooked faster and did not require flipping. Ingram was so pleased with the perforating process that he patented it.[51]

Because White Castle outlets were small and needed quick customer turnover, the chain promoted take-out food, a new concept for most Americans. Customers were encouraged to buy a bag of sliders and eat them elsewhere. Many customers liked this idea, but they complained that the burgers in the bottom of the bag were crushed and cold.

Anderson and Ingram developed a cardboard package, with a heat-resistant lining, to keep each slider warm and intact. Then they created carry-out packaging for White Castle's other menu items.[52]

As part of White Castle's promotional strategy, management hired a spokeswoman and called her "Julia Joyce." Joyce's job was to spread the word about White Castle's quality and cleanliness to women and to promote take-out orders. Joyce often spoke at women's clubs, telling the members about White Castle's high standards and inviting them to inspect the restaurant's premises and operations. She also served them hamburgers, pie, and drinks in carry-out containers. This strategy was quite successful, and thousands of women turned up to inspect White Castle's operations and take food home.[53]

In 1933, Ingram bought Anderson's share of the company. Under Ingram's leadership, White Castle grew slowly but steadily. In 1964, the chain had 100 outlets, and Ingram was proud that he continued to operate on a cash basis. Although the company occasionally needed a short-term loan, it had no mortgages or bonded indebtedness. White Castle, which did not franchise restaurants, remained a family company, with Ingram's son and grandson succeeding him. In 2000, consumers could order sliders at 340 restaurants in the Northeast and Midwest, and frozen sliders were available in many supermarkets.[54]

White Tower was the best-known of White Castle's many imitators. In 1926, Thomas E. Saxe, with the help of his father, opened the first White Tower near the campus of Marquette University in Milwaukee, Wisconsin. Even though the restaurant was open around the clock seven days a week, it had a very limited menu: nickel hamburgers, ham sandwiches, pie, doughnuts, coffee, and soft drinks. Later, a few more items would be added to the menu, but the hamburger was always the main attraction. Within a year, the White Tower chain had six shops in Milwaukee and Racine. Since the Saxes "liked quick nickels better than slow quarters," they emphasized high volume and take-out in their slogans: "Buy a bagful" and "Lunch in a Bag in a Jiffy." In 1928, White Tower expanded into Detroit, opening 30 shops there in one year. White Tower did very well during the Depression, when everybody wanted a cheap meal, and expanded to 130 units despite the hard times. Saxe experimented with drive-in outlets and curb service, but most units catered to pedestrian traffic. The White Tower chain thrived immediately after World War II and into the mid-1950s. Then it began to suffer because its restaurants were in downtown areas but population was shifting to the suburbs. By 1979, the chain had shrunk to 80 White Towers, owned by the Tombrock Corporation, which also operated some Burger Kings and Golden Skillet Chicken franchises.[55]

The dozens of nickel-hamburger chains that sprang up in the 1920s and 1930s competed with the soda fountain for the quick-lunch trade. More importantly, they pioneered and refined the methods that would make fast food and take-out staples of the American diet. Thus, they paved the way for the big chains that would devastate the soda fountain in the future.

Surviving the Depression

When Prohibition ended in 1933, soda fountain managers worried about losing patrons to bars, but soda was cheaper than booze. Overall, the soda fountain industry experienced only a minor decline due to repeal and quickly recovered from the setback. During the Depression, established soda fountains fared better than most retail businesses, primarily because of the luncheonette trade. The small change spent at the soda fountain kept many drugstores afloat during the lean years. Diners unable to afford restaurant prices patronized the fountain, and the small sales added up. Some customers brought sandwiches from home and ordered soup or a drink at the lunch counter. For only a nickel, a soda conjured up memories of better times.

During the Depression, the chain drugstores looked for new ways of promoting their soda fountains. One technique that proved to be profitable was focusing on a particular food for a week or a month. The idea seems to have originated in 1930, when California avocado growers had a bumper crop and asked local drugstores to feature avocados at their soda fountains. In subsequent years, drugstore chains teamed up with citrus growers, dairy farmers, and other groups for special promotions. The National Milk Month and Apple-a-Day promotions were especially popular. Typical milk-month promotions were a Congressional cow-milking contest on the White House lawn and all-you-can-drink buttermilk for a nickel at the soda fountain.[56]

In general, soda fountain owners cooperated with the National Recovery Administration by complying with the Code of Fair Competition for the Restaurant Industry, which regulated employee wages, working hours, overtime, and so forth. To help fountain owners survive the Depression, the Commerce Department set up a model soda fountain at a drugstore in Washington, D.C., and demonstrated how a fountain could be updated for a small investment. It also conducted an extensive survey of soda fountain-luncheonettes in retail stores and concluded that a well-managed fountain substantially increased sales throughout the entire store. On average, the sales volume of drugstores with soda fountains was 64.2% higher than that of stores without fountains.[57]

Independent druggists obviously understood the importance of the soda fountain because nearly half of them bought new fountains or updated their old ones during the Depression. During the three worst years of the Depression, more than 3,600 drugstores without fountains added them. In 1938, a Dun & Bradstreet survey of nearly 600 drugstores found that a typical soda fountain returned a net profit of 14%. In 1940, another survey showed that, on average, a soda fountain accounted for one-fourth of a drugstore's sales volume. Interestingly, a study by the U.S. Department of Commerce revealed that the most profitable items sold at the soda fountain were syrup beverages, such as Coca-Cola, and fruit drinks, followed closely by ice cream. On the other end of the scale, sandwiches yielded a small profit while fountains generally lost money on hot plate lunches. So, serving a full menu at the soda fountain was not always a wise decision.[58]

Ironically, the soda fountain survived the economic hardships of the Depression but would disappear during one of the most prosperous eras in American history. When the Depression ended, the fountain industry was robust. There were some potential problems on the distant horizon, but it would have taken a fortune teller to see them. A few regional chains of drive-in restaurants and hamburger stands did not seem like a real threat to America's beloved soda fountains.

7

BURSTING BUBBLES

In the 1940s, soda fountains were an American institution popular with all ages and all classes. Like movies and baseball, they were a staple of American popular culture. In 1942, fountain sales of food and beverages totaled more than $1 billion. A rosy future seemed to lie ahead. However, after World War II, lifestyle trends led to the unforeseen demise of the traditional soda fountain. It died a slow death but eventually joined the ranks of the passenger pigeon, the dodo bird, and the dinosaur. Stores that once had boasted the biggest, most ornate soda fountains ripped them out and hauled them to the junkyard. The new suburban, car-loving, self-service, supermarket America didn't need the old-fashioned soda fountain.

At Home and at the Front

In the 1940s, while GI Joe and Rosie the Riveter tended to America's defense needs, bobby soxers mooned over matinee idols and listened to the hottest platters by the coolest crooners. Americans at home and at war loved the soda fountain. Homesick GIs craved fountain treats, and workers on the homefront gulped down quick lunches at the fountain in the corner drugstore or the five-and-dime. After school, teenagers headed for the soda fountain to hang out with their friends.

In the midst of World War II, in Circular No. 153, the United States War Department recognized the importance of soda fountain treats to American GIs. This circular listed six items essential to soldier morale: confections, soft drinks, ice cream, tobacco products, basic toiletries, and cleaning kits. To assure an adequate supply of these items at all stateside military bases, the Office of the Quartermaster General arranged priority clearance and provided Army Exchanges with the necessary ration or allotment certificates. Thousands of new soda fountains were opened at army post exchanges, service clubs, USO clubs, naval training stations, and aboard ships.[1]

It is not surprising that American soft drinks, candy, and ice cream were so important to GIs. Soldiers are deprived of many expressions of individuality, such as the choice of clothing and hairstyles. Those stationed overseas are also deprived of material representations of their

43

homeland, such as the familiar architecture of Main Street and their hometown newspapers. Moreover, they usually feel isolated because they are surrounded by a populace that does not speak English. In such circumstances, familiar objects and favorite foods become almost sacred. They are symbols of home and also tangible proof that home is worth fighting for. Hence, familiar treats were essential to American troop morale, especially at overseas bases.[2]

The Red Cross placed a high priority on providing ice cream and soft drinks to GIs overseas. In "leave clubs" throughout Europe and the South Pacific, the Red Cross operated soda fountains and snack bars, serving American food to homesick soldiers. Red Cross workers also served ice cream and soft drinks at evacuation stations, airports, and bivouac areas whenever possible. Since the troops wanted real American ice cream, the Red Cross workers made it themselves, going to great lengths to find the right ingredients. Often, the ice cream freezers were old and needed frequent repairs, but the workers persevered. In many areas, electrical service was sporadic. In Italy, for example, the Red Cross operated seven small ice cream plants despite frequent interruptions of electricity. When all these plants were operating at full capacity, they produced a thousand gallons per day.[3]

In England, the Red Cross could not make ice cream due to rationing and the lack of refrigeration. So, the American Red Cross Rainbow Club in London operated a soda fountain that served soft drinks only. American bottled sodas could not be transported overseas due to the limited space available on ships, but fountain syrups could be shipped. To increase the supply of sodas near the frontlines, General George Catlett Marshall advised his army commanders to arrange for the construction of Coca-Cola bottling plants. As a result, more than 60 new Coke plants were built in various allied theaters, including the Pacific and North Africa. Pepsi president Walter Mack objected to Coca-Cola's overseas monopoly and demanded to build foreign plants, too. He felt that Pepsi was being left out because Jim Farley, the president of Coca-Cola Export, was a prominent Democrat and a good friend of the army's quartermaster general. Despite Mack's protests, the army brass remained loyal to Coke. However, the navy allowed Pepsi to build a plant on Guam, which was not operational until after the war ended.[4]

America's fighting men ate prodigious amounts of soda fountain treats whenever they were available. It was not uncommon for GI's to consume four or five ice cream sodas at one sitting in the USO and Red Cross clubs. Ravenous soldiers returning from the front sometimes wolfed down sundaes, milkshakes, and ice cream sodas all at one meal. The Office of War Information (OWI) reported that the best-selling beverages on army bases were soft drinks, coffee, milk, and malted milk. Coca-Cola management pledged that every man in uniform could buy a bottle of Coke for a nickel, regardless of the cost to the company. The Pepsi-Cola company gave away free Pepsi to soldiers at the three biggest canteens for military personnel.[5]

When the OWI declared that the American army was the best behaved in the country's history, some pundits attributed it to the GI's preference for non-alcoholic drinks. Government officials promoted the soda fountain as a wholesome alternative to the bar for all young people, in or out of uniform. When religious leaders expressed concern about the mingling of young men and women working in defense plants, First Lady Eleanor Roosevelt advised the workers to drink ice cream sodas and stay away from bars.[6]

Like all protracted wars, World War II created shortages of foodstuffs. For the soda fountain owner, the most serious were the shortfalls of sugar, chocolate, vanilla, and ice cream. Beginning in December 1942, the War Production Board ordered manufacturers of ice cream and ice cream mix, except those that supplied military bases or were located in war-boom towns, to reduce their output, due to the critical shortage of butter. The quota was adjusted from month to month to reflect the current situation in the dairy industry. Soda fountains coped with the ice cream shortage by promoting other desserts and by selling half-and-half sundaes, which combined one scoop of ice cream with one scoop of sherbet. Since everyone knew the reason for the ice cream shortage, customers generally were understanding when their favorite fountain ran out of their favorite flavor.[7]

The shortages of both raw chocolate and vanilla beans were due to the disruption of international shipping. In 1942, U.S. chocolate manufacturers processed only 60% of the amount they had produced the preceding year. Also in 1942, the government banned the production of heavy cream, which eliminated whipped cream from the soda fountain. When sugar was rationed, soda fountain owners scrambled to reformulate their recipes using substitutes, like maple syrup, molasses, and corn syrup. Sugar rationing limited the supply of sweetened soft drinks, prompting fountains to promote tart drinks, like old-fashioned phosphates.[8]

Supplying the military was given priority over domestic needs in all sectors. The demand for soda fountains for military bases and service clubs quickly depleted the inventories of the major fountain manufacturers. In addition to supplying soda fountains for Uncle Sam, several fountain manufacturers produced other items needed for defense purposes. Retail stores had to keep their old fountains in working order, since it was very difficult for a civilian business to buy a new one. Small appliances, like mixers, were also in short supply. Even paper cups were scarce because the military used so many of them.[9]

Ironically, while foodstuffs and equipment were in short supply, there were more soda fountain customers than ever before, with more money to spend, since defense plants running at top capacity virtually eliminated unemployment. The defense plants' manpower needs created a labor shortage for other sectors, like retail businesses. As men left for the armed services or the defense plants, soda fountain managers had trouble finding good help. The obvious solution was to train women to man the counter. In 1945, a national survey of fountain managers found that 87% of them were relying chiefly on female employees. However, more than half of the managers said that they preferred males behind the counter.[10]

Self-service was another solution to the shortage of fountain help. The Walgreens chain was an innovator in self-service soda fountains, beginning with its stores in boom towns where customers were plentiful but labor was scarce. Walgreens simply removed the stools from the counter and installed glass cases, packed with cracked ice, for displaying salads and other cold lunches. The customers picked up their own trays, silverware, and glasses. Walgreens found that these self-service fountains could accommodate almost double the number of customers during the lunch rush. The War Manpower Commission publicized Walgreens' success with self-service and encouraged other fountains to try it.[11]

While most fountain operators coped stoically with the wartime shortages, the problems proved to be too much for some retailers. Approximately 17% of drugstore soda fountains closed during World War II, and most of these never reopened.[12]

More Competition

As the 1950s began, the soda fountain industry seemed to be healthy. The wartime food shortages were a bad memory, fountain manufacturers had plenty of new models to sell, and the economy was strong. The GIs had returned home, and there was a new emphasis on family life. The Americans who had fought the Axis powers and manned the defense plants wanted to return to normalcy. They were tired of dealing with the world's problems. The war had forced them out of their homes to fight or work on the assembly lines. Now they wanted to cocoon at home with their families and make up for lost time. After the war's privations, they also wanted luxuries, like televisions and big cars. Although these trends did not seem particularly ominous for the soda fountain, its demise was just over the horizon. American families were moving to the suburbs, where 85% of new homes would be built in 1948-1958. American lifestyles and shopping habits were changing. The supermarket and the shopping center were replacing Main Street's traditional retail stores. By the mid-1950s, the USA would have more than 17,000 supermarkets and 1,800 shopping centers, with many more under construction.[13]

During World War II, industry focused on the war effort, consumers postponed major purchases, and a huge pent-up demand developed for big-ticket items. When the war ended, Americans went on a car-buying spree, snapping up new models at full list price as fast as they came off the assembly lines. New car sales jumped from 69,500 in 1945 to 5.1 million in 1949. Television sales were also remarkable, soaring from 7,000 in 1946 to more than five million per year, on average, in the 1950s. Parents embraced TV because it was cheap entertainment that did not require hiring a babysitter or getting dressed up. During the 1950s, there were about 15 million new housing starts, mostly in the suburbs, where savvy contractors, epitomized by William J. Levitt, were building small, standardized houses for young families. Like Henry Ford, Levitt understood that Americans were willing to trade style and variety for affordability, in order to own a product that they really wanted.[14]

In the years immediately after World War II, soda fountain operators struggled with low profit margins. Without wartime price controls, wholesale food prices skyrocketed, but competition for customers prevented the fountain operator from raising his prices accordingly. Fountain profits were further reduced because the operator had to pay high wages for labor. At some fountains, the scarcity of clerks led to violations of health regulations, which produced bad publicity for the entire industry. Meanwhile, drive-in restaurants and roadside stands were popping up everywhere, luring patrons away from the soda fountain. The quick-lunch trend had started before World War II, but in the 1950s people wanted even speedier service. Rather than sit at the soda fountain, a driver could pull into a drive-in or roadside stand, grab a burger, and eat lunch as he drove. By 1961, the USA had more than 40,000 drive-in restaurants, accounting for one-third of all restaurant income. According to a survey, neighborhood families and teenagers accounted for the lion's share of drive-in sales.[15] The big cars popular after World War II meshed well with the trend toward cocooning by providing a unique family space. They could be a living room on wheels when the family went to the drive-in movie or a dining room on wheels when the family decided to eat on the go.

In 1949, a survey of soda fountain owners on the West Coast found that fountain sales in drive-in restaurants had increased, but fountain sales had declined in other types of outlets. The survey attributed this trend to several factors: population was shifting to the suburbs, drive-ins were giving fast service, Americans were traveling more, and drive-ins had learned how to use signage and lighting to attract more customers. Although this survey only covered five states, it was obvious that drive-in restaurants were popular across the USA. They were especially popular with teenagers, who now jumped in their cars to go cruising instead of walking to the soda fountain on Main Street.[16]

In 1946, Liquid Carbonic announced a major expansion program, including a new million-dollar factory for making soda fountains. Then, only seven years later, the company stopped manufacturing fountains. This led both the mainstream press and trade papers to report the "impending demise" of the soda fountain. However, L. G. Blessing, president of the Bastian-Blessing Company, remained optimistic. He stated that sales of fountain equipment had recently shown a strong recovery and that stores with the foresight to buy a new soda fountain would prosper. Bastian-Blessing, which had already expanded its manufacturing facilities, planned further increases in production.[17]

Despite optimistic pronouncements from executives like Blessing, it was obvious that drive-ins were hurting traditional food service. In 1953, the National Restaurant Association's annual convention focused on take-home service as a means of stimulating business. Traditional sit-down restaurants were in a slump because people preferred to eat in their cars or in front of the television. Convention speakers called take-home food service "the hottest restaurant trend in years" and offered advice on how to operate such a service. Other segments of the food industry also noted the trend toward eating in front of the television and introduced new convenience products, including the frozen heat-and-eat TV dinner.[18] While many social commentators argued that television harmed family life, it had a home-centering influence in that it encouraged families to stay home and eat on TV trays. Thus, it fit in with the trend toward cocooning.

In the mid-1950s, a few entrepreneurs saw the potential for large fast-food chains, although it is likely that no one envisioned how very important they would become. Immediately after World War II, independent drive-ins were the industry norm. Then in 1954, the two biggest hamburger chains—McDonald's and Burger King—opened their first units. That fateful year a milkshake-mixer salesman named Ray Kroc arranged to franchise restaurants patterned after Maurice and Richard McDonald's very successful hamburger drive-in in San Bernardino, California. Labor problems had prompted the McDonalds to develop a system that could serve customers quickly with a minimum of employees. Kroc opened his first McDonald's in Des Plaines, Illinois, and the chain grew to 100 outlets in only four years. Under Kroc's aggressive leadership, McDonald's expanded rapidly and there were 710 outlets by 1965.[19]

McDonald's biggest competitor can also trace its origins to 1954. In Miami, David Egerton opened an Insta Burger King, a unit in a new chain headquartered in Jacksonville, Florida. Three months later, he persuaded James McLamore to become his partner. The two men were experienced restaurateurs who believed that consumers wanted inexpensive food, quick service, and cleanliness. They opened seven Insta Burger Kings but were unable to make them profitable. Then in 1957 they severed their ties with the Jacksonville chain, dropped Insta from the name, and introduced a large burger they called the Whopper. The chain grew slowly at first, as McLamore and Egerton sold exclusive rights to large territories and allowed territory owners to operate with a great deal of leeway. In 1967, Pillsbury bought Burger King and began to impose more standardization on the franchisees. In 1989, when Pillsbury was acquired by Grand Metropolitan PLC, Burger King had 5,500 outlets. Naturally, the success of McDonald's and Burger King spawned dozens of smaller chains that imitated their methods.[20]

Burger chains weren't the only competition for soda fountain customers. For decades, soda fountains had enjoyed a virtual monopoly on the sale of ice cream. In addition to buying ice cream concoctions to eat at the fountain, customers bought hand-packed cartons to take home. Then grocery stores began to install refrigerated display cases to sell cold foods, including ice cream. At first, grocery store sales of ice cream were limited because home refrigerators had no freezer compartment. So customers who bought ice cream from the grocery could store it for a day, at most. However, as home refrigeration improved, so did the grocery store's ice cream sales. In 1951, for the first time, grocery stores sold more ice cream than drugstores did.[21]

In the mid-1950s, sales of soda fountain equipment increased slightly and fountain profits rebounded somewhat. In 1956, for the first time in a decade, the number of drugstores with a soda fountain was larger than it had been the year before. But that same year, grocery stores and supermarkets accounted for 48% of all ice cream sales, while only 14% was sold at drugstores. Three years later, a marketing survey found that ice cream was America's favorite dessert and most people preferred to eat it at home, either with dinner or as an after-dinner snack. This same survey revealed that in 1959 only 6% of ice cream had been purchased in drugstores, while a whopping 71% had been sold by supermarkets and grocery stores.[22]

Although supermarkets and grocery stores were the soda fountain's main competition for ice cream sales, roadside stands were also a factor. The Dairy Queen (DQ) chain was started by J. F. "Grandpa" and H. A. "Alex" McCullough, owners of the Homemade Ice Cream Company in Green River, Illinois. DQ expanded slowly under the McCulloughs' leadership but picked up steam after World War II ended and a salesman named Harry Axene took over the management. The number of DQ outlets soared from eight in 1945 to 1,400 in 1950. In 1948 Axene severed most of his ties with DQ and formed a partnership with Leo Maranz. The new partners started the Tastee Freez chain, which quickly grew to more than 1,500 outlets. Thomas Carvel opened an ice cream store in Hartsdale, New York, in 1934 and was operating three stores when World War II began. After the war, he expanded by opening new stores and by selling franchises. Carvel Dari-Freeze Stores had more than 500 outlets in 1956. In addition to the chains, thousands of independent ice cream stands dotted America's highways.[23]

While roadside chains were taking ice cream sales away from drugstores, supermarkets were a threat in virtually every department because they were selling cosmetics, toiletries, nonprescription drugs, and other traditional drugstore goods. Moreover, they were selling these items at discounted prices, making it urgent for drugstores to lower overhead. Since traditional soda fountains were expensive to install and operate, this put more pressure on drugstores to close their fountains. Self-service departments, like cosmetics and nonprescription drugs, could be stocked by low-skilled, low-paid workers, but soda fountains required trained employees. Selling eyeliner and aspirin was more profitable for the typical drugstore.

A few grocery stores had experimented with self-service as early as the 1910s, and the chain stores' adoption of open display was a giant step toward self-service. Another leap in that direction occurred in 1937, when a simple invention dramatically changed America's shopping habits. Grocer Sylvan N. Goldman, who had noticed that his customers stopped shopping when their wicker baskets became full or too heavy, invented the rolling shopping cart. Improvements in cash register checkout systems in the late 1940s also facilitated the switch to self-service. By 1953, more than one-third of chain drugstores had self-service in at least a few departments. Five years later, that number had climbed to 55 percent.[24]

Walgreens, the nation's largest drugstore chain, experimented with self-service during World War II and began to adopt it chain-wide in the 1950s. In the early 1940s, Walgreens executives chose three stores—big, medium-sized, and very small—to test self-service. After a year, they decided that self-service hadn't made any significant improvement in profitability. Then in 1949, Walgreens management learned that a West Coast chain, Save-On Drugstores, was having great success with self-service. After observing this chain's methods, Walgreens executives decided that self-service was the wave of the future. From 1950 to 1960, Walgreens' profits grew dramatically, largely due to adopting self-service and offering a wider selection of merchandise. In the early 1960s, Walgreens' accountants found that soda fountains and lunch counters were not as profitable as other departments. Therefore, the chain began to remove them from older drugstores and leave them out of new ones.[25]

Traditionally, soda fountains had enjoyed a virtual monopoly on the sale of soft drinks. But gradually sales of bottled drinks began to undermine sales at the fountain. In 1900, America's annual bottled soft drink consumption was only 12 bottles per capita. By 1960, this number had risen to 185 bottles, and it reached an amazing 485 bottles in 1974! Americans were buying bottled drinks at supermarkets and many other outlets. In the early 1950s executives at Pepsi-Cola decided to make take-home sales the centerpiece of their new marketing strategy. Since Coca-Cola had always sold much better than Pepsi at soda fountains, they saw bottled drinks as their best bet for higher profits. Dr Pepper, which had limited fountain sales, also focused on bottling as it expanded to become a national brand after World War II. In keeping with the general trend, Coca-Cola's bottle volume skyrocketed after the war, accounting for 80 percent of all Coke sales in 1952.[26]

The first soft drink vending machines offered little competition for the soda fountain because they had serious defects. But they gradually improved until they became a major point-of-sale. Bottles often became jammed inside the early machines, and coin receivers could not distinguish wooden nickels, metal slugs, or even cardboard circles from real coins. Moreover, coin-operated coolers relied on ice for refrigeration until the early 1930s, when mechanical refrigeration became practical. Then in 1936, Vendo Red Top introduced a new dispensing device in which a lever rotated an opening to stationary bottles. Since the bottles didn't move, they didn't get jammed. The following year, Coca-Cola teamed up with Vendo and began to recommend the use of coin-operated coolers to its distributors. Ten years later, Coca-Cola and Westinghouse Electric jointly introduced a vending machine that dispensed Coke in a cup and could make change. By the mid-1960s canned sodas were also being sold in vending machines. In 1967, nearly 1.2 million machines were vending soft drinks in the United States. [27]

The Final Chapter

By 1965, soda fountains could be found in only one-third of city drugstores and about half of the drugstores in small towns (less than 10,000 population). The vast majority of city fountains were in chain stores, because independent city drugstores simply didn't have the high traffic volume required to support a soda fountain. In 1969, *Efficient Drug Store Management* stated unequivocally that "the traditional soda fountain should be thrown out" because it did not belong in the modern drugstore. The old-fashioned, ornate fountain took up too much space and entailed high overhead, making it incompatible with the latest trends in retailing and food service.[28]

As the market for old-fashioned soda fountains shrank, the trend toward small, plain fountains accelerated. Because the new no-frill fountains took up little space, any drive-in or roadside stand could serve fountain drinks without the drawbacks of a traditional soda fountain. The latest models were starkly utilitarian, stainless-steel boxes that merely dispensed soft drinks, without even a hint of the panache and romance of an old-fashioned soda fountain. Stylistically, fountains had come full circle—from a merely functional piece of equipment to an ornate, showy centerpiece and then back to an unadorned dispensing apparatus. During the evolutionary process, form had often trumped function, but ultimately the practical triumphed over the decorative. Once again, profitability had mandated a fundamental change in the soda fountain.

The newest fountain models were strictly utilitarian because the faster, busier America no longer felt a need for the neighborhood soda fountain. Lifestyles were changing. Main Street America was undergoing painful, forced change. Urban neighborhoods were declining as many families moved to suburbia, where people emerged from their homes to hop into their cars to run to the supermarket or shopping center. The latest fountain models were designed for the drive-ins and fast-food outlets patronized by eat-on-the-run suburbanites. The old-fashioned soda fountain, a distinctly American institution, was being replaced by another American institution—fast food.

The contrasts between soda fountains and fast food outlets were marked and revealing. Soda fountains were inviting and restful, enticing customers to relax and enjoy a treat. The store owner wanted his fountain to create a lush, luxurious ambiance that drew people in and encouraged them to linger. Therefore, the most popular colors for soda fountain décor were muted, subtle tones that suggested tranquility, graciousness, and prosperity. Each fountain was unique, even if it was not custom-built. The soda jerk was an important part of the ambiance because he (or she) helped to give the fountain its unique personality. He chatted with the customers and flirted with the opposite sex. He knew the names of the regulars, asked about their families, and joked with them. A trip to the neighborhood soda fountain was fun. It was also comforting and pleasant because it was a friendly, familiar place.

To a large extent, fast-food outlets are the antithesis of the soda fountain. In lieu of a friendly face, the customer is greeted by a stranger who, except in rare instances, seems either bored or rushed. The customer gets his food in a sack or on a tray—the epitome of self-service. The soda fountain's décor encouraged the customer to linger, but fast food décor makes him slightly uneasy. Bright, jarring colors and uncomfortable furniture encourage him to eat quickly. The warm familiarity of the neighborhood soda fountain has been replaced by the familiarity of standardization. A Burger King in a strange town looks very much like the one at home, but both are impersonal.

In many ways, fast food is the culmination of the trends toward standardization and self-service. It's impossible to pinpoint when either trend began, but it's obvious that the proliferation of chain stores played a major role in both. From self-service, standardized chain stores, it was only a small step to today's fast-food chains.

Many social commentators lamented the decline of Main Street and the loss of thriving urban neighborhoods, both related to the mass migration to the suburbs. Sociologists debated whether the new public spaces, like malls and food courts, nourished the soul and fostered community life as well as Main Street's warm, welcoming institutions had. They worried that the standardized, impersonal environment of Anywhere USA lacked the vitality of Main Street and failed to nurture the civic spirit. But most consumers were oblivious to such esoteric issues. Occasionally they might sense that something was missing in their lives and feel a tinge of nostalgia, but for the most part they couldn't put their finger on exactly what they had lost.

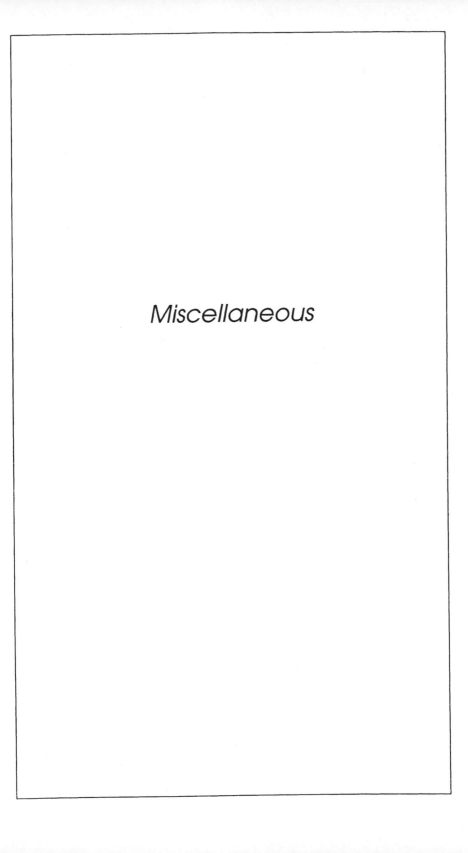

Miscellaneous

THE REAL SCOOP

The ice cream scoop, or dipper, was a supremely important piece of soda fountain equipment. Therefore, it is surprising that the soda fountain was a drugstore fixture for many years before the scoop was invented. The first ice cream scoop was patented soon after the ice cream soda was invented, and both first appeared in Pennsylvania. Perhaps this was merely coincidence, but there's no doubt that the scoop was very handy in making ice cream sodas. It was also indispensable in filling cones and making attractive sundaes.

In 1878, the first patent for an ice cream scoop was issued to William Clewell, a confectioner in Reading, Pennsylvania. Clewell's pewter-gray device, which looked like a candle snuffer, scooped up a cone-shaped serving of ice cream. The dispenser twisted a key-shaped mechanism on the top that released the serving into a dish. Clewell's dipper was awkward to operate because it required both hands, but it dominated the market for about two decades. In 1894, Edson Clemant Baugham patented a one-handed scoop, which featured a spring-handle that operated the release mechanism, permitting quick and easy dipping. Baugham's design was manufactured and marketed by the Kingery Company of Cincinnati, Ohio.

Scoops with round bowls became popular in the early 1900s. One of the first was the Clipper Disher, invented by Rasmus Nielsen and produced by the H. S. Geer Manufacturing Company of Troy, New York. Nielsen proved to be a prolific dipper inventor, patenting at least ten designs over the years. Edwin Walker of Erie, Pennsylvania, was another creative designer, patenting nine scoops as well as cork screws, lemon squeezers, ice shavers, and milk shake machines.

Raymond B. Gilchrist of Newark, New Jersey, invented and manufactured a variety of dippers, including round, oval, and cone-shaped models. Gilchrist promoted his scoops as "better than need be" and even advertised that his dippers cost more than his competitors' products, because he was confident that they were worth the higher price. Many soda fountain owners agreed.

One of the best-selling dippers of all time was the Zeroll, patented by Sherman Kelly in 1934. The Zeroll was a one-piece, non-mechanical dipper that featured a handle filled with a defrosting fluid. As the server gripped the handle, the heat from his hand warmed the fluid, which slightly thawed the ice cream, making it easier to dish up the frozen product. The Zeroll was very popular during the Depression because it rolled the ice cream, rather than packing it down, making a serving look larger than it really was. Zeroll production was halted during World War II, due to the shortage of aluminum, but the company was revived by Kelly's son and other investors when peace returned. Today, a Zeroll-style microwave scoop, which the user heats in the microwave for a few seconds, is on the market.

Specialty scoops were designed for specific purposes, such as filling ice cream cones or making banana splits. Gilchrist marketed an oval disher that produced a scoop of ice cream just the right size and shape for a banana split. At least two companies manufactured scoops designed to dish up triangular servings of ice cream, perfect for pie a la mode. A surprisingly large number of scoops produced square or rectangular portions for making ice cream sandwiches. The Economy, patented by E. S. Millo, was designed for filling paper cups with ice cream. The No-Pak disher had a hole in the bowl that kept the ice cream from packing down too tightly. Frederick W. Vollens manufactured a scoop that molded the ice cream into the shape of a wiener to fit into a tubular wafer for a novelty called a Cold Dog. The most unusual form was probably the Manos Manufacturing Company's heart-shaped dipper, which came with a set of heart-shaped dishes for serving the unique scoops.

When soda fountains became virtually extinct, some dipper manufacturers were forced to close their plants, but many models are still made and marketed today for both commercial and home use. Old scoops from the fountain's heyday are valuable collector's items that evoke the days when the neighborhood drugstore was a lively community center.

HASH-HOUSE GREEK

Over the years, eateries spawned a language all their own, which came to be called "hash-house Greek." Cooks and waiters, like workers in many fields, developed their own special jargon to facilitate their work. Many of the terms were a verbal shorthand used to communicate orders quickly, but hash-house Greek was more than that. It was a colorful argot used for the entertainment of customers and the amusement of the workers, to brighten up their tedious workday. In a few cases, it was also intended to spare the customer embarrassment—for example, when someone tried to leave without paying his check.

Hash-house Greek was used to transmit orders from waiters to cooks in the early 1850s and probably even earlier. One early source stated that such jargon was most often heard in log-cabin restaurants out West. Soda dispensers developed their own lingo, which naturally featured slang terms for popular fountain treats. When soda fountains expanded to become lunch counters, the vocabulary also expanded to include terms commonly used in short-order eateries. By the mid-1930s, chain drugstores and department stores frowned upon the use of slang at their lunch counters because it was associated with low-class eateries. However, in 1939, *The New York Times* said that "the prime requisite" for a being soda jerk was "the ability to bandy words." *Drug Store Management* disagreed and stated flatly, "[T]he most capable fountain operators . . . do not permit the use of slang under any conditions." Nevertheless, the lingo survived for decades.

The origins of many of the slang terms are self-explanatory because they are obviously abbreviations or shortened spellings. Other terms refer to a distinguishing characteristic of the food, such as "hot stuff" for coffee. A few terms were borrowed from another lingo. For instance, Seven-Up was called a "natural" because crap shooters who roll a seven or eleven on the first turn have a "natural." Some terms were more obvious when they were coined than they are now. For example, anyone who watched Popeye cartoons knew that Wimpy loved hamburgers, but today's youngsters may not make that connection. Likewise, young people are unlikely to know that John Wayne was an actor who played tough guys in movies and, therefore, a difficult customer was "John Wayne" or "Duke," which was Wayne's nickname.

Some origins may have been apparent when the terms were coined but are obscure now—such as B.M.T. for bacon and tomato sandwich and I.R.T. for lettuce and tomato sandwich. B.M.T. was the common abbreviation for the Brooklyn-Manhattan Transit Company, while I.R.T. stood for the Interborough Rapid Transit Company. Using these two abbreviations for sandwiches may have been rational at the time, but the connection is obscure today. Similarly, "to the left" for lemon syrup and "to the right" for cherry syrup are puzzling today but would have been logical in the fountain's heyday, because those two flavors were usually located on either side of the cola-syrup pump. A few of the terms originated as puns. For example, "down" meant toast, so "tuna down" was a tuna salad sandwich on toast. Because "tuna down" sounded like something one would do to the radio, "radio" also meant tuna salad on toast.

Some slang terms were used more or less universally, while others were used in specific geographic areas and were unknown in other parts of the country. Not surprisingly, there were multiple terms for many common menu items. For example, "honest," "virgin," "virgin Coke," "virtue," and "make it virtuous" all referred to cherry Coca-Cola. The root of the last four was the slang usage of "cherry" for virginity, but "honest" had a different origin. It referred to the legend about George Washington cutting down a cherry tree and being praised for his honesty when he did not lie about his misdeed.

One of the most common slang terms was "soda jerk," which first appeared as "soda jerker," referring to the jerking motion made by the dispenser when he pulled on the spigot handles. "Soda jerker" appeared in print as early as 1883 in *Groceryman and Peck's Bad Boy*, one of a series of popular books by humorist George Wilbur Peck, who later became the governor of Wisconsin. Although consumers had no problem with "soda jerk," the soda fountain industry did. *Let's Sell Ice Cream*, published by the Ice Cream Merchandising Institute, stated that the term was insulting because "jerk" meant "halfwit" or "moron." Just as no doctor would call himself a "pill pusher," no soda dispenser should call himself a "jerk," reasoned the book's author. Some industry publications promoted "fountaineer" and "fizzician" as occupational titles that sounded more professional, but neither caught on.

Let's Sell Ice Cream also included advice by Richard C. Reager, chairman of the speech department at Rutgers University. Reager told drugstore employees to avoid grunts, groans, mispronunciations, argumentative words, and lazy, careless speech, such as dropping a word's final consonant. He also instructed them to talk quietly, use a pleasant tone, and "smile with your voice." In large type, he forbade the use of WISECRACKS, PUNS, ATTEMPTS AT HUMOR, FORCED GREET-

INGS, and SLANG. If the survival of a large vocabulary of hash-house Greek is any indication, Reager's advice fell on many deaf ears.

ABBOTT & COSTELLO: A serving of franks and beans.
ABC: A bowl of alphabet soup.
ACTOR or BAD ACTOR: A ham sandwich.
ADAM AND EVE: Two fried eggs. (In some locations, this meant two poached eggs.)
ADAM AND EVE ON A RAFT: Two fried eggs on toast. (In some locations, this referred to poached eggs.)
ADAM AND EVE ON A RAFT—SINK 'EM: Two fried eggs, with broken yolks, on toast.
ADAM AND EVE ON A RAFT—WRECK 'EM: Two scrambled eggs on toast.
ADAM'S ALE: Water.
A JACK: A grilled American cheese sandwich.
ALL BLACK: A chocolate soda with chocolate ice cream.
ALL HOT: Baked potato.
ALL THE WAY: Make a sandwich with lettuce, tomato, and all the trimmings.
AMMO or AMMUNITION: Beans.
AND ANOTHER: A cup of coffee.
AN IN: An ice cream soda.
APPLE IN: A pineapple ice cream soda.
APPLE SHAKE: A pineapple milk shake.
ARIZONA: Buttermilk.
ARMORED COW: Canned milk.
ATLANTA SPECIAL: Coca-Cola.
AVIATOR: A customer who does not tip.
AXLE GREASE: Butter.

BABY: Small glass of milk.
BACON AND: An order of bacon and eggs.
BALE OF HAY: Shredded wheat cereal.
BARKED PIE: A two-crust pie.
BARKER: A hot dog.
BAR MOP: Dish towel.
BEAGLE: A hot dog.
BEAN JOCKEY: Waiter or waitress.
BELCH WATER: Seltzer water.
BELLYWASH: Soup.
BERRIES: Eggs.

BIB: Napkin.

BICARB: Bicarbonate of soda.

BIDDIES: Eggs.

BIDDIES ON A RAFT: Eggs on toast.

BIDDY BREAD: French toast.

BILGE: Soup.

BIRD SEED: A generic term for cereal. (In some locations, this meant grapenuts cereal.)

BLACK AND WHITE: A glass of chocolate malted milk with vanilla ice cream. (In some locations, this meant a cup of black coffee with cream or a chocolate soda with vanilla ice cream or a scoop of chocolate ice cream topped with marshmallow syrup.)

BLACK BOTTOM: Chocolate ice cream with chocolate syrup.

BLACK COW: Chocolate milk. (In some locations, a root beer float.)

BLACK-OUT: A dish of vanilla ice cream smothered with chocolate syrup.

BLACK STICK: A chocolate ice cream cone.

BLANCHE: An incompetent waitress.

BLANKETS: Pancakes.

BLAST IT: Heat it up.

BLONDE: A cup of coffee with cream.

BLOOD: Ketchup.

BLOWOUT PATCHES: Pancakes.

B.L.T.: Bacon, lettuce, and tomato sandwich.

B.M.T.: Bacon and tomato sandwich.

BLUE BOTTLE: Seltzer water or bromo seltzer.

BOILED LEAVES: Hot tea.

BOSSY: Beef.

BOSSY IN A BOWL: Beef stew.

BOTTOM: Ice cream in a drink.

BOULEVARD: Generic term for an ice cream soda.

BOVINE EXTRACT: Milk.

BOWL OF FIRE or BOWL OF RED: An order of chili.

BOW-WOW: A hot dog.

BREAK IT AND SHAKE IT: Put an egg in a drink.

BREATH: Onion.

BRIDE AND GROOM: Two fried eggs.

BRIDE AND GROOM ON A RAFT: Two fried eggs on toast.

BRIDGE: Four of anything. (It takes four people to play bridge.)

BRONX VANILLA: Garlic.

BROWN: Chocolate syrup.

BROWN BOULEVARD: A chocolate ice cream soda.

BROWN WASH: Weak coffee.

B.T.: Bacon and tomato sandwich.

BUBBLE DANCER: Dishwasher.

BUCKET OF HAIL: A glass of ice.

BULLDOG: A large hot dog.

BULLETS: Beans.

BUN PUP: A hot dog.

BURN IT: Cook the order well done. (In some locations, cook it quickly.)

BURN ONE: Make a chocolate malted milk.

BURN ONE ALL THE WAY: Make a chocolate malted milk with chocolate ice cream.

BURN ONE AND LET IT SWIM: Make a chocolate malted milk float.

BURN ONE WITH A CACKLE: Make an egg malted milk.

BURN THE BRITISH: Toast an English muffin.

BUTTONS: Small, round crackers.

CACKLEBERRIES: Eggs.

CACKLEBERRIES AND GRUNT: An order of bacon and eggs.

CACKLERS: Eggs.

CAKES HAM: An order of pancakes with ham.

CAMPERS: Customers who stay for a long time.

CANARY: Lemon Coca-Cola.

CANARY ISLAND SPECIAL: A vanilla soda with chocolate ice cream.

CANNED COW: Condensed milk.

CANNIBAL: A hamburger cooked rare.

CAR FARE: A tip.

CARNATION: An onion.

CAT BEER: Milk.

CAT'S EYES: Tapioca.

CHALK: Chocolate syrup.

CHASER OF ADAM'S ALE: A glass of water.

CHEWED FINE: A hamburger.

CHEWED FINE WITH A BREATH: A hamburger with onions.

CHICAGO: A pineapple ice cream soda or pineapple sundae.

CHINA: Rice pudding.

CHINA CHOW: Chow mein. (In some locations, this referred to chop suey.)

CHINA CLIPPER: Dishwasher.

CHIP: A pat of butter.

CHOC COKE: Chocolate Coca-Cola.

CHOC HIGH or CHOC MALT: Chocolate malted milk.

CHOCOLATE ALL AROUND: A chocolate soda with chocolate ice cream.

CHOKE ONE: Cook a hamburger.

CHOKER HOLES: Doughnuts.

CHOW SLINGER: Waiter or waitress.

CHUMP: Customer.

CITY COKE or CITY JUICE: Water.

C.J. WHITE: Cream cheese and jelly sandwich on white bread.

CLEAR ONE: A glass of water.

CLEAN UP THE KITCHEN: Prepare an order of hash.

CLOWN: Hot dog.

C&O: Cream cheese and olive sandwich.

C.O. COCKTAIL or C.O. HIGHBALL: A dose of castor oil in soda water.

COFF: Coffee.

COFFEE AND: A cup of coffee and a doughnut.

COKE MUSH: A Coca-Cola ice cream soda.

COKE STRETCHER: A customer who made a small purchase and sat at the fountain for a long time.

COKETTE: A girl who hangs out at the soda fountain.

COLD BAG or COLD ENGLISH: A glass of iced tea.

COLD ON: A la mode. For example, "cold on apple" meant apple pie a la mode.

COLD SPOT: A glass of iced tea.

COMBO: A combination salad or sandwich.

COMMUNIST: Ketchup.

CONEY ISLAND BLOODHOUND or CONEY ISLAND CHICKEN: A hot dog.

COUNTER JUMPING: Working at a soda fountain or lunch counter.

COW or COW JUICE: Milk.

COW BETWEEN SHEETS: An order for a roast beef sandwich.

COWBOY: A Denver or western sandwich. (In some locations, a western omelet.)

COWBOY WITH SPURS: Denver or western sandwich with french fries.

COWCUMBER: A pickle.

COW FEED: Salads.

COW GREASE: Butter.

COW TRUCK: Dairy products in general.

CRAPS: Sugar cubes.

CRASH: Scrambled eggs.

CREAM DE GOO: Milk toast.

CREAM IT: Cook the order well done.

CREMATE IT: Toast the bread.

CROW: Chocolate pie.

CROWD: Three of anything. (Two's company; three's a crowd.)

CRUMBS: Small children.

CUP OF MUD: A cup of coffee.

C&W: Cream cheese and walnut sandwich.

DAGWOOD: A large sandwich.

DAGWOOD SPECIAL: A banana split.

DANDY: A chocolate sundae.

DEADEYES: Poached eggs.

DEADS: Dirty dishes.

DEATH IN THE AFTERNOON: A bowl of chili with beans.

DECK: The top of the counter or table.

DEEP-SIX IT: Throw it out.

DER UFFS: Two eggs. (A corruption of the French "deux oeufs.")

DEUCE: A table with two customers.

DICE: Sugar cubes.

DILLY: Lime-flavored soda.

DISH BREAKER or DISHCLOTH: Dishwasher.

DISH JUGGLER: Waiter or waitress.

DISHWATER: Soup.

DOG AND MAGGOT: Cheese and crackers.

DOG BISCUITS: Crackers.

DOG SOUP: Water.

DOLLY VARDEN: A generic term for ice cream soda.

DO THE SPLITS: Make a banana split.

DOUBLE-DECKER: A two-scoop ice cream cone.

DOUGH WELL DONE WITH COW TO COVER: Bread and butter. (In some locations, this meant an order of buttered toast.)

DOWN: Toast.

DRAGGER: Customer who does not tip.

DRAGGING: Part of an order is missing. For example, the toast is dragging.

DRAG ONE THROUGH GEORGIA: Fill an order for a chocolate Coca-Cola.

DRAW ONE or DRAW ONE BLACK or DRAW ONE IN THE DARK or DRAW SOME MUD: Pour a cup of coffee.

DRESS A PIG: Fill an order for a ham sandwich.

DRESS A PIG TO TRAVEL: Fill an order for a ham sandwich to go.

DROP: A generic term for ice cream sundae.

DRUGSTAURANT: A drugstore soda fountain with a large menu.

DUKE: A tough customer.

DUNKER: Doughnut.

DUST: Malted milk powder.

DUSTY MILLER: A chocolate sundae with a dusting of malted milk powder. (In some locations, this meant a scoop of vanilla ice cream topped with chocolate syrup, marshmallow syrup, and malted milk powder.)

DUSTY ROAD: A chocolate sundae with a dusting of malted milk powder.

ECHO: Repeat order.

EGG CREAM: A chocolate soda with a dash of milk.

ELEPHANT DANDRUFF: Corn flakes cereal.

ENGLISH: A cup of hot tea.

EVE WITH THE LID ON: Apple pie.

EYEFUL: Grapefruit.

EYE OPENER: A dose of castor oil in sarsaparilla.

FARMER'S LUNCH: Banana split.

FILET: A la mode. (In some locations, a filet was a slice of fudge cake.)

FISH EGGS: Tapioca.

FIX THE PUMPS: Code between two male workers for "Look at the girl with the large breasts."

FIZZ or FIZZ WATER: Soda water.

FLATS: Pancakes.

FLOATER: A glass of malted milk with a scoop of ice cream.

FLOP 'EM: Fry two eggs until the yolks are firm.

FLOWER: An onion.

FLUFF AND FOLD: Give a customer special attention.

FODDER: Salads.

FOUNTAINEER: Soda jerk.

FOUR IN A BOAT: Four scoops of ice cream in a dish.

FOUR-TOP: A table for four people.

FREAK: Orange-flavored soda.

FREEZE ONE: Make a chocolate frosted.

FRESH: Lemon-flavored soda.

FRESH GREEN: Lime-flavored soda.

FROSTED: A glass of malted milk.

FROST ONE: Make a frosted Coca-Cola. (In some locations, make a frosted chocolate soda.)

FROWN: Lemon Coca-Cola.

FRUICE: Fruit juice.

FRY ONE: Fry an egg with an unbroken yolk.

FULL HOUSE: Grilled cheese, bacon, and tomato sandwich.

GAC: Grilled American cheese sandwich.

GALVANIZED GUERNSEY: Canned milk.

GEDUNK: Eat a sundae.

GEE: Glass

GENTLEMAN WILL TAKE A CHANCE: The customer is ordering hash.

GEORGE EDDY: Customer who does not tip.

GLOB: Generic term for an ice cream sundae.

GLUE: Oatmeal.

GO FOR A WALK: Prepare a take-out order.

GOO or GOOK or GOOZLUM: Syrup.

GOOBER: Peanut butter sandwich.

GORP: Eat greedily or sloppily.

GRAB JOINT: A lunch counter or other quick-lunch eatery.

GRAFERS: Graham crackers.

GRAND ON A PLATE: Serving of baked beans.

GRASS: A salad or lettuce.

GRAVEL: Grapenuts cereal.

GRAVEYARD STEW: Milk toast.

GREASE: Butter.

GREAT UNKNOWN: A bowl of hash.

GRIND ONE: Make an orangeade.

GROUNDHOG or GROWL: A hot dog.

GUMMER: A customer, especially an elderly person, who takes a long time to eat.

HAIL: Ice cubes.

HALF MALT: A small glass of malted milk.

HALITOSIS: Onion.

HAM AND: An order of ham and eggs.

HAM STEAK WITH: A hamburger with onion.

HAM STEAK WITHOUT: A hamburger without onion.

HANDFUL: Five of anything. HANDFUL PLUS ONE: Six of anything. HANDFUL PLUS A PAIR: Seven. HANDFUL PLUS A CROWD: Eight. HANDFUL PLUS A BRIDGE: Nine.

HANG A DRAW: Fill an order for a glass of root beer.

HANG A FROWN: Fill an order for lemon Coke.

HANG A MUDDY: Fill an order for chocolate Coca-Cola.

HANG A VAN: Fill an order for vanilla Coca-Cola.

HANG ONE: Fill an order for a Coca-Cola.

HAY: A salad.

HAYSTACK: An order of strawberry pancakes.

H.C.: Ham and cheese sandwich.

HEADLIGHTS: Two eggs sunny-side up.

HEAT ONE: Make a cup of hot chocolate.

HEAVENLY DEW: Generic term for soft drink.

HEAVY ON THE HAIL: Add extra ice.

HEMORRHAGE: Ketchup.

HEN FRUIT SAND: An egg sandwich.

HIGH & DRY: A sandwich without condiments.

HITCH OLD DOBBIN TO A BUN: Make a hamburger.

HOBOKEN SPECIAL: A pineapple soda with chocolate ice cream.

H2O COCKTAIL: A glass of water.

HOLD THE GRASS: Make a sandwich without lettuce.

HOLD THE HAIL or HOLD THE HAIR: Make a drink without ice.

HOLLYWOOD: Chocolate Coca-Cola.

HONEST: Cherry Coke.

HOPE: Oatmeal.

HOPS: Malted-milk extract.

HOT BAG: A cup of hot tea.

HOT CHA: Hot chocolate.

HOTS: Pancakes.

HOT SCOTCH: Hot butterscotch syrup.

HOT STUFF: A cup of coffee.

HOT SUN: A hot butterscotch sundae.

HOT TOP: A cup of hot chocolate.

HOUND or HOUND ON AN ISLAND: A hot dog.

HOUSEBOAT: A banana split.

HUDDLE SODA: One soda with two straws, often ordered by a courting couple.

HUDSON RIVER ALE: Water.

HUG ONE: Fill an order for fresh-squeezed orange juice.

HUMPTY-DUMPTY: Scrambled eggs.

HUSKY: A large hot dog.

IN: A generic term for ice cream soda.

INK or IODINE: Coffee.

IN THE AIR: A large glass.

IN THE ALLEY: A side order.

IN THE HAY: Strawberry ice cream soda or milk shake.

IN THE WEEDS: The fountain or counter is swamped with customers.
IN THE WINDOW: Refers to an order that has been cooked and is ready
    to go.
I.R.T.: Lettuce and tomato sandwich.

JACK: Grilled cheese sandwich.
JACK BACK: Grilled cheese and bacon sandwich.
JAVA: Coffee.
JEEP: A novice or inept soda jerk.
JENNIE: Waitress.
JOE: Coffee.
JOE POT: A pot of coffee.
JOHN WAYNE: A tough customer.

L.A.: A la mode.
LACEY CUP: Cup of hot chocolate.
LEADER: The special of the day.
LEAVES: Lettuce.
LEG OFF A PAIR OF DRAWERS: Pour one cup of coffee.
LEMON SUDS: Lemon cream pie.
LET IT WALK: Make this order to go.
LET THE SUNSHINE IN: Fry an egg with an unbroken yolk.
LICK AND SMELL: Grab a light lunch.
LIFESAVER: A doughnut.
LIGHTHOUSE: Ketchup bottle.
LOAD OF: A plate of anything.
LONG COKE: A large glass of Coca-Cola.
LONG STACK: A large order of pancakes.
LOOSENERS: An order of prunes.
L.T.: A lettuce and tomato sandwich.
LUMBER: Toothpicks.
LUNGS: Smokers.

MAGGOT: A generic term for cheese.
MAIDEN'S DELIGHT: Cherries.
MAKE IT VIRTUOUS: Fill an order for a cherry Coke.
MAKE ONE OLD STYLE: Fill an order for a glass of root beer.
MALT TOSSER: Soda jerk.
MAMA: Marmalade.
MANHATTAN COCKTAIL: Castor oil in soda water.
MARY GARDEN or M.G. COCKTAIL: Citrate of magnesia.
MASHED T-BONE: A hamburger.

MAY or MAYO: Mayonnaise.

M.D.: Dr Pepper.

MIDNIGHT: A cup of black coffee.

MIKE AND IKE: Salt and pepper shakers.

MILK SHAKER: Soda jerk.

MILLION ON A PLATTER: A serving of baked beans.

MODE: A scoop of ice cream.

MOISTURE: Water.

MOKE: Coffee.

MOO or MOO JUICE: Milk.

MOO WITH GOO: An ice cream sundae with extra syrup.

MUD: Chocolate pudding. (In some locations, "mud" meant chocolate soda pop or chocolate ice cream.)

MUG OF MURK: A cup of coffee.

MURK—NO COW: A cup of black coffee.

MURPHY: Potato.

MURPHY WITH A WREATH: A plate of ham, potatoes, and cabbage.

MYSTERY: A bowl of hash. (In some locations, "mystery" referred to a chocolate and vanilla sundae.)

NAKED STEAK: Plain hamburger.

NATURAL: Seven-Up.

NERVOUS PUDDING: Jello. (In some locations, this referred to jelly.)

NOAH'S BOY: Ham.

NO COW: A cup of coffee without cream.

NONSKIDS: Waffles.

NOSE WARMER: Hot consommé served in a cup.

NUX: Hot tea.

OH-GEE: Orangeade.

O.J.: Orange juice.

OLD-FASHIONED or OLD STYLE: Root beer.

ON: Generic term for an ice cream sundae.

ONE DOWN: An order of toast.

ONE FROM MANHATTAN: A bowl of clam chowder.

ONE FROM THE ALPS: Swiss cheese sandwich.

ONE IN: Chocolate ice cream soda.

ONE IN ALL THE WAY: A chocolate soda with chocolate ice cream.

ONE IN SHAKE: Chocolate milk shake.

ONE IN THE HAY: A strawberry milk shake.

ONE ON: A chocolate sundae. (In some locations, an order of toast or a hamburger.)

ONE ON STRAW: A strawberry sundae.

ONE ON THE CITY or ONE ON THE HOUSE: A glass of water.

ONE ON THE COUNTRY: A glass of buttermilk.

ONE UP: Hot dog. (In some locations, a cup of hot chocolate.)

ON THE HOOF: Cook the meat rare.

ON WHEELS: A take-out order.

OPENERS: An order of prunes.

ORDERETTE: A small order.

PAINT: Ketchup.

PAIR: Two orders of the same item, such as two hamburgers.

PAIR OF DRAWERS: Two cups of coffee.

PALLBEARER: Busboy.

PARTY: Four orders of the same item, such as four hamburgers.

PATCH: Strawberry ice cream.

P.C.: Chocolate milk.

PEARL DIVER: Dishwasher.

PEST: Assistant soda fountain manager.

P.I.: Pineapple juice.

PIG BETWEEN TWO SHEETS: A ham sandwich.

PIN A ROSE ON IT: Put an onion on a sandwich.

PINK STICK: A strawberry ice cream cone.

PITTSBURGH!: The toast is burning.

PLAIN VANILLA: A soda fountain manager who's been demoted.

PLATTER OF SATURDAY NIGHTS: A serving of baked beans.

POOCH: Hot dog.

POP BOY: A novice or inept soda jerk.

POPEYE: Spinach.

POP ONE: Fill a glass with Coca-Cola.

POT MASSAGER: Dishwasher.

POTOMAC PHOSPHATE: Water.

POT RASTLER: Dishwasher.

PRIDDLE: A pan of water used for washing the counter or tables.

PROFESSOR: A soda jerk.

P.T.: A pot of hot tea.

PULL ONE: Fill a glass with milk.

PULL ONE MUDDY: Fill a glass with chocolate milk.

P.W.G.: Pretty waiter girl.

RABBIT FOOD: A salad.

RADIO: Tuna salad sandwich made with toasted bread.

RED: Cherry Coke.

RED BALL: Orangeade.

RED EYES: An order for two eggs cooked sunny-side up.

RED LEAD: Ketchup.

RHINELANDER: A chocolate soda with vanilla ice cream.

RIFFLE: Refill the order.

ROOT BEER SPECIAL: Castor oil in root beer.

RUMBA: A milk shake.

RUNNER: A take-out order.

RUSH IT: Put Russian dressing on a salad.

SALTIES: Salted peanuts.

SALT-WATER MAN: Man who makes ice cream for the fountain.

SALVE: Butter.

SAND: Salt.

SATURDAY NIGHT SPECIAL: Code between two male workers for "This girl is available." (In some locations, a Saturday night special was seltzer water.)

SCANDAL SOUP: Tea.

SCOTCH: Butterscotch syrup.

SCRAMBLED T-BONE: A hamburger.

SCUTTLE OF JAVA: A cup of coffee.

SEABOARD: A take-out order.

SEA DUST: Salt.

SET UP: Make a banana split.

SHAKE ONE: Make a milk shake.

SHAKE ONE IN THE HAY: Make a strawberry milk shake.

SHIMMY or SHIVERIN' LIZ: Gelatin or jello.

SHIVERIN' EVE: Apple jelly.

SHOT: A glass of Coca-Cola.

SHOOT A GRADE A: Fill an order for a glass of milk.

SHOOT A RED: Fill an order for cherry Coca-Cola.

SHOOT ONE: Fill an order for Coca-Cola.

SHOOT ONE FROM THE SOUTH: Mix a Coca-Cola using extra syrup to give it a stronger taste.

SHOOT ONE HOLLYWOOD: Fill an order for chocolate Coca-Cola.

SHOOT ONE RED: Fill an order for cherry Coke.

SHOOT ONE VAN: Fill an order for vanilla Coke.

SHOOT ONE YELLOW or SHOOT ONE AND SPIKE IT: Fill an order for lemon Coke.

SHORT COKE: A small glass of Coca-Cola.

SHORT STACK: A small order of pancakes.

SHOT: A small glass of Coca-Cola.

SHOT IN THE ARM: A glass of Coca-Cola.

SHOT OF CAFFEINE: A cup of coffee.

SHOT OUT OF THE BLUE BOTTLE: Bromo-seltzer.

SHRAPNEL: Grapenuts cereal.

SHRUBBERY: Salad.

SIDE OF MAMA: Marmalade.

SINKER: Doughnut.

SINKER AND SUDS: A doughnut and a cup of coffee.

SISSY: Vanilla Coca-Cola.

SISSY NUT: Cream cheese on date-nut bread.

SISSY STICK: A straw.

SKID GREASE: Butter.

SKY JUICE: Water.

SLIP AND SLUG: A doughnut and a cup of coffee.

SLIVERS: French fried potatoes.

SLUG: Doughnut.

SLUG AND WHISTLE: A doughnut and a cup of coffee.

SMEAR: Butter.

SNAPPERS: A serving of baked beans.

SNEEZONING: Pepper.

SNOWSHOE: A cup of hot chocolate.

SNOW WHITE: Seven-Up.

SORORITY SAUCE: Ketchup.

SOUR: Coca-Cola with lime.

SPARKLE ONE: Draw a seltzer water.

SPIKE ONE: Fill an order for a glass of lemon phosphate.

SPIKER: A glass of lemon phosphate.

SPLA: Whipped cream.

SPLASH: A generic term for soup.

SPLASH OF RED NOSE: Tomato soup.

SPLASH OF SPLIT PEAS: Pea soup.

SPLIT: A banana split.

SPLIT ONE: Make a banana split.

SPOIL 'EM: Prepare an order of scrambled eggs.

SPRINKLE: Spirits of ammonia.

SPRINKLE IT: Add spirits of ammonia.

SQUEAL: Ham.

SQUEEZE: Lemonade. (In some locations, "squeeze" meant Coca-Cola with lemon or lime.)

SQUEEZE ONE: Fill an order for limeade. (In some locations, orange juice.)

SQUIRT or SQUIRTER: Soda jerk.

STACK: An order of pancakes.

STACK AND: An order of pancakes and a fried egg.

STACK OF VAN: A dish of vanilla ice cream.

STACK OF WHEAT: An order of whole wheat toast.

STACK ONE: An order of toast.

STACK WITH PIGS: An order of pancakes with sausage.

STARS AND STRIPES: Bacon and eggs.

STICK: An ice cream cone.

STIFF: As a noun, a customer who does not tip. As a verb, fails to leave a tip.

STRAIGHT KELLY: Orange juice.

STRAIGHT MALT: Vanilla malted milk.

STRAIGHT SHAKE: A vanilla milk shake.

STRAW HIGH or STRAW MALT: Strawberry malted milk.

STRAW IN or STRAWN: A strawberry ice cream soda.

STRAW ON: A strawberry sundae.

STRAWS: French fried potatoes.

STRETCH IT: Pour a large drink.

STRETCH ONE: Fill an order for a large Coca-Cola.

STRETCH SWEET ALICE: Fill an order for a large glass of milk.

SUBMARINE: A doughnut.

SUBWAY: A tip.

SUDS: Root beer.

SUICIDE: A glass of Coca-Cola topped off with a squirt of every flavor available at the fountain.

SUN-KISSED: Orange juice.

SWEEP THE KITCHEN: Prepare an order of hash.

SWEET ALICE: Milk.

TAKE A FLOWER: Put onion on a sandwich.

THOMAS: Waiter.

TIN COW or TIN TITTY: Canned milk.

TOAST AND: An order of toast and a cup of coffee.

TOOLS: Silverware.

TO THE LEFT: Lemon syrup.

TO THE RIGHT: Cherry syrup.

TO TRAVEL: A take-out order.

TRAY TROTTER: Waiter or waitress.

TREED: There are so many customers that the workers can't handle the rush.

TRILBY: A ham sandwich with onion.

TRIPLE THREAT: Three scoops of ice cream.

TUNA DOWN or TUNE IN ONE: A tuna salad sandwich on toast.

TWICE-LAID: Food that has been warmed up.

TWINS: Salt and pepper shakers.

TWIST IT, CHOKE IT, AND MAKE IT CACKLE: Mix an egg into a chocolate malted milk.

TWO CENTS PLAIN: A glass of seltzer water.

TWO DOWN or TWO FLOPPED or TWO WITH THEIR EYES CLOSED: An order for two fried eggs with firm yolks.

TWO IN THE WATER, EASY: An order for two soft-boiled eggs.

TWO IN THE WATER, HARD: An order for two hard-boiled eggs.

TWO LOOKING AT YOU: An order for two eggs sunny-side up.

TWO ON A SLICE OF SQUEAL: An order for two fried eggs and a slice of ham.

VAN: Vanilla Coca-Cola.

VAN HIGH or VAN MALT: Vanilla malted milk.

VANILLA: Code used by male employees, meaning "there's a pretty girl at the counter."

VAN ON: A vanilla sundae.

VERMONT: Maple syrup.

VIRGIN or VIRGIN COKE or VIRTUE: Cherry Coca-Cola.

WALK A SHOT: Mix a Coca-Cola with extra syrup to give it a stronger taste.

WALKAWAY: A take-out order.

WALLOWING WILLIE: A sloppy eater who leaves a mess that must be cleaned up.

WARTS: Olives.

WEAPONS: Silverware.

WESTERN: Chocolate Coca-Cola.

WHEAT STACK: An order of whole wheat toast.

WHISTLE: A cup of coffee.

WHISTLE BERRIES: An order of baked beans.

WHITE BREAD: Soda fountain manager. This was also code for "Look busy, the manager's coming."

WHITE COW: A vanilla milk shake.

WHITE HORN: A vanilla ice cream cone.

WHITE ON: An order of toasted white bread.

WHITE ONE: A small glass of milk.

WHITE ONE THROUGH GEORGIA: A small glass of chocolate milk.

WHITE STACK: An order of toasted white bread.

WHITE STICK: A vanilla ice cream cone.

WIMPY: A hamburger.

WORKING: A reminder that a waitress is waiting for an order.

WRECK: Scrambled eggs.

WRECK 'EM: Cook an order of scrambled eggs.

YELLOW: Lemon Coca-Cola.

YELLOW PAINT: Mustard.

YESTERDAY, TODAY, AND FOREVER: An order of hash.

YUM-YUM: Sugar.

ZEPPELIN: A hot dog.

ZEPPELIN IN A FOG: Sausage or hot dog served with mashed potatoes.

NUMBERS

1/2: Small order of any item.

2: Glass of milk.

2 1/2: Small glass of milk.

5: Large glass of milk. (In some locations, a five-cent glass of any beverage.)

10: A ten-cent drink or a large glass.

13: Look alert, the big boss is coming!

14: Special order.

16: Coca-Cola. (In some locations, 16 was cherry Coke.)

19: A banana split.

21: Limeade. (In some locations, 21 was orangeade.)

22: The customer hasn't paid his check.

23: Scram. Stop bothering me.

30: That's all. That's the end of the order.

31: Lemonade. (In some locations, 31 was orangeade.)

33: A dose of bromo seltzer.

33 Red: A glass of cherry Coke.

41: A glass of lemonade. (In some locations, 41 was orangeade or milk.)

48 1/2: Terminated or fired.

51: A cup of hot chocolate.

52: Two cups of hot chocolate.

55: A glass of root beer.

80: A glass of water. (82: Two glasses of water; 83: Three glasses of water; etc.)

81: The customer needs service. (In some locations, 81 meant a glass of water.)

86: The kitchen is out of the item ordered. (In some locations, 86 meant disregard the previous order.)

87 1/2: There's a pretty girl at the counter.

95 or 96: The customer is trying to leave without paying.

97: My customer's in a hurry.

98: The assistant soda fountain manager. Also code for "The assistant manager is nearby."

99: The soda fountain manager. Also code for "Look busy, the manager is around."

400W: Maple syrup.

CELLULOID SODA FOUNTAINS

Old-fashioned soda fountains are rarely seen in drugstores or restaurants today, but many have been preserved on film as attractive backdrops for movie scenes. Glimpses of yesterday's marble marvels may be seen in many flicks, including those listed here.

AGE OF CONSENT (1932) Starring Dorothy Wilson, Arline Judge, Richard Cromwell, and Eric Linden. Mike and Betty are college students engaged to be married, but their plans are derailed when Mike has a fling with a waitress, Dora, who becomes pregnant. Dora's father demands that Mike marry her, and Mike agrees. However, when Dora realizes how much Mike loves Betty, Dora declares that she won't marry him, clearing the way for him to wed his true love.

ANGELS WITH DIRTY FACES (1938) Starring James Cagney, Pat O'Brien, Humphrey Bogart, Ann Sheridan, and George Bancroft. In this classic melodrama, two playmates grow up to represent conflicting worlds: O'Brien enters the priesthood and Cagney becomes a gangster, who eventually is sentenced to the electric chair.

ANNAPOLIS FAREWELL (1935) Starring Sir Guy Standing, Tom Brown, Richard Cromwell, and Rosalind Keith. This is a sentimental tale about a retired naval officer who loves the service so much that he spends all his time hanging around the United States Naval Academy.

BABES IN ARMS (1939) Starring Mickey Rooney, Judy Garland, and Charles Winninger. In this musical, based on a Rodgers and Hart play, the children of retired vaudevillians put on a show to prove that they have talent.

BABES ON BROADWAY (1943) Starring Judy Garland, Mickey Rooney, Ray Macdonald, and Virginia Weidler. Young Broadway hopefuls stage a show for charity and, after many setbacks, are discovered by a big-time producer.

179

BACK TO THE FUTURE (1985) Starring Michael J. Fox, Christopher Lloyd, Crispin Glover, Lea Thompson, and Billy Zane. A crazy scientist invents a time-travel machine, and teenager Marty McFly takes a journey from the 1980s back to the 1950s.

BENNY AND JOON (1993) Starring Johnny Depp, Jeremiah Chechik, Mary Stuart Masterson, and Aidan Quinn. An auto mechanic who must look after his mentally-ill sister stumbles onto the perfect companion for her: a male misfit who fancies himself to be the reincarnation of Buster Keaton.

THE BEST YEARS OF OUR LIVES (1946) Starring Fredric March, Myrna Loy, Teresa Wright, Dana Andrews, and Virginia Mayo. In this film classic that won seven Oscars, three veterans return home after World War II and struggle to adjust to civilian life.

THE BIG SQUIRT (1937) Starring Charley Chase, Lucille Lund, Leora Thatcher, and Eddie Featherstone. In this two-reel short, the main character is a soda jerk and mystery buff who becomes involved in tracking down a criminal.

THE BLACK LEGION (1936) Starring Humphrey Bogart, Erin O'Brien-Moore, Dick Foran, and Ann Sheridan. A factory worker joins a Ku Klux Klan-type organization after he loses a promotion to a co-worker named Dombrowski. When he realizes the true nature of the group, he denounces it. This "message movie" was based on real events.

BLONDE DYNAMITE (1950) Starring Leo Gorcey, Huntz Hall, Gabriel Dell, and Adele Jergens. The Bowery Boys set up an escort business at Louis' Sweet Shop and get mixed up with crooks.

BORN TO DANCE (1936) Starring Eleanor Powell, James Stewart, Una Merkel, and Buddy Ebsen. Powell plays a dancer who goes to New York and gets her big break on Broadway. She falls in love with a naval officer played by Stewart.

CAUGHT PLASTERED (1931) Starring Bert Wheeler, Robert Woolsey, Dorothy Lee, and Jason Robards. Two men help an old woman save her failing drugstore from financial ruin and become involved with bootleggers.

COLLEGE (1927) Starring Buster Keaton and Ann Cornwall. A nerdy student, who works as a soda jerk to pay for college, strives to become a star athlete in order to impress his girlfriend.

COME CLEAN (1931) Starring Stan Laurel, Oliver Hardy, Gertrude Astor, and Mae Bush. In this short, two married men go to the soda fountain to buy ice cream, encounter a lady of the night, save her from suicide, and take her home with them.

CRIME IN THE STREETS (1956) Starring James Whitmore, John Cassavetes, Sal Mineo, and Mark Rydell. Rival street gangs terrorize a tenement neighborhood, and one of the angry teenagers plots a murder.

DANCING SWEETIES (1930) Starring Grant Withers, Sue Carol, and Edna Murphy. Two ambitious dancers get married and then separate because the wife is unable to perform complicated dance routines. At the end of the film, they are reunited.

A DATE WITH JUDY (1948) Starring Wallace Beery, Jane Powell, Elizabeth Taylor, and Robert Stack. Two teenaged girls have a crush on the same college guy, who has a summer job as a soda jerk at the corner drugstore.

ESCAPE TO WITCH MOUNTAIN (1975) Starring Eddie Albert, Ray Milland, Kim Richards, and Ike Eisenmann. In this fantasy-mystery, two children with extraordinary powers try to discover their origins. They are pursued by the evil Milland, who has dastardly plans for their special powers.

FIGHTING BLOOD (1923) Starring Gale Galen, Clara Horton, Arthur Rankin, Ena Gregory, and M. C. Lyman. In this film serial based on a book by H. W. Witwer, Galen works as a soda dispenser at a small-town drugstore. After he punches an abusive customer named Knockout Kelly, a fight promoter convinces Galen to become a professional boxer. Galen has a successful fighting career and makes a fortune from a soft drink he concocts.

FOR HIS SON (1912) Starring Charles Hill Mailes, Alfred Paget, Blanche Sweet, and Charles West. In this silent film directed by D. W. Griffith, a doctor becomes wealthy after inventing a cocaine-laced beverage called "Dopokoke." Sadly, many people, including his own son, become addicted to the drink.

THE FRESHMAN (1925) Starring Harold Lloyd, Jobyna Ralston, and Brooks Benedict. Lloyd plays a nerdy college freshman who is ridiculed by his classmates. He decides to change his image by trying out for the football team.

FROM BROADWAY TO CHEYENNE (1932) Starring Rex Bell, Marceline Day, Robert Ellis, Matthew Betz, and Gabby Hayes. A cowboy detective takes on a gang of big-city con men trying to set up a protection racket out west.

THE GOLDWYN FOLLIES (1938) Starring Adolphe Menjou, Andrea Leeds, Kenny Baker, the Ritz Brothers, Bobby Clark, and Edgar Bergen. Menjou plays a movie producer who hires Leeds to critique his movies from an average person's perspective. Baker, who plays a soda jerk, sings the classic "Love Walked In."

GOOD NEWS (1947) Starring June Allyson, Peter Lawford, Patricia Marshall, Joan McCracken, and Mel Torme. In this musical, a college football hero pursues a snobbish sorority girl but eventually falls in love with his brainy French tutor.

HAS ANYBODY SEEN MY GAL? (1952) Starring Charles Coburn, Piper Laurie, Rock Hudson, and Gigi Perreau. An elderly millionaire feels that, in his youth, he made the wrong choice between love and money. He tries to make amends by giving a large sum of money to the family of the woman he almost married. Then he pretends to be poor and moves in with this family.

THE HEARTBREAKER (1930) Starring Eddie Foy Jr. and Oliva Shea. In this two-reel musical, Foy plays a singing soda jerk who is popular with female customers.

HEY BOY! HEY GIRL! (1959) Starring Louis Prima, Keely Smith, and the Witnesses. In this low-budget musical, singer Smith agrees to join Prima and the Witnesses if they will perform at a church bazaar. Prima sings "A Banana Split for My Baby (and a Glass of Water for Me)."

HIS BIG AMBITION (1930) Starring Lucien Littlefield and Lucille Ward. Pa Potter works as a soda jerk at a drugstore but yearns to become a doctor in this two-reel comedy, which was part of the Potters serial.

IT'S A WONDERFUL LIFE (1946) Starring Jimmy Stewart, Donna Reed, and Lionel Barrymore. Stewart plays a small-town business-man who works hard all his life but thinks that he has failed and contemplates suicide, until an angel shows him how much good he has done.

JUDGE HARDY AND SON (1939) Starring Mickey Rooney, Lewis Stone, Cecilia Parker, Fay Holden, and Ann Rutherford. Judge Hardy and Andy grow closer as they cope with Mrs. Hardy's sudden illness and try to save an elderly couple's home from fore-closure.

KING CREOLE (1958) Starring Elvis Presley, Carolyn Jones, Dolores Hart, Walter Matthau, and Dean Jagger. Elvis plays a young night-club singer on his way to stardom in New Orleans' French Quarter. When his father is attacked and nearly killed by two thugs, Elvis seeks revenge.

LITTLE BIG MAN (1970) Starring Dustin Hoffman, Faye Dunaway, and Martin Balsam. In this epic, a 121-year-old man recounts his expe-riences as a young pioneer, medicine-show hustler, adopted Indian, Wild Bill Hickok's pal, and survivor of Custer's Last Stand.

THE LITTLE BIG SHOT (1935) Starring Sybil Jason, Glenda Farrell, Edward Everett Horton, Jack LaRue, and J. Carrol Nash. After a gangster's daughter is orphaned, she is cared for by two con men.

LOLITA (1997) Starring Jeremy Irons, Melanie Griffith, and Dominique Swain. In this tawdry tale, a middle-aged college professor marries a woman because he is infatuated with her adolescent daughter. After the mother is killed in a car accident, he becomes obsessed with the girl.

LOOK WHO'S LAUGHING (1941) Starring Edgar Bergen, Jim Jordan, Marion Jordan, Lucille Ball, and Harold Peary. Bergen's plane acci-dently lands in Wistful Vista, where he becomes involved in a squabble with Fibber McGee and Molly. This flimsy plot provides a showcase for several popular radio characters, including the Great Gildersleeve.

THE LORDS OF FLATBUSH (1974) Starring Martin Davidson, Perry King, Sylvester Stallone, Henry Winkler, and Paul Mace. High-school tough guys in Brooklyn, circa 1957, have problems with girls, adults, and school.

LOVE FINDS ANDY HARDY (1938) Starring Mickey Rooney, Judy Garland, Fay Holden, Ann Rutherford, Lana Turner, and Gene Reynolds. Young Hardy faces an adolescent male's dream dilemma: choosing between two girlfriends.

MAGIC TOWN (1947) Starring James Stewart, Jane Wyman, and Kent Smith. A pollster decides that the small town of Grandview is a perfect microcosm of the USA.

MEN O'WAR (1929) Starring Stan Laurel, Oliver Hardy, Anne Cornwall, and Gloria Greer. In this short comedy, Laurel and Hardy flirt with two girls in the park and take them to a soda fountain for a treat, even though they do not have much money. Fortuitously, there is a slot machine nearby and Laurel wins a jackpot.

MISCHIEF (1985) Starring Doug McKeon, Catherine Mary Stewart, Kelly Preston, and Chris Nash. Set in the 1950s, this coming-of-age movie features McKeon as a lovesick nerd, hungering after a very popular girl. Nash plays his world-wise buddy.

MURDER, INCORPORATED (1960) Starring Stuart Whitman, May Britt, Henry Morgan, and Peter Falk. A couple gets into trouble with a powerful crime syndicate and struggles to escape its murderous grip.

MURPHY'S ROMANCE (1985) Starring Sally Field and James Garner. A young divorcee makes a fresh start in a small Arizona town, where she meets an older, widowed pharmacist.

MY BEST GAL (1944) Starring Jane Withers, Jimmy Lydon, and Frank Craven. Young show-biz hopefuls, including one who works at a drugstore, plan to make it big on Broadway.

MY SISTER EILEEN (1955) Starring Betty Garrett, Janet Leigh, Jack Lemmon, and Bob Fosse. Two small-town girls from Ohio, seeking careers and romance, move to the Big Apple. They live in a basement apartment in Greenwich Village, and the older sister tries to protect the younger one from undesirable boyfriends.

NOW, VOYAGER (1942) Starring Bette Davis, Claude Rains, Paul Henreid, and Gladys Cooper. Davis plays a dowdy, reclusive spinster who is dominated by her stern, blue-blood mother. After Davis receives psychiatric treatment, she becomes a confident, assertive woman and has a doomed love affair with a married architect.

ORCHESTRA WIVES (1942) Starring George Montgomery, Ann Rutherford, and Glenn Miller and his Band. A small-town girl, played by Rutherford, impulsively marries Montgomery, who plays the trumpet in a touring swing band. The flimsy plot is merely an excuse for Miller's orchestra to perform.

OUR TOWN (1940) Starring William Holden, Martha Scott, Frank Craven, and Fay Bainter. This American classic explores the cycle of life in a typical New England town, Grover's Corners.

PAPA'S DELICATE CONDITION (1963) Starring Jackie Gleason, Glynis Johns, and Charles Ruggles. In this nostalgic tale set in Texas at the turn of the century, Gleason plays a tipsy railroad inspector.

THE PLAINSMAN (1936) Starring Gary Cooper, Jean Arthur, Charles Bickford, and Gabby Hayes. The bad guys conspire to sell guns to the Indians in this Cecil B. DeMille western. The complex plot involves Wild Bill Hickok, Calamity Jane, Buffalo Bill, General George Custer, Abraham Lincoln, and other historical figures.

PLEASANTVILLE (1998) Starring William H. Macy, Joan Allen, Jeff Daniels, Tobey Maguire, and Reese Witherspoon. Two teens from the 1990s are sucked into their television set and find themselves trapped in a 1950's sitcom, complete with doting, well-intentioned parents and old-fashioned values.

PRINCESS O'ROURKE (1943) Starring Olivia de Havilland, Robert Cummings, Charles Coburn, Jack Carson, and Jane Wyman. In this World War II comedy, an ace pilot falls in love with a princess and their romance causes diplomatic complications.

SAFETY LAST (1923) Starring Sam Taylor, Harold Lloyd, and Mildred Davis. In this silent comedy, Lloyd plays an ambitious young go-getter, determined to make good in the big city. To impress his girlfriend, he enters a contest to climb a skyscraper.

SATURDAY'S HEROES (1937) Starring Van Heflin, Marian Marsh, Richard Lane, and Alan Bruce. Heflin plays a cocky college football player who is angry because he must live on a small scholarship while the college makes big bucks selling tickets to the games. The college president vows to stop the exploitation of student athletes and to form an organization to reform college sports.

SECOND TIME AROUND (1961) Starring Debbie Reynolds, Andy Griffith, Steve Forrest, and Juliet Prowse. Reynolds plays a widow who is stranded in Arizona, decides to run for sheriff, and is pursued by two suitors.

SHOPWORN ANGEL (1938) Starring Margaret Sullavan, James Stewart, and Walter Pidgeon. A naive soldier falls in love with a worldly, hard-boiled actress, who gradually softens under his influence.

SHOULD MARRIED MEN GO HOME? (1928) Starring Stan Laurel, Oliver Hardy, Edna Marion, and Viola Richard. In this comedy short, Laurel and Hardy flirt with two young women, who suggest that they go to the soda fountain for a drink. The men agree, even though they don't have enough money, and have to leave a watch to pay the tab.

SLIGHTLY DANGEROUS (1943) Starring Lana Turner, Robert Young, and Walter Brennan. Turner plays a soda jerk who is bored with small-town life. Impulsively, she moves to New York City, changes her name, and poses as an heiress. When her former boss sees her photo in the newspaper, he goes to the city to convince her to come back home.

THE SODA JERKER (1917) Starring Harry Watson Jr. and Maxfield Morse. The title character in this one-reel comedy is an inept soda jerk who concocts bad-tasting drinks and causes an explosion.

THE SODA WATER COWBOY (1927) Starring Wally Wales, Beryl Roberts, and J. P. Lockney. Wales plays a soda jerk who yearns for adventure and is fired for reading Western novels on the job. He heads out West, joins a traveling medicine show, captures a gang of outlaws, and romances a beautiful girl.

SOFT DRINKS AND SWEET MUSIC (1935) Starring Georgie Price, Sylvia Froos, and Billy Leonard. Price plays an aspiring song writer working as a soda jerk until he makes it big.

THE SOPHOMORE (1929) Starring Eddie Quillan and Sally Withers. Quillan plays a college boy who works at a soda fountain, falls in love with Withers, and becomes a football hero.

SUMMER OF '42 (1971) Starring Jennifer O'Neill, Gary Grimes, and Jerry Houser. In this initiation story set during World War II, teenager Grimes has a crush on O'Neill, a beautiful war bride.

THEY WON'T FORGET (1937) Starring Claude Rains, Otto Kruger, Allyn Joslyn, and Lana Turner. When a pretty high school girl is murdered in a Southern town, a well-known Northern lawyer comes to defend the man arrested for the crime.

THINGS TO DO IN DENVER WHEN YOU'RE DEAD (1995) Starring Andy Garcia, Gabrielle Anwar, Christopher Walken, Christopher Lloyd, and Treat Williams. In this violent underworld saga, two innocent people are killed when five thugs botch an assignment. This angers the mob boss, who then orders a hit man to murder his incompetent underlings.

TO EACH HIS OWN (1946) Starring Olivia de Havilland, John Lund, Roland Culver, and Mary Anderson. In this tear-jerker, de Havilland plays an unwed mother who gives up her baby for adoption and later becomes involved in his life.

TRUE-HEART SUSIE (1919) Starring Lillian Gish, Robert Harron, and Clarine Seymour. D. W. Griffith wrote and directed this melodrama about a farm girl who sells her cow in order to pay her boyfriend's college expenses, but he proves to be an ungrateful cad.

TRUE TO THE NAVY (1930) Starring Clara Bow, Fredric March, Sam Hardy, and Eddy Featherstone. Bow, who works at a soda fountain, has an on-again, off-again romance with a sailor played by March.

THE VILLAGE CUT-UP (1919) Starring Bryant Washburn and Shirley Mason. Bryant is a small-town soda jerk who decides to seek his fortune in New York City. He finds a job at a drugstore in the city but soon is fired because business is slow. He finds a new job at another fountain, proves to be a valuable employee, buys a roadster, and romances a lovely librarian.

THE WEST POINT STORY (1950) Starring James Cagney, Virginia Mayo, Doris Day, and Gordon Macrae. A down-on-his-luck Broadway showman is hired to direct a musical revue starring cadets at the U.S. army academy.

WHAT'S HIS NAME (1914) Starring Max Figman, Lolita Robertson, and Fred Montague. A soda jerk marries a girl who becomes a movie star. Her fame causes problems in their marriage, but they eventually find happiness together.

WILLY WONKA AND THE CHOCOLATE FACTORY (1971) Starring Gene Wilder, Jack Albertson, and Peter Ostrum. In this film adaptation of Roald Dahl's *Charlie and the Chocolate Factory*, a young boy finds a golden ticket that entitles him to a guided tour of a most unusual candy factory.

WIRELESS LIZZIE (1926) Starring Walter Hiers and Jack Duffy. Hiers, who operates a soda fountain, tries to impress his girlfriend by demonstrating a new invention, a remote-controlled car.

YOU JUST CAN'T WAIT (1919) Starring Ralph Graves and Vivian Martin. A soda dispenser quits his job in a small New England town and moves to New York City, where he finds works at an antique store. When he loses $300 of his boss's money in a poker game, he sneaks away and finds another job as a soda dispenser. Each week, he sends part of his wages to the antique dealer. He also romances Nell Fanshawe, a soda "dispenserette" played by Martin.

YOU WERE MEANT FOR ME (1948) Starring Jeanne Crain, Dan Dailey, and Oscar Levant. Crain marries a band leader, played by Dailey, but soon tires of the constant travel with his touring band. The two seem destined to be unhappy, until Dailey finds a job that allows them to settle down.

NOTES

Abbreviations

Carbonated Drinks = CD
Confectioners' and Bakers' Gazette = CBG
Confectioners' Gazette = CG
Fast Food = FF
Fountain and Fast Food = FFF
Ice Cream Trade Journal = ICTJ
Soda Fountain and Quick Food Service = SFQFS
Soda Fountain Magazine = SFM
The Pharmaceutical Era = PE
The Soda Fountain = SF

Chapter 1

1. John J. Riley, *A History of the American Soft Drink Industry* (Washington, DC: American Bottlers of Carbonated Beverages, 1958), 15. Uno Boklund, *Torbern Bergman as Pioneer in the Domain of Mineral Waters* (Stockholm, Sweden: Almquist & Wiksell, 1956), 108-09.

2. Riley, *op. cit.*, 16. Boklund, *op. cit.*, 109-10. Thomas Chester, *Carbonated Beverages: The Art of Making, Dispensing, and Bottling Soda Water, Mineral Waters, Ginger Ale, and Sparkling Liquors* (New York: Matthews, 1882), 3.

3. Riley, *op. cit.*, 16, 19. Chester, *op. cit.*, 4.

4. Joseph Priestly, *Directions for Impregnating Water with Fixed Air in Order to Communicate to It the Peculiar Spirit and Virtues of Pyrmont Water* (Washington, DC: American Bottlers of Carbonated Beverages, 1945 Reprint), 5-6.

5. Torbern Bergman, *On Acid of Air: Treatise on Bitter, Seltzer, Spa, and Pyrmont Waters and Their Synthetical Preparation* (Stockholm, Sweden: Almquist & Wiksell, 1956 Reprint), 9-27. Boklund, *op. cit.*, 110-13. Chester, *op. cit.*, 4. Riley, *op. cit.*, 18.

6. Robert E. Schofield, ed., *A Scientific Autobiography of Joseph Priestley, 1733-1804* (Cambridge, MA: MIT, 1966), 131-32. Priestley, *op. cit.*, 8-9. Chester, *op. cit.*, 4. F. W. Gibbs, *Joseph Priestley: Revolutions of the 18th Century* (Garden City, NY: Doubleday, 1967), 57.

7. Schofield, *op. cit.*, 131-32. Priestley, *op. cit.*, 10-11. Gibbs, *op. cit.*, 57-59.

8. Schofield, *op. cit.*, 130-31. Gibbs, *op. cit.*, 60.

9. Riley, *op. cit.*, 3. William Kirkby, "Thomas Henry, Apothecary, and the Origin of Artificial Mineral Waters," *PE*, June 23, 1898: 946-48.

10. Priestley, *op. cit.*, 16. Chester, *op. cit.*, 3. Riley, *op. cit.*, 17.

11. Chester, *op. cit.*, 4. Riley, *op. cit.*, 27, 30.

12. Carl Bridenbaugh, *Cities in Revolt: Urban Life in America, 1743-1776* (New York: Knopf, 1955), 166, 326. J. C. Furnas, *The Americans: A Social History of the United States, 1587-1914* (New York: Putnam's, 1969), 193.

13. Thomas Cooper, *The Emporium of Arts and Sciences* (Philadelphia: Kimber & Richardson, 1813), 474-75, 479. Chandros Michael Brown, *Benjamin Silliman: A Life in the Young Republic* (Princeton, NJ: Princeton UP, 1989), 207.

14. Furnas, *op. cit.*, 193-94. Brown, *op. cit.*, 206-07. Mary Cable, *American Manners and Morals* (New York: American Heritage, 1969), 110.

15. Brown, *op. cit.*, 207. Riley, *op. cit.*, 38. Furnas, *op. cit.*, 194.

16. J. Thomas Scharf and Thompson Westcott, *History of Philadelphia 1609-1884* (Philadelphia: Everts, 1884), 943. Bridenbaugh, *op. cit.*, 166, 368.

17. Riley, *op. cit.*, 39.

18. *Ibid.*, 41.

19. Brown, *op. cit.*, 206, 208.

20. *Ibid.*, 206.

21. *Ibid.*, 209-10.

22. *Ibid.* "An Act to Prohibit the Importation of Certain Goods, Wares, and Merchandize," *Acts Passed at the First Session of the Ninth Congress of the United States of America*, Vol. 8, 80-85.

23. Brown, *op. cit.*, 210, 213, 231, 234.

24. *Ibid.*, 220, 230-31.

25. *Ibid.*, 231.

26. *Ibid.*, 233.

27. *Ibid.*, 233-34, 236.

28. *Ibid.*, 236. Leslie Dorsey and Janice Devine, *Fare Thee Well: A Backward Look at Two Centuries of Historic American Hostelries, Fashionable Spas, and Seaside Resorts* (New York: Crown, 1964), 23. John Mariani, *America Eats Out: An Illustrated History of Restaurants, Taverns, Coffee Shops, Speakeasies, and Other Establishments That Have Fed Us for 350 Years* (New York: Morrow, 1991), 12.

29. Brown, *op. cit.*, 238-39. L. A. Becker, "The Soda Fountain Industry," *PE*, Feb. 1913: 63.

30. Brown, *op. cit.*, 239.

31. *Ibid.*, 244-45.

32. *Ibid.*, 243, 45.

33. *Ibid.*, 244.

34. *Ibid.*, 241, 243-45.

35. J. Ritchie Garrison, Bernard L. Herman, and Barbara McLean Ward eds., *After Ratification: Material Life in Delaware, 1789-1820* (Newark, DE: U of Delaware P, 1988), 131.

36. Brown, *op. cit.*, 231, 240, 242.

37. *Ibid.*, 242-43, 246.

38. *Ibid.*, 245, 246, 256.

39. *Ibid.*, 250.

40. *Ibid.*, 250-52.

41. *Ibid.*, 285-86.

42. *Ibid.*, 254-55.

43. *Ibid.*, 255-56.

44. *Ibid.*, 256-58.

45. *Ibid.*, 284-85.

46. *Ibid.*, 254. Michael Karl Witzel and Gyvel Young-Witzel, *Soda Pop!* (Stillwater, MN: Voyageur, 1998), 24-25.

47. Riley, *op. cit.*, 50-51. Elaine Forman Chase, ed., *The Diary of Elizabeth Drinker*, Vol. 3 (Boston: Northeastern UP, 1991), 2071. Witzel and Young-Witzel, *op. cit.*, 24-25.

48. John Redman Coxe, *The Emporium of Arts and Sciences* (Philadelphia: Delaplaine, 1812), 387-90. Thomas Cooper, *The Emporium of Arts and Sciences* (Philadelphia: Kimber & Richardson, 1814), 454-56. Riley, *op. cit.*, 44-45.

49. James Cutbush, *The American Artist's Manual, or Dictionary of Practical Knowledge* (Philadelphia: Johnson & Warner and R. Fisher, 1814), n.p.

50. Adlard Welby, *A Visit to North America and the English Settlements in Illinois* (London: Drury, 1821), 31.

51. Riley, *op. cit.*, 53-55. "Fountains of a By-gone Era," *SFM*, Oct. 1937: 12.

52. Chester, *op. cit.*, 5-7.

53. Chester, *op. cit.*, 4. Eleanor Alexander, "A Uniquely American Watering Hole: The Drug Store Soda Fountain at the Turn of the Twentieth Century," Master's thesis, University of Delaware, 1986, 3-4. "Why 'Soda' Water?" *CD*, Oct. 1877: 21-22.

54. Alexander, *op. cit.*, 15-18.

55. *Ibid.*

56. *Ibid.*, 17. Joseph F. Barker, "History of Boston's Soda Fountain Trade," *PE*, May 1, 1892: 289.

57. Joseph L. Morrison, "The Soda Fountain," *American Heritage*, Aug. 1962: 10-19. Alexander, *op. cit.*, 19-22.

58. Glenn Sonnedecker, ed., *Kremers and Urdang's History of Pharmacy*, Rev. ed. (Philadelphia: Lippincott, 1963), 276.

Chapter 2

1. Morrison, *op. cit.*, 11. Chauncey M. DePew, ed., *One Hundred Years of American Commerce*, Vol. 2 (New York: Haynes, 1895), 471. "Sketch of the House of Lippincott," *PE*, Jan. 2, 1908: 27. "How Matthews Stands for Purity and Progress in the Fountain Industry," *SF*, May 1907: 25.

2. Morrison, *op. cit.*, 11.

3. *Ibid.* Grace Mayer, *Once Upon a City* (New York: Macmillan, 1958), 394.

4. Morrison, *op. cit.*, 11. "Old Ben," *CG*, Dec. 1909: 26-27.

5. Morrison, *op. cit.*, 11. "Old Ben," 26. William Loren Katz, ed., *Anti-Negro Riots in the North, 1863* (New York: Arno and the New York Times, 1969), iii-iv, 7.

6. DePew, *op. cit.*, 470-71. Riley, *op. cit.*, 64. Becker, *op. cit.,* 65.

7. DePew, *op. cit.*, 472. "How Matthews Stands for Purity," 25.

8. Morrison, *op. cit.*, 10. Charles Panati, *Panati's Extraordinary Endings of Practically Everything and Everybody* (New York: Harper & Row, 1989), 32-33.

9. Panati, *op. cit.*, 32-33. Morrison, *op. cit.*, 10.

10. Riley, *op. cit.*, 72. "How Matthews Stands for Purity," 25.

11. "The Lippincotts in Their New Home," *SF*, Dec. 1908: 50.

12. DePew, *op. cit.*, 473. "The Soda Apparatus Made by Chas. Lippincott & Co.," *PE,* July 15, 1893: 92. "Sketch of the House of Lippincott," 27.

13. DePew, *op. cit*, 470-71. Becker, *op. cit.*, 65. "Alvin D. Puffer, Veteran Fountain Manufacturer, Dies Suddenly from Over-exertion," *SF*, Jan. 1907: 48.

14. DePew, *op. cit.*, 471. Riley, *op. cit.*, 65-66.

15. "Good-bye to Old Hudnut's," *PE*, May 2, 1895: 565. "Twenty-five Years Ago at the Hudnut Fount," *SF*, Feb. 1915: 27-28.

16. "Twenty-five Years Ago at the Hudnut Fount," 28.

17. "Good-bye to Old Hudnut's," 565. "A Druggist's Visit to New York," *PE*, May 1, 1894: 410.

18. "Alvin D. Puffer," 48.

19. Becker, *op. cit.*, 65. Joseph F. Barker, "History of Boston's Soda Fountain Trade," *PE*, May 1, 1892: 290.

20. Becker, *op. cit.*, 65. Barker, *op. cit.*, 290-91.

21. DePew, *op. cit.*, 471. Becker, *op. cit.*, 65.

22. Becker, *op. cit.*, 65. Barker, *op. cit.*, 290-91.

23. Charlotte Gale and David M. Gale, "The Drugstore Soda Fountain: A Study and Catalog of 19th-Century Soda Tokens," T*he Numismatist*, Jan. 1983: 13-18. Barker, *op. cit.*, 290.

24. Barker, *op. cit.*, 290-91.

25. Becker, *op. cit.*, 65. Barker, *op. cit.*, 291.

26. Becker, *op. cit.*, 65.

27. Barker, *op. cit.*, 291-92.

28. *Ibid.* "Development of Soda Apparatus," *SF*, Dec. 1906: 16.

29. Becker, *op. cit.*, 65-66. Barker, *op. cit.*, 292. "Reminiscenes of Pioneer Days," *SF*, July 1906: 19. DePew, *op. cit.*, 471.

30. Becker, *op. cit.*, 66. Barker, *op. cit.*, 292.

31. Becker, *op. cit.*, 66. Barker, *op. cit.*, 292. Frederick Stansbury, "The Evolution of the Soda Water Industry in New York City," *PE*, May 15, 1892: 329, 334.

32. "Boston," *CBG*, Mar. 1902: 24.

33. DePew, *op. cit.*, 473-74.

34. "Injunction against R. M. Green and Sons Suspended," *PE*, July 23, 1896: 116. "Robert M. Green and Sons Win Their Suit with the American Soda Fountain Company," *PE*, Jan. 28, 1897: 113. "News Department," *PE*, Jan. 13, 1898: 67.

35. "The First Hundred Years—What Now?" *SF*, Nov. 1927: 84. Barker, *op. cit.*, 292-93. Stansbury, *op. cit.*, 334. Becker, *op. cit.*, 66.

36. Barker, *op. cit.*, 292-93. Stansbury, *op. cit.*, 334. "Detroit's Prize Fountain," *PE*, June 18, 1896: 778.

37. "From Our Special Correspondent: New York State," *PE*, July 15, 1893: 68.

38. Sam Bowers Hilliard, *Hog Meat and Hoecake: Food Supply in the Old South, 1840-1860* (Carbondale, IL: Southern Illinois UP, 1972), 53. Warren S. Tryon, ed., *A Mirror for Americans, Volume One* (Chicago: U of Chicago P, 1952), 194-95.

39. Fred L. Holmes, *Side Roads: Excursions into Wisconsin's Past* (Madison, WI: State Historical Society of Wisconsin, 1949), 79.

40. "Devil's Food, No Doubt!" *Missouri Historical Review*, July 1944: 474. "The Soda Fountain Business of St. Louis," *PE*, June 1, 1892: 369.

41. "Soda Water in Chicago," *PE*, June 16, 1892: 409-10.

42. *Ibid.*

43. *Ibid.*

44. *Ibid.*

45. *Ibid.*, 410-11.

46. *Ibid.* "Dispensing Soda in Chicago," *PE*, June 11, 1896: 746.

47. Jacqueline Williams, *Wagon Wheel Kitchens: Food on the Oregon Trail* (Lawrence, KS: UP of Kansas, 1993), 75. Teresa Griffin Viele, *Following the Drum: A Glimpse of Frontier Life* (Lincoln, NE: U of Nebraska P, 1984), 149. Everett Dick, *The Sod-House Frontier* (Lincoln, NE: U of Nebraska P, 1979), 63, 384.

48. Sally Foreman Griffith, ed., *The Autobiography of William Allen White*, 2nd ed., Rev. and abridged (Lawrence, KS: UP of Kansas, 1990), 6.

49. Elizabeth Margo, *Women of the Gold Rush* (New York: Indian Head, 1955), 162-64. *The First Los Angeles City and County Directory, 1872* (Los Angeles: Ritchie, 1963), 29. Naomi Swett, "Soda Pioneers on the Pacific Coast," *SF*, Mar. 1923: 37. *Directory of City of Seattle and Vicinity, 1879* (Seattle: Hanford and McClaire, 1879), 17.

50. Becker, *op. cit.*, 64-65. *Arctic Soda Apparatus* (Boston: Tufts, 1873), passim. Mary Anne Hines, Gordon Marshall, and William Woys Weaver, *The Larder Invaded: Reflections on Three Centuries of Philadelphia Food and Drink* (Philadelphia: Library Company of Philadelphia and Historical Society of Philadelphia, 1987), 99.

51. *The Matthews Catalogue and Price List of Apparatus, Materials, and Accessories for Making and Dispensing Carbonated Beverages* (New York: Matthews Apparatus, 1891), passim.

52. "Fountain Business of St. Louis," 369.

53. *Matthews Catalogue*, 30-31. Mayer, *op. cit.*, 395.

54. *CD*, Jan. 1878: 29.

55. *Matthews Catalogue*, 27.

56. *Ibid.* "A Druggist's Visit to New York," *PE*, May 1, 1894: 410.

57. *Matthews Catalogue*, passim.

58. *Arctic Soda Apparatus*, passim. *Catalogue of Puffer's Frigid Soda and Mineral Water Apparatus* (Boston, MA: Puffer, 1878), passim.

59. James D. McCabe, *A Collector's Reprint: The Illustrated History of the Centennial Exposition* (Philadelphia: National, 1975), 302, 310. Becker, *op. cit.*, 66.

60. McCabe, *op. cit.*, 309-10, 329, 341-42.

61. John Maass, *The Glorious Enterprise: The Centennial Exhibition of 1876 and H. J. Schwarzmann, Architect-in-Chief* (Watkins Glen, NY: American Life, 1973), 118-19.

62. McCabe, *op. cit.*, 330, 341-42.

63. McCabe, *op. cit.*, 342. Scharf and Westcott, *op. cit.*, 847. John Leng, *America in 1876: Pencillings during a Tour in the Centennial Year, with a Chapter on the Aspects of American Life* (Dundee, England: Dundee Advertiser Office, 1877), 22.

64. DePew, *op. cit.*, 472. Maass, *op. cit.*, 126.

65. "Fountain Business of St. Louis," 370.

66. *Ibid.*, 372.

67. "The Soda Fountain," *PE*, Apr. 21, 1898: 590. W. B. Addington and D. F. Addington, "Soda Water," *PE*, June 1889: 217. "The Soda Fountain," *PE*, Feb. 15, 1890: 7-8.

68. "Soda Water in Chicago," 411.

69. "Soda Water Apparatus," *CD*, Oct. 1877: 10.

70. Mayer, *op. cit.*, 394.

71. "The Street Venders of New York," *Scribner's Monthly*, Dec. 1870: 123. "Soda Water on the East Side," *PE*, June 11, 1896: 745.

72. "Soda Water in Confectionery Stores," *PE*, June 11, 1896: 734. "Soda Water on the East Side," 745.

73. Mayer, *op. cit.*, 79.

74. Harry Golden, *Only in America* (New York: World, 1958), 63-64.

Chapter 3

1. Mary Gay Humphreys, "The Evolution of the Soda Fountain," *Harper's Weekly*, Nov. 21, 1891: 924.

2. *PE*, Aug. 27, 1896: 281. "Soda Water," *PE*, Apr. 21, 1898: 592.

3. "The Soda Season," *PE*, June 1, 1894: 502.

4. Riley, *op. cit.*, 114.

5. "Soda Water Notes," *PE*, July 1, 1893: 46. "Riker's Altar to Thirst," *PE*, June 4, 1896: 715-16.

6. "New Names for Soda Beverages," *PE*, June 11, 1896: 747. "Popular Drinks," *PE*, July 1, 1894: 10.

7. Charles Panati, *Panati's Parade of Fads, Follies, and Manias* (New York: Harper Collins, 1991), 14-15.

8. *Ibid.*, 12-14. Cable, *op. cit.*, 268.

9. Panati, *Fads*, 12-14. Cable, *op. cit.*, 268. Arthur Train, *Puritan's Progress* (New York: Scribner's, 1931), 306-08.

10. "Soda Water and Wheelmen," *PE*, June 11, 1896: 747. "For the Soda Fountain," *PE*, Mar. 28, 1895: 415. "He Catches the Cyclists," *PE*, Aug. 20, 1896: 259.

11. "Some Soda Water Fountain Statistics," *PE*, Sept. 14, 1899: 362. "New Names," 747.

12. "Some Soda Water Fountain Statistics," *Scientific American*, Aug. 12, 1899: 99.

13. *Ibid.*

14. Riley, *op. cit.*, 113.

15. Riley, *op. cit.*, 114.

16. Clement B. Lowe, "Pharmacy in Philadelphia," *PE*, Feb. 20, 1908: 229-30.

17. "Where the Famous Smith True Fruit Flavors Are Manufactured," *SF*, Apr. 1907: 48. "Buildings in Which the Famous Smith True Fruit Flavors Are Manufactured," *PE*, Apr. 18, 1907: 386.

18. "Growth of J. Hungerford Smith Company," *SF*, Jan. 1921: 85. "J. Hungerford Smith's Double Anniversary," *SF*, Oct. 1916: 45.

19. "Soda Water and Its Syrups: Three Representative Fountains," *New York Daily Tribune*, July 27, 1884: 10.

20. *Ibid.*

21. *Ibid.*

22. "Soda Water in Chicago," 414. Jane Mobley, *Prescription for Success: The Chain Drug Story* (Kansas City, MO: Hallmark, 1991), 6.

23. "Soda Water in Chicago," 414. "Soda Water and Its Syrups," 10.

24. "Strange Sight for English Tourists," *PE*, July 16, 1896: 92. Alexander, *op. cit.*, 87. Stansbury, *op. cit.*, 335.

25. D. W. Saxe, *Saxe's New Guide, or Hints to Soda Water Dispensers* (Chicago: Saxe, 1893), 65-68.

26. Saxe, *op. cit.*, 68. "Arts of the Mixer," *PE*, June 4, 1896: 715. "It Paid Addington," *PE*, June 11, 1896: 746.

27. John Ayto, *The Glutton's Glossary* (New York: Routledge, 1990), 156. L. Patrick Coyle, *The World Encyclopedia of Food* (New York: Facts on File, 1982), 337, 345-46. "Kuomiss," *PE*, June 1889: 215.

28. "Horlick's Achievement," *PE*, Aug. 24, 1905: 189.

29. "Malted Milk Question Is Discussed Once More," *PE*, May 16, 1907: 478.

30. C. R. Johnson, "Malted Milk: A Business Romance," *SF*, Mar. 1927, 23, 62, 64. "Malted Milk: The New National Drink," *SF*, Mar. 1928: 41, 76.

31. E. F. White, "A Chat about Soda Water," *Supply World*, Apr. 1900: 18-19. *American Soda Book of Receipts and Suggestions* (Boston: American Soda Fountain, n.d.), 132. *A Standard Dictionary of the English Language* (New York: Funk & Wagnalls, 1890, 1893), 1124.

32. *James W. Tufts' Arctic Soda-Water Apparatus: Book of Directions* (Boston, MA: Tufts, 1890), 58.

33. Saxe, *op. cit.*, 64-65.

34. "Father of Ice Cream Sodas," Apr. 1906: 17.

35. Fred Sanders, "How I Invented Ice Cream Soda," *CBG*, Nov. 1907: 19-20. "The Three Principal Claimants to the Honor of Inventing Ice Cream Sodas," *SF*, Nov. 1913: 18.

36. "How Ice Cream Soda Was Invented in 1858," *SF*, Apr. 1911: 47.

37. "Three Principal Claimants," 17-18.

38. Carl J. Palmer, *History of the Soda Fountain Industry* (Washington, DC: Soda Fountain Manufacturers, 1947), 20-21.

39. "Ice Cream Soda's Birth Due to Pioneer's Happy Inspiration," *SF*, Feb. 1910: 115-17.

40. "Robert McCay Green," *SF*, June 1920: 81. "Congratulations to R. M. Green," *SF*, May 1912: 28. "A Golden Anniversary in the Fountain Trade," *SF*, May 1924: 31.

41. *Directions for Making Soda Water and Other Aerated Beverages* (New York: Matthews, 1871), 40. *PE*, Sept. 14, 1899: 363.

42. *PE*, Sept.14, 1899: 363.

43. Alexander, *op. cit.*, 75. Stansbury, *op. cit.*, 329, 335-36.

44. *PE*, Sept. 14, 1899: 262-63.

45. "The First Hundred Years," 84.

46. "Hot Soda," *PE*, Nov. 15, 1892: 318.

47. "Hot Beverages," *PE*, Nov. 15, 1892: 34. "The Aetna No. 1 Hot Soda Apparatus," *PE*, Dec. 1, 1892: 58. "Art Tile Soda Fountains," *PE*, Jan. 1, 1892: 16.

48. *James W. Tufts' Arctic Soda-Water Apparatus: Book of Directions*, 74.

49. "Hot Soda," 319.

50. "Recalls Early Days of Ice Cream Soda," *SF*, Dec. 1924: 27. "Recalls Old Days of Soda Fountain," *SF*, Oct. 1924: 36. "Hot Soda," 319.

51. Barker, *op. cit.*, 294.

52. E. C. Tracey, "Hot Soda Progress," *SF*, Jan. 1906: 20-21.

53. *American Soda Book*, 15, 52.

54. David N. Laband and Deborah Henry Heinbuch, *Blue Laws: The History, Economics, and Politics of Sunday-Closing Laws* (Lexington, MA: Lexington, 1987), 30-32.

55. William Addison Blakely, *Legislative, Elective, Judicial American State Papers Bearing on Sunday Legislation* (New York: National Religious Liberty Association, 1890), 272, 276, 282.

56. *Ibid.*, 272, 277, 279.

57. *Ibid.*, 288-90, 297, 318, 319.

58. "An Important Decision: The Sale of Soda Water on Sunday Is Not Illegal," *PE*, Sept. 26, 1895: 401.

59. Clyde D. Foster, *Evanston's Yesterdays* (Evanston, IL: n.p., 1956), 89-91. William Lyon Phelps, *Autobiography with Letters* (New York: Oxford UP, 1939), 919-20.

60. "Still Another Origin for the Sundae," *SF*, Nov. 1913: 52.

61. "One Version of the Origin of the Name 'Sundae,'" *SF*, Nov. 1906: 36. "Speculation as to the Origin of Sundae," *SF*, Apr. 1906: 25.

62. Palmer, *op. cit.*, 40.

63. George Philip Krapp, *The English Language in America*, Volume One (New York: Century, 1925), 142.

64. "Stop Me If You've Heard This One Before," *ICTJ*, July 1927: 68.

65. Holmes, *op. cit.*, 77-78. H. L. Mencken, *The American Language: An Inquiry into the Development of English in the United States* (New York: Knopf, 1963), Supplement I, 376-77.

66. Eric Partridge, *Origins: A Short Etymological Dictionary of Modern English* (London: Routledge & Paul, 1958), 681. "Origin of the Sundae," *ICTJ*, Aug. 1908: 22. Mencken, *op. cit.*, 377.

67. "The Home Town of College Ices," *SF*, Dec. 1919: 75.

Chapter 4

1. *Beverage World: 100 Year History 1882-1982 and Future Probe* (Great Neck, NY: Keller, 1982), 43.

2. "Dr. Thompson's Tonic," *Blair & Ketchum's Country Journal*, Mar. 1986: 12-13. Dorothy Jewell, "When Moxie Came in a Bottle," *Modern Maturity*, Apr.-May 1983: 4. John F. Mariani, *The Dictionary of American Food and Drink* (New York: Hearst, 1994), 204. Frank N. Potter, *The Book of Moxie* (Paducah, KY: Collector, 1987), 162.

3. Mariani, *Dictionary*, 204. Mark Pendergrast, *For God, Country, and Coca-Cola: The Unauthorized History of the Great American Soft Drink and the Company That Makes It* (New York: Scribner's, 1993), 17. Witzel and Young-Witzel, *op. cit.*, 54. Potter, *op. cit.*, 19, 53.

4. Witzel and Young-Witzel, 53-54. "Dr. Thompson's Tonic," 12. Frank N. Potter, *The Moxie Mystique* (Virginia Beach, VA: Donning, 1981), 44.

5. Witzel and Young-Witzel, 54, 57. "Dr. Thompson's Tonic," 12-13. Jewell, *op. cit.*, 4. Potter, *Book of Moxie,* 82-83, 88. Potter, *Mystique*, 43, 49. Hal Morgan, *Symbols of America* (New York: Steam, 1986), 119.

6. Jeffrey L. Rodengen, *The Legend of Dr. Pepper/Seven-Up* (Ft. Lauderdale, FL: Write Stuff, 1995), 14, 21. Harry E. Ellis, *Dr Pepper: King of Beverages* (Dallas, TX: Dr Pepper, 1979), 30.

7. Rodengen, *op. cit.*, 21-22. Ellis, *op. cit.*, 9, 12, 29.

8. Rodengen, *op. cit.*, 22-23. Hannah Campbell, *Why Did They Name It?* (New York: Fleet, 1964), 65. Ellis, *op. cit.*, 10-11.

9. Rodengen, *op. cit.*, 23. Ellis, *op. cit.*, 14.

10. Rodengen, *op. cit.*, 22.

11. Rodengen, *op. cit.*, vii, 23, 25-27, 29. Ellis, *op. cit.*, 39, 115. "Mr. O'Hara's Nickel Drink," *Fortune*, Oct. 1947: 108-10. Paula Kepos, ed., *International Directory of Company Histories*, Vol. 9 (Detroit: St. James P, 1994), 177.

12. Rodengen, *op. cit.*, 29-30, 36-38. "Mr. O'Hara's Nickel Drink," 111.

13. Rodengen, *op. cit.*, 37.

14. Ellis, *op. cit.*, 145.

15. Rodengen, *op. cit.*, 37, 47-48. Ellis, *op. cit.*, 256.

16. Rodengen, *op. cit.*, 49-50.

17. Pendergrast, *op. cit.*, 19, 20-27, 64.

18. *Ibid.*, 20-21. Furnas, *op. cit.*, 441-42.

19. Pendergrast, *op. cit.*, 20-21.

20. *Ibid.*, 21.

21. J. C. Louis and Harvey Z. Yazijian, *The Cola Wars* (New York: Everest House, 1980), 18. Pendergrast, *op. cit.*, 22.

22. Pendergrast, *op. cit.*, 22-23.

23. Louis and Yazijian, *op. cit.*, 16. Pendergrast, *op. cit.*, 23.

24. *Ibid.*, 15. Pendergrast, *op. cit.*, 23-24.

25. Pendergrast, *op. cit.*, 24-25.

26. Witzel and Young-Witzel, *op. cit.*, 75-76.

27. *Ibid.*, 76. Elizabeth Candler Graham and Ralph Roberts, *The Real Ones: Four Generations of the First Family of Coca-Cola* (Fort Lee, NJ: Barricade, 1992), 14-15.

28. Louis and Yazijian, *op. cit.*, 16. E. J. Kahn, Jr., *The Big Drink* (London: Max Reinhardt, 1960), 103-04.

29. Pendergrast, *op. cit.*, 26-27.

30. Louis and Yazijian, *op. cit.*, 15, 16, 18. Randy Schaeffer and Bill Bateman, *Coca-Cola* (Philadelphia: Courage, 1995), 11.

31. Pendergrast, *op. cit.*, 31-32

32. Witzel and Young-Witzel, *op. cit.*, 76, 83. Schaeffer and Bateman, *op. cit.*, 11. Pendergrast, *op. cit.*, 30.

33. Louis and Yazijian, *op. cit.*, 22.

34. Witzel and Young-Witzel, *op. cit.*, 83.

35. Pendergrast, *op. cit.*, 35.

36. Louis and Yazijian, *op. cit.*, 22.

37. Witzel and Young-Witzel, *op. cit.*, 85. Schaeffer and Bateman, *op. cit.*, 12.

38. Witzel and Young-Witzel, *op. cit.*, 88-89. Louis and Yazijian, *op. cit.*, 19, 21. Schaeffer and Bateman, *op. cit*, 12.

39. Bob Stoddard, *Introduction to Pepsi Collecting* (Pomona, CA: Double Dot Enterprises, 1991), vi. Louis and Yazijian, *op. cit.*, 49. Carolyn Wyman, *I'm a Spam Fan: America's Best-Loved Foods* (Stamford, CT: Longmeadow, 1993), 96.

40. Bob Stoddard, *Pepsi-Cola: 100 Years* (Santa Monica, CA: General Publishing Group, 1997), 18-19. Louis and Yazijian, *op. cit.*, 49. Wyman, *op. cit.*, 96. Kepos, *op. cit.*, vol. 10: 450.

41. Stoddard, *op cit.*, 46, 49-50, 52-53, 56-57, 61. Louis and Yazijian, *op. cit.*, 49-50. Kepos, *op. cit.*, vol. 10: 450-51.

42. Kepos, *op. cit.*, vol. 10: 451. Louis and Yazijian, *op. cit.*, 50. Muris, Scheffman, and Spiller, *op. cit.*, 17. Walter Mack and Peter Buckley, *No Time Lost* (New York: Atheneum, 1982), 119.

43. Louis and Yazijian, *op. cit.*, 50-51. "Pepsi-Cola's Walter Mack," *Fortune*, Nov. 1947: 128, 130. Mack and Buckley, *op. cit.*, 120-21.

44. "Pepsi-Cola's Walter Mack," 130-31, 176. Mack and Buckley, *op. cit.*, 131-33.

45. "Pepsi-Cola's Walter Mack," 176, 178, 181-82.

46. *Ibid.*, 182, 184. Mack and Buckley, *op. cit.*, 148.

47. Edward Arber, ed., *Travels and Works of Captain John Smith*, vol. 1 (Edinburgh: John Grant, 1910), 57. Edward R. Emerson, *Beverages, Past and*

Present, vol. 2 (New York: Putnam's, 1908), 457, 474. Mark Edward Lender and James Kirby Martin, *Drinking in America: A History* (New York: Free, 1982), 4-5. John Hull Brown, *Early American Beverages* (Rutland, VT: Tuttle, 1966), 21.

48. Lender and Martin, *op. cit.*, 5, 7-8. Emerson, *op. cit.*, 458, 463.

49. W. H. Daniels, ed., *The Temperance Reform and Its Great Reformers* (New York: Nelson and Phillips, 1877), 9. Lender and Martin, *op. cit.*, 17. Paul Sann, *The Lawless Decade* (New York: Bonanza, 1957), 21, 23. Leo Markun, *Mrs. Grundy: A History of Four Centuries of Morals in Great Britain and the United States Intended to Illuminate Present Problems* (New York: Appleton, 1930), 362. Fairfax Downey, *Our Lusty Forefathers* (New York: Scribner's, 1947), 4-6.

50. Cable, *op. cit.*, 74. Lender and Martin, *op. cit.*, 1, 16.

51. J. C. Furnas, *The Life and Times of the Late Demon Rum* (New York: Putnam's, 1965), 37-42. Lender and Martin, *op. cit.*, 36-37.

52. Stuart C. Henry, *Unvanquished Puritan: A Portrait of Lyman Beecher* (Grand Rapids, MI: Eerdmans, 1973), 92-94. Vincent Harding, *A Certain Magnificence: Lyman Beecher and the Transformation of American Protestantism 1775-1863* (Brooklyn, NY: Carlson, 1991), 203-06.

53. Harding, *op. cit.*, 204-06, 210. Brown, *Early American Beverages*, 77.

54. Mary Caroline Crawford, *Social Life in Old New England* (Detroit: Tower, Reprint, 1971), 134.

55. William Andrus Alcott, *Forty Years in the Wilderness of Pills and Powders, or the Cogitations and Confessions of an Aged Physician* (Boston, MA: Jewett, 1859), 85-86.

56. Harding, *op. cit.*, 210. Furnas, *Demon Rum*, 53-54.

57. Cable, *op. cit.*, 255. Furnas, *Demon Rum*, 55, 122, 133-34.

58. Furnas, *Demon Rum*, 88-90, 95-97. Lender and Martin, *op. cit.*, 76-78.

59. Sann, *op. cit.*, 23. Furnas, *Demon Rum*, 89-90, 147-55.

60. *Ibid.*, 67-68.

61. *Ibid.*, 168-71. Lender and Martin, *op. cit.*, 42-43.

62. Furnas, *Demon Rum*, 166, 168-71. Lender and Martin, *op. cit.*, 44-45.

63. Julie Roy Jeffrey, *Frontier Women*, Rev. ed. (New York: Hill & Wang, 1998), 223. Lender and Martin, *op. cit.*, 84.

64. Furnas, *Demon Rum*, 242-52. Jeffrey, *op. cit.*, 222-25. Lender and Martin, *op. cit.*, 90-91. Sann, *op. cit.*, 24-25.

65. Furnas, *Demon Rum*, 284-85. Lender and Martin, *op. cit.*, 90-92, 110.

66. Cable, *op. cit.*, 299. Furnas, *Demon Rum*, 285-86. Lender and Martin, *op. cit.*, 110.

67. Sann, *op. cit.*, 25.

68. "The Great Temperance Movement," *Scribner's Monthly*, 1874: 111-12.

69. Furnas, *Demon Rum*, 301, 303. Martin and Lender, *op. cit.*, 126-27. Richard Erdoes, *Saloons of the Old West* (Salt Lake City, UT: Howe, 1985), 241.

70. Cable, *op. cit.*, 299. Otto L. Bettmann, *The Good Old Days—They Were Terrible* (New York: Random, 1974), 129, 132. Erdoes, *op. cit.*, 240. Sann, *op. cit.*, 24. Lender and Martin, *op. cit.*, 104.

71. Furnas, *Demon Rum*, 309. Cable, *op. cit.*, 298. Erdoes, *op. cit.*, 115-16. Moritz Busch, *Travels between the Hudson and the Mississippi 1851-1852* (Lexington, KY: UP of Kentucky, 1971), 39. Madelon Powers, *Faces Along the Bar: Lore and Order in the Workingman's Saloon, 1870-1920* (Chicago: U of Chicago P, 1998), 208-09, 223-24.

72. Furnas, *Demon Rum*, 304-05. Bettmann, *op. cit.*, 129.

73. Cable, *op. cit.*, 299. Bettmann, *op. cit.*, 129-30. Jeffrey, *op. cit.*, 222. Mariani, *America Eats Out*, 40. Erdoes, *op. cit.*, 11.

74. Raymond Calkins, *Substitutes for the Saloon* (Boston, MA: Houghton-Mifflin Company, 1901), 217-18. Powers, *op. cit.*, 222-23. "Southern Woman Predicts a Glorious Future for Soda Fountains," *SF*, Apr. 1908: 19.

75. "Comment," *PE*, Nov. 15, 1892: 289-90. "Fountains Solve the Problem," *SF*, May 1908: 20. "No More High Balls in Detroit," *SF*, May 1908: 20. Barker, *op. cit.*, 294.

76. "Don'ts for the Fountain," *PE*, May 1, 1892: 294.

77. Michael Batterberry and Ariane Batterberry, *On the Town in New York from 1776 to the Present* (New York: Scribner's, 1973), 153-54. "Soda Water in Chicago," 412. "Soda's Conquest in New Orleans," *SF*, July 1906: 15. Pendergrast, *op. cit.*, 116.

78. Wyman, *op. cit.*, 91. Joyce Jorgensen, ed., *Encyclopedia of Consumer Brands*, vol. 1 (Detroit: St. James, 1994), 261.

79. *Ibid.* Pendergrast, *op. cit.*, 16. Louis A. Becker, "The Soda Fountain Industry, IV," *SF*, May 1913: 244.

80. Russell H. Conwell, *Acres of Diamonds: How Men and Women May Become Rich* (Philadelphia: Huber, 1890), 14-19. Wyman, *op. cit.*, 91.

81. "The Chas. E. Hires Co.," *PE*, June 15, 1893: 572. Wyman, *op. cit.*, 91. Jorgensen, *op. cit.*, 262.

82. Witzel and Young-Witzel, *op. cit.*, 43. Wyman, *op. cit.*, 91. Jorgensen, *op. cit.*, 262.

83. "Where Root Beer Is Made," *SF*, June 1906: 25. "Story of Hires' Dispensing Keg," *SF*, Jan. 1907: 44. "Hires Automatic Munimaker," *CBG*, Nov. 1908: 26. "Important Apparatus Innovation Devised for the Purpose of Dispensing Hires," *SF*, Nov. 1908: 64.

84. "Philadelphia," *PE*, Oct. 15, 1890: 51. "Hires' Root Beer," *PE*, July 15, 1893: 84.

85. Wyman, *op. cit.*, 91-92. Jorgensen, *op. cit.*, 262. Joseph J. Fucini and Suzy Fucini, *Entrepreneurs: The Men and Women behind Famous Brand Names and How They Made It* (Boston: Hall, 1985), 151-52.

86. William Chazanof, *Welch's Grape Juice: From Corporation to Cooperative* (Syracuse, NY: Syracuse UP, 1977), 4-5. Fucini and Fucini, *op. cit.*, 71.

87. Chazanof, op. cit., 5-7.

88. *Ibid.*

89. *Ibid.*, 10.

90. *Ibid.*, 7.

91. *Ibid.*, 7-8.

92. *Ibid.*, 8.

93. *Ibid.*, 9.

94. *Ibid.*, 10-12.

95. *Ibid.*, 12-13.

96. *Ibid.*, 13-14, 31, 34.

97. *Ibid.*, 16-17, 33, 35.

98. *Ibid.*, 17, 35-37, 39.

99. *Ibid.*, 70, 72. "Handsome New Factory of the Welch Grape Juice Company at Westfield," *SF*, Jan. 1907: 52. "Handsome New Factory of the Welch Grape Juice Co.," *PE*, Jan. 3, 1907: 22. "Welch's Buys the Walker Plant," *SF*, Sept. 1911: 46. Janice Jorgensen, ed., *Encyclopedia of Consumer Brands*, Vol. 1 (Detroit: St. James, 1994), 629. Kepos, *op. cit.*, vol. 9: 178.

100. Wyman, *op. cit.*, 99. Chazanof, *op. cit.*, 73-75, 78-79.

101. Chazanof, *op. cit.*, 75-76, 79-80.

102. *Ibid.*, 81-83. Jorgensen, *op. cit.*, vol. 1: 630. Paul M. Angle, *Crossroads: 1913* (New York: Rand McNally, 1963), 225. Lawrence W. Levine, *Defender of the Faith, William Jennings Bryan: The Last Decade, 1915-1925* (New York: Oxford UP, 1965), 110.

103. Joseph L. Morrison, *Josephus Daniels: The Small-d Democrat* (Chapel Hill, NC: U of North Carolina P, 1966), 65-66. Jorgensen, *op. cit.*, vol. 1: 630. Jonathon Daniels, *The End of Innocence* (Philadelphia: Lippincott, 1954), 127-28.

Chapter 5

1. "Ten Billion Nickels a Year for Soda Water!" *SF*, May 1910: 393-95. "Ice Cream Soda on Trains," *ICTJ*, May 1911: 43. "Americans Spend $500,000,000 a Year for Soda Water," *ICTJ*, June 1910: 33-35.

2. "Fountains in Small Communities," *SF*, Apr. 1907: 25.

3. Shine Phillips, *Big Spring: The Casual Biography of a Prairie Town* (New York: Prentice-Hall, 1943), 36-37.

4. "Ice Water on Wheels," *New York Daily Tribune*, Apr. 19, 1880: 8. Calkins, *op. cit.*, 219.

5. "Will Soda Water Supplant Intoxicants?" *SF*, May 1915: 27. "New Prohibition States Increase Soda Trade," *SF*, Jan. 1916: 19-20, 44. "Non-alcoholic Beer," *SF*, Apr. 1918: 49-50. "Fountain Beverages for Men," *SF*, Aug. 1919: 39. "Washington Saloons Selling Soft Drinks," *SF*, Jan. 1916: 27-28.

6. "The Soda Fountain—the New American Bar," *ICTJ*, Oct. 1910: 24-25. "Hotels Welcome Soda Fountains," *SF*, July 1917: 17-18. "Prohibition and the Fountain," *SF*, Jan. 1919: 27-29. "Two Views of Prohibition," *SF*, May 1916: 22.

7. "Twenty-five Years Ago at the Hudnut Fount," *SF*, Feb. 1915: 28.

8. John Todd Somerset, "Boosting Business," *Drug Topics*, Apr. 1920 [qtd. in Douglas Congdon-Martin, *Drugstore and Soda Fountain Antiques* (West Chester, PA: Schiffer, 1991), 59.]

9. Ronald M. Deutsch, *The New Nuts among the Berries* (Palo Alto, CA: Bull, 1977), 95-96. James D. Hart, *The Oxford Companion to American Literature*, Fourth ed. (New York, Oxford UP, 1965), 435.

10. Deutsch, *op. cit.*, 95-96. Ralph K. Andrist, ed., *The American Heritage History of the Confident Years* (New York: American Heritage, 1969), 361-62.

11. Pendergrast, *op. cit.*, 114, 120.

12. *Homes Commission Report*, 372 (qtd. in Harvey W. Wiley, "Soft Drinks and Dopes," *Good Housekeeping*, Aug. 1912: 242-45).

13. "Cocaine in Soda Fountain Drinks," *PE*, Feb. 20, 1908: 250. "Koca-Nola Company Is Convicted; Shipment of Coca-Cola Is Seized," *SF*, Nov. 1909: 52. "Guilty in Celery Cola Case," *PE*, Apr. 1910: 359. Pendergrast, *op. cit.*, 41, 66, 125.

14. "Coca-Cola Vindicated as a Healthful Drink," *SF*, Feb. 1906: 20. "Chemists All Praise Coca-Cola," *SF*, Apr. 1906: 22-23. "Detailed Resume of Case of the United States vs. 40 Barrels, 20 Kegs of Coca-Cola," *SF*, Apr. 1911: 41-42. "No Cocaine Charge in Coca-Cola Case," *SF*, May 1911: 26. "Government Loses in Coca-Cola Case," *SF*, July 1914: 23. "Supreme Court Reverses the Coca-Cola Decision: A New Trial Ordered," *SF*, June 1916: 44. Pendergrast, *op. cit.*, 90-91, 119-24.

15. "Dangers of Habit-producing Drinks," *SF*, July 1909: 17.

16. "Habit-forming Drugs at Fountains," *SF*, Mar. 1909: 17-18. "Why That Soda Water Tastes So Good!" *SF*, June 1909: 27-28. "Newspapers Attack Dirt at Fountains," *SF*, Sept. 1916: 23-24. "Beer Interests Attack Soft Drinks," *SF*, Jan. 1909: 18.

17. "Denounces Soda Fountain," *PE*, Dec. 6, 1906: 537. "Tckulsky and the Drug Stores," *PE*, Jan. 24, 1895: 118.

18. "The New National Pure Soda Water League," *SF*, Sept. 1908: 27-28. "Masterful Presentation of Objects of the New National Pure Soda Water League," *PE*, Sept. 10, 1908: 344-46. "National Pure Soda Water League," *CBG*, Oct. 1908: 20.

19. "Infantile Paralysis at the Soda Fountain," *SF*, Nov. 1916: 47. "Sanitation at the Fountain," *SF*, Nov. 1918: 14.

20. "Making Soda Water Straws," *SF*, Oct. 1908: 58-59.

21. "Fluted Soda Straws Almost Like Natural," *SF*, Jan. 1907: 46.

22. H. Collins, "Straw Holders—Part II," *The Ice Screamer*, Nov. 1994: 2-7.

23. "Dr. Robinson Advocates Paper Soda Cups," *SF*, Apr. 1913: 59. "Paper Cups Versus Glassware," *SF*, May 1920: 43. "Glassware vs. Paper Cups," *SF*, Mar. 1920: 39. "Skoonas: The New Paper Glasses for Soda Fountains," *SF*, Nov. 1914: 6. "Paper Cup Answers Public Demand," *SF*, June 1915: 55.

24. "Trade Department: Miscellaneous," *PE*, July 1, 1892: 53. "Soda Fountain Supplies," *PE*, July 15, 1892: 43. "WCTU and the Druggists," *PE*, June 25, 1896: 798. "Dangerous WCTU Beverage," *PE*, July 8, 1897: 34. G. R. Schreiber, *A Concise History of Vending in the USA* (Chicago: Vend, 1961), 26.

25. Campbell, *op. cit.*, 197. "Sanitary Idea in Drinking Cups Spreads," *SF*, Nov. 1910: 952. Jorgensen, *op. cit.*, vol. 2: 173.

26. "Massachusetts Banishes All Public Cups," *SF*, Nov. 1910: 952.

27. "Making and Using Sanitary Paper Cups," *SF*, Mar. 1914: 22-23.

28. Campbell, *op. cit.*, 195-96. Charles Panati, *Panati's Extraordinary Origins of Everyday Things* (New York: Harper & Row, 1987), 122-23. Jorgensen, *op. cit.*, 173. "Lily Cup Makers File Suit," *SF*, Mar. 1925: 60. U.S. Patent #1,032,557. U.S. Patent #1,043,854. U.S. Patent #946,242.

29. Jorgensen, *op. cit.*, 173. Michael Gershman, *Getting It Right the Second Time* (Reading, MA: Addison-Wesley, 1990), 25.

30. Jorgensen, *op. cit.*, 173. Furnas, *Americans*, 431. Gershman, *op. cit.*, 27-28.

31. Campbell, *op. cit.*, 198-99. Panati, *Origins*, 123.

32. Campbell, *op. cit.*, 199. Panati, *Origins*, 124.

33. Campbell, *op. cit.*, 199.

34. "Dixie Cup Company Is Voted New Name," *SF*, May 1943: 24. Jorgensen, *op. cit.*, 174. Gershman, *op. cit.*, 30.

35. "The Innovation," *CBG*, Jan. 1904: 39.

36. *Ibid.* "Modern Soda Fountain: What It Is and What It Has Done for the Industry," *SF*, Dec. 1906: 17-19.

37. "Pure Food Era the Inspiration of the Liquid Carbonic's Genuises," *SF*, Dec. 1906: 22. "Development of the Soda Fountain," *CG*, Dec. 1913: 29-30.

38. "Modern Soda Fountain," 18. L. A. Becker, "The Soda Fountain Industry, III," *PE*, Apr. 1913: 186.

39. "The Luncheonette," *SF*, Feb. 1912: 21-22. "Women Shoppers and the Soda Fountain," *CBG*, Apr. 1902: 23.

40. "Uhl Art Steel Soda Shop Furniture," *SF*, Apr. 1915: 50. Ralph Pomery, *The Ice Cream Connection* (London: Paddington, 1975), 232.

41. "The First Hundred Years—What Now?" *SF*, Nov. 1927: 86. "The Manufacture of Carbon Dioxide," *SF*, May 1923: 31. "Development of Soda Apparatus," *SF*, Dec. 1906: 16.

42. "Jacob Baur on Iceless Fountains," *SF*, Aug. 1908: 22.

43. *Ibid.* "Keen Demand for Iceless Fountains," *SF*, Oct. 1908: 51.

44. "Jacob Baur," 22. L. A. Becker, "The Soda Fountain Industry, II," *PE*, Mar. 1913: 126. "Bishop-Babcock-Becker Co. Consolidation," *PE*, Apr. 1911: 158.

45. "Twentieth Century Soda Fountain," *CBG*, Dec. 1902: 26. "Miniature Working Models and the Latest Ideas in Cooling Apparatus," *SF*, Dec. 1906: 23-25. "The Growth of an Idea," *CBG*, Feb. 1903: 28. "Mr. Becker Discourses on the Advent of the Iceless Fountain," *SF*, July 1908: 30. "Mr. Becker Discourses Further upon the Iceless System," *SF*, Sept. 1908: G-H.

46. "The Plant Where 20th Century Fountains Are Manufactured," *SF*, Feb. 1906: 18. Becker, "Soda Fountain Industry, II," 125.

47. "Big New Factory of L. A. Becker Co., Chicago, Which Has Just Been Put into Operation," *PE*, Mar. 1911: 132. "Bishop-Babcock-Becker Company New $8,500,000 Corporation," *SF*, Mar. 1911: 31-32. Becker, "Soda Fountain Industry, II," 126. "L. A. Becker Dead," *SF*, June 1919: 68.

48. Becker, "Soda Fountain Industry, II," 124. "Jacob Baur Dead," *CG*, Aug. 1912: 21.

49. Charles Herman Sulz, *A Treatise on Beverages* (New York: Dick & Fitzgerald, 1888), 158-59.

50. "The Growth of a Great Concern," *SF*, Jan. 1906: 28.

51. "Liquid Light on the Soda Water Business," *CBG*, Feb. 1903: 30. "Farewell to Charged Tanks and Rockers," *SF*, Mar. 1911: 60.

52. "New Home of the Liquid Carbonic Acid Mfg. Co. in Chicago," *CBG*, Mar. 1903: 25-26. "Men, Methods, and Products that Have Created Wonderful Success," *SF*, Mar. 1906: 24-25. "The Liquid Expanding—Mammoth New Chicago Plant a Marvel," *SF*, Mar. 1910: 244, 246. "Remarkable Growth of the Liquid Carbonic Company's Business," *SF*, Mar. 1911: 65-66. "Jacob Baur Happy Over Crowning Triumph in Completion of Million Dollar Plant," *SF*, Dec. 1910: 1025.

53. "The Liquid Expanding," *CG*, Mar. 1910: 30-31.

54. *Ibid.*

55. "Jacob Baur Dead," 21. Becker, "Soda Fountain Industry, II," 125. "Liquid Carbonic Erecting Two New Buildings," *SF*, Dec. 1935: 34. Kepos, *op cit.,* vol. 7: 77.

56. Becker, "Soda Fountain Industry, II," 127. "Bastian-Blessing Plans New Factory," *SFM*, Aug. 1940: 45.

57. "American Soda Fountain Figures," *CBG*, Jan. 1903: 31. "Sixty Years Honest Record," *SF*, Dec. 1906: 26. "Lippincotts Withdraw," *PE*, Jan. 17, 1907: 72. "Daniel J. Puffer Dead at 58," *SF*, June 1911: 44.

58. "Lippincotts Withdraw," 72. "Lippincotts in Trade Once More," *SF*, Jan. 1907: 46. "The Lippincotts in Their New Home," *SF*, Dec. 1908: 50. "A New Lippincott Factory," *CG*, May 1911: 19. "A. H. and F. H . Lippincott Inc. Move," *SF*, Feb. 1912: 50. "The New Lippincott Factory," *CG*, Feb. 1912: 29.

59. "J. Matthews Corporation in Bankruptcy," *PE*, Feb. 1911: 83. "No Interruption to Matthews' Business," *SF*, Feb. 1911: 55-56. "J. Matthews Inc.'s Stock under Hammer," *SF*, Jan. 1912: 42. "John Matthews Rejuvenated," *SF*, Mar. 1912: 50.

60. WWW.SODAFOUNTAIN.COM

61. "Effects of European War on Soda Fountain Industry Now Being Felt," *SF*, Sept. 1914: 15-16.

62. *Ibid.*, 16.

63. *Ibid.*, 15. "Why Sugar Is High," *SF*, Jan. 1917: 43. E. C. Foote, "New Sugar Sources," *SF*, June 1917: 47.

64. "France Allows Saccharin," *SF*, June 1917: 47. Foote, "New Sugar Sources," 47. "Sugar Prices Hold in Peace Talk," *SF*, Jan. 1917: 43. "The Sugar Situation," *SF*, Nov. 1917: 51. "The Sugar Shortage," *SF*, Jan. 1918: 29-30.

65. "The Sugar Situation," *SF*, June 1918: 49. "The Fifty-Percent Sugar Rule," *SF*, July 1918: 23-24. "Sugar Stocks and Prices," *SF*, Jan. 1919: 23-24. "Outlook on Sugar Grows Brighter," *SF*, Dec. 1919: 67. "Prospect for Sugar in 1920," *SF*, Feb. 1920: 35, 38. "Sugar Shows Downard Trend," *SF*, June 1921: 31-32. "Forecast of 1922 Sugar Situation," *SF*, Jan. 1922: 71-72.

66. "Cocoa Imports Now Double 1910 Figures," *SF*, Jan. 1917: 43. "The Chocolate Supply," *SF*, Oct. 1918: 21-22.

67. "Soldiers and Soda Water," *SF*, July 1917: 51. "Sweets for Soldiers and Sailors," *SF*, Dec. 1917: 17.

68. "Making Soda Safe for Soldiers," *SF*, Sept. 1917: 17-18.

69. "Ice Cream Fans on the High Seas," *SF*, Sept. 1923: 31.

70. "Soda for Sammies in London," *SF*, Sept. 1917: 25. "Sammy Demands Soda," *SF*, June 1918: 14.

Chapter 6

1. "U.S. Soda Bars' Income Put at $1,500,000,000," *SF*, Mar. 1930: 3. Paul Sann, *op. cit.*, 21.

2. "Volstead Act Helps Soda Men," *SF*, Dec. 1920: 30. "Drinks for Men," *SF*, June 1920: 21-22.

3. "American Soda Habits Change," *SF*, July 1922: 82. "We Have Tables Reserved for Men," *SF*, Nov. 1922: 25. John Russell Ward, "Shake Hands with the New Competition," *SF*, Apr. 1933: 44.

4. "New Luncheonette Development," *SF*, Nov. 1921: 11. "Is the Nickel Cup of Coffee Doomed?" *SF*, Oct. 1924: 27.

5. J. O. Dahl, *Soda Fountain and Luncheonette Management* (New York: Harper & Brothers, 1930), 24. John Russell Ward, "The Machine Age of Sanitation," *SF*, Sept. 1933: 14-16.

6. "The Evans System of Fountain Management: Refrigeration by Ammonia Replaces Ice," *PE*, Mar. 16, 1903: 338. "Refrigeration without Ice," *PE*, May 4, 1905: 508-09. "Mr. Evans Makes His Own Ice," *SF*, June 1906: 26. "Fountain That Is a Work of Art," *SF*, May 1906: 22. "Dealing with Refrigeration Problem," *SF*, June 1906: 13-14. "Mechanical Refrigeration for Soda Fountains," *ICTJ*, June 1908: 13-15.

7. F. H. Lippincott, "Soda Fountain Mechanically Refrigerated: Application and System," *SF*, Mar. 1915: 21-13. "Sanitation," *SF*, Dec. 1914: 23. B. I. Masurovsky, *Sherbets, Water Ices, and Modern Soda Fountain Operation* (Milwaukee, WI: Olsen, 1933), 145.

8. C. L. Hadley, "We All Vote for Mechanical Refrigeration," *SF*, May 1925: 19. "Economy of Mechanical Refrigeration," *SF*, Feb. 1926: 23-25. Masurovsky, *op. cit.*, 89.

9. Louis A. M. Phelan, "The History of the Counter Freezer Industry," *SFM*, Mar. 1936: 20.

10. *Ibid.*, 20-22, 40-41.

11. Panati, *Origins*, 160. "Air Conditioning Soda Fountains," *SFM*, Aug. 1933: 33-34, 46-47.

12. George Herrick, "Down with the Temperature, Up with the Sales," *SFM*, Apr. 1938: 24-25. Alfred B. Hoppe, "Is Air Conditioning Mandatory?" *SFM*, Apr. 1938: 16-17, 60-61.

13. John P. Nichols, *The Chain Store Tells Its Story* (New York: Institute of Distribution, 1940), 80, 83.

14. *Ibid.*, 21, 81-83, 93. Mobley, *op. cit.*, 22.

15. Nichols, 71, 80. Arthur R. Herrmann, "The Chain Store Invasion," *SF*, Feb. 1932: 25-28.

16. "A Salesman Who Made the Drug Store a Palace," *Sales Management*, Feb. 20, 1932: 250-51, 271. "500 Corner Drugstores," *Fortune*, Sept. 1935: 71. L. A. Becker, "The Soda Fountain Industry, V," *PE*, June 1913: 304-05. Mobley, *op. cit.*, 22.

17. "The World's Biggest Drug Chain," *Fortune*, Oct. 1930: 42. Samuel Merwin, *Rise and Fight Againe* (New York: Albert & Charles Boni, 1935), 14, 19, 22, 26, 38, 44, 52-53.

18. I. E. Lambert, *The Public Accepts: Stories Behind Famous Trademarks, Names, and Slogans* (Albuquerque, NM: U of New Mexico P, 1976), 189-90. Vince Staten, *Do Pharmacists Sell Farms? A Trip Inside the Corner Drugstore* (New York: Simon & Schuster, 1998), 36. Merwin, *op. cit.*, 60-61, 63.

19. Merwin, *op. cit.*, 94, 114. "World's Biggest Drug Chain," 42.

20. Merwin, *op. cit.*, 159-60, 181-96, 207-08.

21. *Ibid.*, 219, 225, 247. "The Drug Chain Bankruptcy Case," *Business Week*, Apr. 12, 1933: 7-8. "Drug Inc.—Too Big," *Business Week*, July 8, 1933: 11-12.

22. "United Gets Its Man," *Time*, May 11, 1942: 84-85. "Fumble?" *Time*, Nov. 14, 1949: 95-96. "Rexall Drug, Inc.," *Business Week*, Feb. 19, 1955: 58. "The Rexall Rx," *Business Week*, Mar. 1, 1982: 85-86. James W. Robinson, *Prescription for Success: The Rexall Showcase International Story and What It Means to You* (Rocklin, CA: Prima, 1999), xv-xvi.

23. "500 Corner Drugstores," 73. "Links in the Chain of Soda Success," *SF*, Mar. 1925: 23.

24. "500 Corner Drugstores," 73.

25. *Ibid.*, 73-74. Mobley, *op. cit.*, 100.

26. "500 Corner Drugstores," 73-74.

27. *Ibid.*, 71-72, 74, 76, 80, 100. Jay P. Pederson, ed., *International Directory of Company Histories*, vol. 20 (Detroit: St. James, 1998), 511.

28. "500 Corner Drugstores," 76-78.

29. *Ibid.*, 75-76. Aimee Morrison, "The Fountain Lunch at Walgreen's," *SF*, Jan. 1929: 26-27, 30.

30. "500 Corner Drugstores," 71-72, 80, 100. Pederson, *op. cit.*, 513.

31. V. E. Moynahan, "The 1936 Annual New Soda Fountain Equipment Reference Review," *SFM*, Feb. 1936: 12-13. Robert Latimer, "Streamline versus Frills," *SFM*, Jan. 1938: 20-21.

32. "The Fountain of Today," *SFM*, Jan. 1936: 10-11.

33. *Ibid.*, 11-12. Philip Langdon, *Orange Roofs, Golden Arches* (New York: Knopf, 1986), 19.

34. "Fountain of Today," 13. Langdon, *op. cit.*, 19.

35. "Fountain of Today," 13-15. Langdon, *op. cit.*, 19.

36. "Fountain of Today," 15. "Backbar Fountains and Fountains without Backbars," *SF*, Dec. 1935: 14-16.

37. "Getting the Trade of Motorists," *SF*, June 1923: 43-44.

38. "What Curb Service Did for This Fountain," *SF*, July 1927: 30.

39. *Ibid.*, 31, 52.

40. Emmett Maum, "Mr. Drive-In," *FFF*, July 1955: 29-30.

41. "Birmingham Has Unique Luncheon Cafe," *SF*, Sept. 1924: 28.

42. Laura E. Whitley, ed., *International Directory of Company Histories*, Vol. 25 (Detroit: St. James), 3.

43. *Ibid.*

44. *Ibid.*, 4.

45. *Ibid.*

46. *Ibid.*, 4-5.

47. Michael Karl Witzel, *Drive-in Deluxe* (Osceola, WI: Motorbooks International, 1997), 16. Jim Heimann, *Car Hops and Curb Service: A History*

of American Drive-in Restaurants, 1920-1960 (San Francisco: Chronicle, 1996), 22, 56.

48. John A. Jakle and Keith A. Sculle, *Fast Food: Roadside Restaurants in the Automobile Age* (Baltimore, MD: Johns Hopkins UP, 1999), 43, 172. Heimann, *op. cit.*, 16, 21, 28. Witzel, *op. cit.*, 14.

49. "Granddaddy of the Hamburger," *FF*, Mar. 1957: 48. E. W. Ingram, Sr., *All This from a Five-cent Hamburger! The Story of the White Castle System* (Princeton, NJ: Princeton UP for the Newcomen Society in North America, 1964), 10. David Gerard Hogan, *Selling 'Em by the Sack* (New York: New York UP, 1997), 25.

50. Ingram, *op. cit.*, 8, 10, 15-16. Hogan, *op. cit.*, 28, 30.

51. *Ibid.*, 11. "Grandaddy," 48.

52. Ingram, *op. cit.*, 12-13.

53. Ingram, *op. cit.*, 14-15.

54. *Ibid.*, 15-16. Tina Grant, ed., *International Directory of Company Histories*, vol. 12 (Detroit: St. James, 1996), 551.

55. Paul Hirshorn and Steven Izenour, *White Towers* (Cambridge, MA: MIT, 1979), 1, 3, 4, 6, 8, 11, 13, 21-23. Jeffrey Tennyson, *Hamburger Heaven: The Illustrated History of the Hamburger* (New York: Hyperion, 1993), 29.

56. Mobley, *op. cit.*, 20-21, 102.

57. "Concerning the Codes!" *SFM*, Sept. 1934: 28-29, 32. Waldon Fawcett, "Fountain Flashes from Washington: Federal Aid for Fountain Operators," *SFM*, Mar. 1933: 35-38. Weldon Fawcett, "Uncle Sam Sets Up a Model Fountain," *SFM*, Apr. 1933: 35-37, 43. Weldon Fawcett, "Fountain Flashes from Washington: Uncle Sam's Fountain Findings," *SFM*, May 1933: 37-39, 46-47.

58. L. C. Blessing, "Hammer versus Drug Store Fountains," *SFM*, May 1942: 12-13. Herman C. Nolen and Harold H. Maynard, *Drug Store Management* (New York: McGraw-Hill, 1941), 7, 353, 354-55, 485.

Chapter 7

1. "Ice Cream and Soft Drinks Essential to Soldiers," *SFQFS*, Oct. 1943: 40. "Fountains in the USO," *SFQFS*, June 1942: 16-17.

2. Sidney W. Mintz, *Tasting Food, Tasting Freedom: Excursions into Eating Culture and the Past* (Boston, MA: Beacon, 1996), 27-28.

3. "Fountains Under Fire, *SFQFS*, Sept. 1944: 16-17, 41.

4. *Ibid.*, 17. Mintz, *op. cit.*, 26. Kepos, *op. cit.*, Vol. 10: 226. "Pepsi-Cola's Walter Mack," 184. Mack and Buckley, *op. cit.*, 152-53.

5. "Four Scoops in a Row," *SFQFS*, Jan. 1943: 32. Mack and Buckley, *op. cit.*, 153.

6. *Ibid.* "Ice Cream Sodas to the Rescue," *SFQFS*, Nov. 1942: 37.

7. "The Government Says Ice Cream Must Be Cut 20% December and January," *SFQFS*, Dec. 1942: 10. "Ice Cream Rationing Is Started," *SFQFS*, Dec. 1942: 19. "Rationing the Fountain-Luncheonette," *SFQFS*, Feb. 1943: 9, 22. "And Now Ice Cream," *SFQFS,* Feb. 1943: 10-11. "The Government Says Ice Cream Cut to 65%," *SFQFS,* Feb. 1943: 23.

8. "Whipping Cream Order," *SFQFS*, Dec. 1942: 10. "Cream Order Permanent," *SFQFS*, Feb. 1943: 10. "Chocolate Is Scarce!" *SFQFS*, July 1942: 10-11. "January Ice Cream Quota Cut to 50 Percent," *SFQFS*, Jan. 1943: 18-20.

9. "One Year after Pearl Harbor," *SFQFS*, Dec. 1942: 8-9, 30-34. C. E. Henderson, "Keep 'Em Serving for the War's Duration," *SFQFS*, Feb. 1942: 10-11.

10. J. J. Clark, "Personnel: Uncle Sam versus Fountain Operators," *SFQFS*, Aug. 1941: 12-13. "Can They Step in the Boys' Shoes?" *SFQFS*, Nov. 1942: 8-9, 34-35. Vin Moynahan, "How Are They Filling the Boys' Shoes?" *SFQFS*, July 1945: 14-15.

11. "Walgreen's Finds Self-Service a Success," *SFQFS*, Aug. 1943: 17. "Ken Wallace Says Self-Service Is the Answer," *SFQFS*, May 1943: 12-13, 35-36.

12. Sonnedecker, *op. cit.*, 277.

13. J. Ronald Oakley, *God's Country: America in the Fifties* (New York: Dembner, 1990), 114, 125, 127.

14. *Ibid.*, 9-10, 97, 112-14.

15. Jim Horan, "Operators Are Lowering Food Margins to Meet the Higher Food Costs," *SFQFS*, Dec. 1947: 20-21. Ross Cole, "How Much Have Fountain Prices Gone Up? Plenty," *SFQFS*, Nov. 1948: 40, 69. "It's the Consensus—Volume Is Up but Profits Are Down—Here's Why," *SFQFS*, Aug. 1952: 28-29. "Drive-ins Booming," *Financial World*, Sept. 20, 1961: 6.

16. "Drive-in Volume Up," *SFQFS*, Aug. 1949: 26-27.

17. "Liquid Plans New Fountain Factory and Equipment Plant," *SFQFS*, Jan. 1946: 56. "L. G. Blessing Says Fountain Business Expanding," *FFF*, June 1953: 66-67.

18. "Take-Home Service Is Big Topic at NRA Convention," *FFF*, June 1953: 26-27. Oakley, *op. cit.*, 107.

19. Mariani, *America Eats Out*, 164-65. Oakley, *op. cit*, 237-38.

20. James W. McLamore, *The Burger King: Jim McLamore and the Building of an Empire* (New York: McGraw-Hill, 1998), 21-22, 26, 44-46. James Trager, *The Food Chronology: A Food Lover's Compendium of Events and Anecdotes, from Prehistory to the Present* (New York: Holt, 1995), 154, 626. Tina Grant, ed., *International Directory of Company Histories*, vol. 17 (Detroit, MI: St. James, 1997), 69-72.

21. "Where the Ice Cream Industry Sold Its Gallonage in 1956," *ICTJ*, Dec. 1957: 11.

22. *Ibid.*, 10-11. "Latest Drug Store Survey," *ICTJ*, Sept. 1957: 10. "Preliminary Findings of the Latest Study on Consumer Attitudes toward Ice Cream," *ICTJ*, Jan. 1960: 12-13, 85-86.

23. *The Cone with the Curl on Top: Celebrating Fifty Years, 1940-1990* (Minneapolis: International Dairy Queen, 1990), 11-12, 25, 30, 36. Anne Cooper Funderburg, *Chocolate, Strawberry, and Vanilla: A History of American Ice Cream* (Bowling Green, OH: Bowling Green State University Popular Press, 1995), 150. "Ice Cream Parlay," *Fortune* 48 (July 1953): 166.

24. Trager, *op. cit.*, 402, 490. Mobley, *op. cit.* 30, 40, 110, 124.

25. Lloyd Gladwell, *Starting and Managing a Small Retail Drugstore* (Washington, DC: Small Business Administration, 1966), 42. Pederson, *op. cit.*, 512-13. Mobley, *op. cit.*, 43.

26. *Beverage World*, 43. Waverly Root and Richard de Rochement, *Eating in America: A History* (Hopewell, NJ: Ecco, 1981), 417. Timothy J. Muris, David T. Scheffman, and Pablo T. Spiller, *Strategy, Structure, and Antitrust in the Carbonated Soft Drink Industry* (Westport, CT: Quorum, 1993), 19. "Mr. O'Hara's Nickel Drink," 108, 161.

27. Jasper Guy Woodroof and G. Frank Phillips, *Beverages: Carbonated and Noncarbonated* (Westport, CT: Avi, 1974), 207-08, 340, 343.

28. Gladwell, *op. cit.*, 42. Frank L. Ferguson, *Efficient Drug Store Management* (New York: Fairchild, 1969), 202.

SELECTED BIBLIOGRAPHY

Journals

Carbonated Drinks
Confectioners' and Bakers' Gazette
Confectioners' Gazette
Fast Food
Fountain and Fast Food
Ice Cream Trade Journal
The Pharmaceutical Era
The Soda Fountain
Soda Fountain and Quick Food Service
Soda Fountain Magazine

Books

Adkins, William S. *The National Soda Fountain Guide.* St. Louis, MO: National Druggist, 1913.

Alexander, Eleanor. "A Uniquely American Watering Hole: The Drug Store Soda Fountain at the Turn of the Twentieth Century." Master's thesis, U of Delaware, 1986.

American Soda Book of Receipts and Suggestions. Boston, MA: American Soda Fountain, n.d.

Andrist, Ralph K., ed. *The American Heritage History of the Confident Years.* New York: American Heritage, 1969.

Angle, Paul M. *Crossroads: 1913.* New York: Rand McNally, 1963.

Arber, Edward, ed. *Travels and Works of Captain John Smith.* 2 vols. Edinburgh: John Grant, 1910.

Arctic Soda Apparatus. Boston, MA: James W. Tufts, 1873.

Armour, Richard. *Drug Store Days: My Youth among the Pills and Potions.* New York: McGraw-Hill, 1959.

Batterberry, Michael, and Ariane Batterberry. *On the Town in New York from 1776 to the Present.* New York: Charles Scribner's Sons, 1973.

Bergman, Torbern. *On Acid of Air: Treatise on Bitter, Seltzer, Spa, and Pyrmont Waters and Their Synthetical Preparation.* Reprint. Stockholm, Sweden: Almquist & Wiksell, 1956.

Berrey, Lester V., and Melvin Van Den Bark. *American Thesaurus of Slang.* New York: Thomas Y. Crowell Company, 1953.

Boklund, Uno. *Torbern Bergman as Pioneer in the Domain of Mineral Waters.* Stockholm, Sweden: Almquist & Wiksell, 1956.

Bridenbaugh, Carl. *Cities in Revolt: Urban Life in America, 1743-1776.* New York: Knopf, 1955.

Brown, Chandros Michael. *Benjamin Silliman: A Life in the Young Republic.* Princeton, NJ: Princeton UP, 1989.

Brown, John Hull. *Early American Beverages.* Rutland, VT: Charles E. Tuttle, 1966.

Busch, Moritz. *Travels between the Hudson and the Mississippi 1851-1852.* Trans. and ed. Norman H. Binger. Lexington, KY: UP of Kentucky, 1971.

Cable, Mary. *American Manners and Morals.* New York: American Heritage, 1969.

Calkins, Raymond. *Substitutes for the Saloon.* Boston, MA: Houghton-Mifflin, 1901.

Campbell, Hannah. *Why Did They Name It?* New York: Fleet, 1964.

Catalogue of Puffer's Frigid Soda and Mineral Water Apparatus. Boston, MA: N.p., 1878.

Chase, Elaine Forman, ed. *The Diary of Elizabeth Drinker.* Vol. 3. Boston: Northeastern UP, 1991.

Chazanof, William. *Welch's Grape Juice: From Corporation to Cooperative.* Syracuse, NY: Syracuse UP, 1977.

Chester, Thomas. *Carbonated Beverages: The Art of Making, Dispensing, and Bottling Soda Water, Mineral Waters, Ginger Ale, and Sparkling Liquors.* New York: John Matthews, 1882.

The Cone with the Curl on Top: Celebrating Fifty Years, 1940-1990. Minneapolis: International Dairy Queen, 1990.

Conwell, Russell H. *Acres of Diamonds: How Men and Women May Become Rich.* Philadelphia: John Y. Huber, 1890.

Coxe, John Redman. *The Emporium of Arts and Sciences.* Philadelphia: Joseph Delaplaine, 1812.

Crawford, Mary Caroline. *Social Life in Old New England.* Reprint. Detroit: Tower, 1971.

Cutbush, James. *The American Artist's Manual, or Dictionary of Practical Knowledge.* Philadelphia: Johnson, Warner, and Fisher, 1814.

Dahl, J. O. *Soda Fountain and Luncheonette Management.* New York: Harper and Brothers, 1930.

Daniels, Jonathon. *The End of Innocence.* Philadelphia: Lippincott, 1954.

Daniels, W. H., ed. *The Temperance Reform and Its Great Reformers.* New York: Nelson and Phillips, 1877.

DePew, Chauncey M., ed. *One Hundred Years of American Commerce.* 2 vol. New York: Haynes, 1895.

Deutsch, Ronald M. *The New Nuts among the Berries.* Palo Alto, CA: Bull, 1977.

Dick, Everett. *The Sod-house Frontier.* Lincoln, NE: U of Nebraska P, 1979.

Dispenser's Formulary, or Soda Water Guide. New York: Haynes, 1915.

Dorsey, Leslie, and Janice Devine. *Fare Thee Well: A Backward Look at Two Centuries of Historic American Hostelries, Fashionable Spas, and Seaside Resorts.* New York: Crown, 1964.

Downey, Fairfax. *Our Lusty Forefathers.* New York: Scribner's Sons, 1947.

Dunn, Jerry. *Idiom Savant: Slang as It Is Slung.* New York: Henry Holt , 1997.

Ellis, Harry E. *Dr Pepper: King of Beverages.* Dallas, TX: Dr Pepper, 1979.

Emerson, Edward R. *Beverages, Past and Present.* 2 vol. New York: Putnam's Sons, 1908.

Ferguson, Frank L. *Efficient Drug Store Management.* New York: Fairchild, 1969.

Forbes, B. A. *Money-making Hints for Soda Fountain Owners.* New York: Haynes, 1907.

Fulton, John, and Elizabeth H. Thomson. *Benjamin Silliman, 1779-1864: Pathfinder in American Science.* New York: Schuman, 1947.

Funderburg, Anne Cooper. *Chocolate, Strawberry, and Vanilla: A History of American Ice Cream.* Bowling Green, OH: Bowling Green State U Popular P, 1995.

Furnas, J. C. *The Americans: A Social History of the United States, 1587-1914.* New York: Putnam's Sons, 1969.

——. *The Life and Times of the Late Demon Rum.* New York: Putnam's Sons, 1965.

Garrison, J. Ritchie, Bernard L. Herman, and Barbara McLean Ward, eds. *After Ratification: Material Life in Delaware, 1789-1820.* Newark, DE: U of Delaware, 1988.

Gershman, Michael. *Getting It Right the Second Time.* Reading, MA: Addison-Wesley, 1990.

Gibbs, F. W. *Joseph Priestley: Revolutions of the 18th Century.* Garden City, NY: Doubleday, 1967.

Gladwell, Lloyd. *Starting and Managing a Small Retail Drugstore.* Washington, DC: Small Business Administration, 1966.

Graham, Elizabeth Candler, and Ralph Roberts. *The Real Ones: Four Generations of the First Family of Coca-Cola.* Fort Lee, NJ: Barricade, 1992.

Griffith, Sally Foreman, ed. *The Autobiography of William Allen White,* 2nd ed. Rev. and abridged. Lawrence, KS: UP of Kansas, 1990.

Heimann, Jim. *Car Hops and Curb Service: A History of American Drive-in Restaurants, 1920-1960.* San Franciso: Chronicle, 1996.

Hilliard, Sam Bowers. *Hog Meat and Hoecake: Food Supply in the Old South, 1840-1860.* Carbondale, IL: Southern Illinois UP, 1972.

Hirshorn, Paul, and Steven Izenour. *White Towers.* Cambridge, MA: MIT, 1979.

Hogan, David Gerard. *Selling 'Em by the Sack.* New York: New York UP, 1997.

Ingram, E. W., Sr. *All This from a Five-cent Hamburger! The Story of the White Castle System.* Princeton, NJ: Princeton UP for the Newcomen Society in North America, 1964.

International Directory of Company Histories. 25 vol. Detroit: St. James, 1994, 1995, 1998.

Jakle, John A., and Keith A. Sculle. *Fast Food: Roadside Restaurants in the Automobile Age.* Baltimore, MD: Johns Hopkins UP, 1999.

James W. Tufts. *Patentee and Manufacturer of Arctic Soda Water Apparatus.* N.p., 1887.

Jorgensen, Janice, ed. *Encyclopedia of Consumer Brands.* 3 vol. Detroit: St. James P, 1994.

Kahn, E. J., Jr. *The Big Drink.* London: Max Reinhardt, 1960.

Katz, William Loren, ed. *Anti-Negro Riots in the North, 1863.* New York: Arno and the New York Times, 1969.

Lambert, I. E. *The Public Accepts: Stories behind Famous Trademarks, Names, and Slogans.* Albuquerque, NM: U of New Mexico P, 1976.

Langdon, Philip. *Orange Roofs, Golden Arches.* New York: Knopf, 1986.

LaWall, Charles H. *Four Thousand Years of Pharmacy: An Outline History of Pharmacy and the Allied Sciences.* Philadelphia: Lippincott, 1927.

Lender, Mark Edward, and James Kirby Martin. *Drinking in America: A History.* New York: Free, 1982.

Let's Sell Ice Cream. Washington, DC: The Ice Cream Merchandising Institute, 1947.

Levine, Lawrence W. *Defender of the Faith, William Jennings Bryan: The Last Decade, 1915-1925.* New York: Oxford UP, 1965.

Louis, J. C., and Harvey Z. Yazijian. *The Cola Wars.* New York: Everest, 1980.

Mack, Walter, and Peter Buckley. *No Time Lost.* New York: Atheneum, 1982.

Mariani, John F. *America Eats Out: An Illustrated History of Restaurants, Taverns, Coffee Shops, Speakeasies, and Other Establishments That Have Fed Us for 350 Years.* New York: Morrow, 1991.

——. *The Dictionary of American Food and Drink.* New York: Hearst, 1994.

Markun, Leo. *Mrs. Grundy: A History of Four Centuries of Morals in Great Britain and the United States Intended to Illuminate Present Problems.* New York: Appleton, 1930.

Masurovsky, B. I. *Sherbets, Water Ices, and Modern Soda Fountain Operation.* Milwaukee, WI: Olsen, 1933.

Matthews' Catalogue and Price List of Apparatus, Materials, and Accessories for Making and Dispensing Carbonated Beverages. New York: Matthews Apparatus, 1891.

McCabe, James D. *A Collector's Reprint: The Illustrated History of the Centennial Exhibition.* Philadelphia: National Publishing, 1975.

McLamore, James W. *The Burger King: Jim Lamore and the Building of an Empire.* New York: McGraw-Hill, 1998.

Merwin, Samuel. *Rise and Fight Againe.* New York: Boni, 1935.

Michael, P. *Ices and Soda Fountain Drinks.* London: MacLaren, n.d.

Miller, T. Michael. *Artisans and Merchants of Alexandria, Virginia, 1784-1820.* Two Vol. Bowie, MD: Heritage, 1991-92.

Mobley, Jane. *Prescription for Success: The Chain Drug Story.* Kansas City, MO: Hallmark Cards, 1991.

Morgan, Hal. *Symbols of America.* New York: Steam, 1986.

Morrison, Joseph L. *Josephus Daniels: The Small-d Democrat.* Chapel Hill, NC: U of North Carolina P, 1966.

Muris, Timothy J., David T. Scheffman, and Pablo T. Spiller. *Strategy, Structure, and Antitrust in the Carbonated Soft Drink Industry.* Westport, CT: Quorum, 1993.

Nichols, John P. *The Chain Store Tells Its Own Story.* New York: Institute of Distribution, 1940.

Nolen, Herman C., and Harold H. Maynard. *Drug Store Management.* New York: McGraw-Hill, 1941.

Oakley, J. Ronald. *God's Country: America in the Fifties.* New York: Dembner, 1990.

Palmer, Carl J. *History of the Soda Fountain Industry.* Washington, DC: Soda Fountain Manufacturers' Association, 1947.

Panati, Charles. *Panati's Extraordinary Endings of Practically Everything and Everybody.* New York: Harper & Row, 1989.

——. *Panati's Extraordinary Origins of Everyday Things.* New York: Harper & Row, 1987.

——. *Panati's Parade of Fads, Follies, and Manias.* New York: Harper Perennial, 1991.

Parks, Mal, ed. *Soda Fountain Handbook.* New York: Hearst Magazines, 1942.

Pendergrast, Mark. *For God, Country, and Coca-Cola: The Unauthorized History of the Great American Soft Drink and the Company That Makes It.* New York: Scribner's Sons, 1993.

Phillips, Shine. *Big Spring: The Casual Biography of a Prairie Town.* New York: Prentice-Hall, 1943.

Potter, Frank N. *The Book of Moxie.* Paducah, KY: Collector, 1987.

——. *The Moxie Mystique.* Virginia Beach, VA: Donning, 1981.

Powers, Madelon. *Faces along the Bar: Lore and Order in the Workingman's Saloon, 1870-1920.* Chicago: U of Chicago P, 1998.

Priestley, Joseph. *Directions for Impregnating Water with Fixed Air in Order to Communicate to It the Peculiar Spirit and Virtues of Pyrmont Water.* Reprint. Washington, DC: American Bottlers of Carbonated Beverages, 1945.

Riley, John J. *A History of the American Soft Drink Industry.* Washington, DC: American Bottlers of Carbonated Beverages, 1958.

Robinson, James W. *Prescription for Success: The Rexall International Story and What It Means to You.* Rocklin, CA: Prima, 1999.

Rodengen, Jeffrey L. *The Legend of Dr Pepper/Seven-Up*. Ft. Lauerdale, FL: Write Stuff, 1995.

Root, Waverly, and Richard de Rochement. *Eating in America: A History*. Hopewell, NJ: Ecco, 1981.

Sann, Paul. *The Lawless Decade*. New York: Bonanza, 1957.

Saxe, D. W. *Saxe's New Guide or Hints to Soda Dispensers (Confidential)*. Chicago: Saxe Guide, 1893.

Scharf, J. Thomas, and Thompson Westcott. *History of Philadelphia, 1609-1884*. Philadelphia: Everts, 1884.

Schofield, Robert E., ed. *A Scientific Autobiography of Joseph Priestley, 1733-1804*. Cambridge, MA: MIT, 1966.

Schreiber, G. R. *A Concise History of Vending in the USA*. Chicago: Vend, 1961.

Smith, Wayne. *Ice Cream Dippers: An Illustrated History and Collector's Guide to Early Ice Cream Dippers*. Walkersville, MD: Smith, 1986.

Soda Water: How to Make and Serve It with Profit. Chicago: Liquid Carbonic, 1905.

Sonnedecker, Glenn, ed. *Kremers' and Urdang's History of Pharmacy*. Rev. ed. Philadelphia: Lippincott, 1963.

Staten, Vince. *Do Pharmacists Sell Farms? A Trip Inside the Corner Drugstore*. New York: Simon & Schuster, 1998.

Stoddard, Bob. *Introduction to Pepsi Collecting*. Pomona, CA: Double Dot, 1991.

——. *Pepsi-Cola: 100 Years*. Santa Monica, CA: General Publishing Group, 1997.

Tennyson, Jeffrey. *Hamburger Heaven: The Illustrated History of the Hamburger*. New York: Hyperion, 1993.

Trager, James. *The Food Chronology: A Food Lover's Compendium of Events and Anecdotes, from Prehistory to the Present*. New York: Holt, 1995.

Train, Arthur. *Puritan's Progress*. New York: Scribner's, 1931.

Viele, Teresa Griffin. *Following the Drum: A Glimpse of Frontier Life*. Lincoln, NE: U of Nebraska P, 1984.

Ward, John Russell. *Soda Fountain Profits*. Stamford, CT: Dahl, 1935.

Welby, Adlard. *A Visit to North America and the English Settlements in Illinois, with a Winter Residence at Philadelphia*. London: Drury, 1821.

Witzel, Michael Karl. *Drive-in Deluxe*. Osceola, WI: Motorbooks, 1997.

Witzel, Michael Karl, and Gyvel Young-Witzel. *Soda Pop!* Stillwater, MN: Voyageur, 1998.

Woodroof, Jasper Guy, and G. Frank Phillips. *Beverages: Carbonated and Noncarbonated*. Westport, CT: AVI, 1974.

Wyman, Carolyn. *I'm a Spam Fan: America's Best-loved Foods*. Stamford, CT: Longmeadow, 1993.

1. Column fountains often resembled architectural columns or fire hydrants.

2. The Nautilus, a rectangular box fountain manufactured by Matthews, dispensed up to eight syrups and could be ordered with a façade of either Italian marble or Tennessee marble. (*The Matthews Catalogue and Price List of Apparatus, Materials, and Accessories for Making and Dispensing Carbonated Beverages*, 1891)

3. This cottage fountain by Tufts dispensed 12 flavors of soda water: coffee, nectar, catawba, ginger, chocolate, pineapple, cream, vanilla, raspberry, lemon, seltzer, and congress. (*Arctic Soda Apparatus*, 1873)

4. The Matthews trade catalogue boasted that The France featured six different kinds of marble plus gold, silver, and bronze ornamentation for only $625. (*The Matthews Catalogue and Price List of Apparatus, Materials, and Accessories for Making and Dispensing Carbonated Beverages*, 1891)

5. The Albion, manufactured by Tufts, was a single-faced marble fountain popular in the 1870s. (*Arctic Soda Apparatus*, 1873)

6. The Adriatic was a double-faced apparatus that combined the rectangular box and tower styles. It was almost six feet tall and cost $1,000. (*The Matthews Catalogue and Price List of Apparatus, Materials, and Accessories for Making and Dispensing Carbonated Beverages*, 1891)

7. An intricate bas-relief was typical of soda fountains manufactured by The Low Art Tile Company.

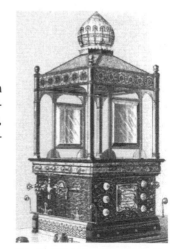

8. The Japan, made by Matthews, was more than six feet tall and cost $1,380. (*The Matthews Catalogue and Price List of Apparatus, Materials, and Accessories for Making and Dispensing Carbonated Beverages*, 1891)

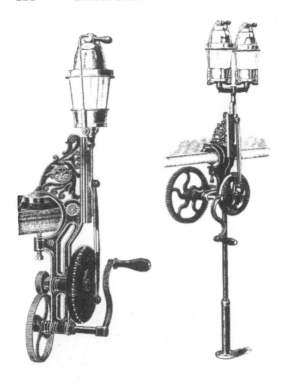

9. These hand-cranked Lightning Shaker milk-shake machines were manufactured by Tufts.

TODAY when you're shopping — when you're tired and half exhausted—drop in here for a refreshing drink of soda or a luscious confection. Don't hurry, but stay till you're rested. Please feel very much "at home" in our soda department.

A Suggestion

Banana Split. A generous cone of vanilla ice cream, resting on a prime, ripe banana — split lengthwise. Topped with fresh, chopped nuts — a cap of whipped cream and a rich red cherry.

15 Cents

J. F. Brown,
810 Market St., New York, N.Y.

10. Soda fountains in the shopping district often catered to women.

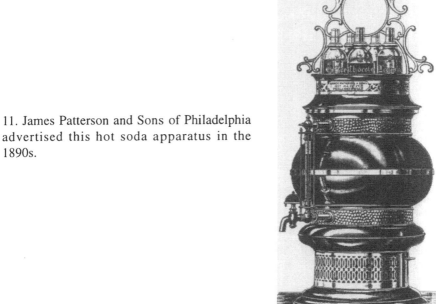

11. James Patterson and Sons of Philadelphia advertised this hot soda apparatus in the 1890s.

12. This National Automatic Fountain, an ancestor of modern vending machines, dispensed Crystal Spring Water in a paper cup for a nickel.

13. This street spa was more attractive than the average street stand selling soda water. Made of chestnut and white oak, it cost $450. (*The Matthews Catalogue and Price List of Apparatus, Materials, and Accessories for Making and Dispensing Carbonated Beverages*, 1891)

14. Wall fountains typically had a superstructure and a large mirror. (*The Matthews Catalogue and Price List of Apparatus, Materials, and Accessories for Making and Dispensing Carbonated Beverages*, 1891)

15. "King of Beverages" was an early Dr Pepper slogan. (Dr Pepper Museum and Free Enterprise Institute, Waco, Texas)

16. This photo of the soda fountain in George S. Royer's drugstore on Main Street in Ephrata, Pennsylvania, was taken circa 1925. (The Historical Society of Cocalico Valley)

17. Four soda jerks stood ready to wait on customers at this fountain in Knoxville, Tennessee, in 1936. (The Coca-Cola Company)

18. This decorative tile fountain was located in a Houston, Texas, pharmacy in the 1930s. (The Coca-Cola Company)

19. The menu at this soda fountain included Coca-Cola, oyster stew, chopped egg salad, pig 'n bun, sundaes, and a variety of sandwiches. (The Coca-Cola Company)

20. This soda fountain at Field's Cut Rate Drugs in Dallas, Texas, was a typical 1950s lunch counter. (Texas/Dallas History and Archives Division, Dallas Public Library)

INDEX